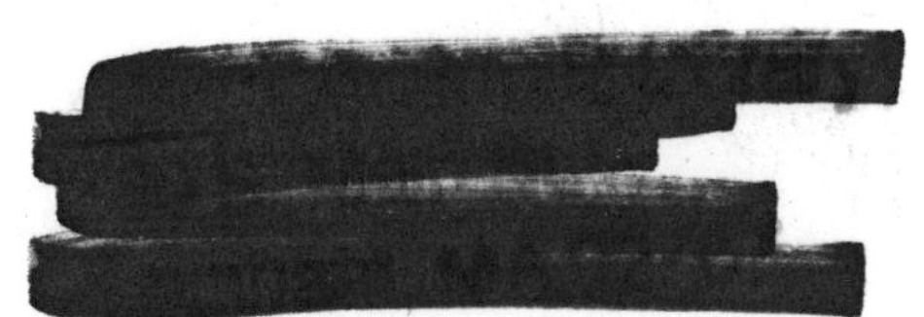

HEALING AT THE SPEED OF SOUND™

HEALING AT THE SPEED OF SOUND™

How What We Hear Transforms Our Brains and Our Lives

Don Campbell and Alex Doman

Hudson
Street
Press

HUDSON STREET PRESS
Published by Penguin Group
Penguin Group (USA) Inc., 375 Hudson Street, New York, New York 10014, U.S.A. • Penguin Group (Canada), 90 Eglinton Avenue East, Suite 700, Toronto, Ontario, Canada M4P 2Y3 (a division of Pearson Penguin Canada Inc.) • Penguin Books Ltd., 80 Strand, London WC2R 0RL, England • Penguin Ireland, 25 St. Stephen's Green, Dublin 2, Ireland (a division of Penguin Books Ltd.) • Penguin Group (Australia), 250 Camberwell Road, Camberwell, Victoria 3124, Australia (a division of Pearson Australia Group Pty. Ltd.) • Penguin Books India Pvt. Ltd., 11 Community Centre, Panchsheel Park, New Delhi – 110 017, India • Penguin Books (NZ), 67 Apollo Drive, Rosedale, Auckland 0632, New Zealand (a division of Pearson New Zealand Ltd.) • Penguin Books (South Africa) (Pty.) Ltd., 24 Sturdee Avenue, Rosebank, Johannesburg 2196, South Africa

Penguin Books Ltd., Registered Offices: 80 Strand, London WC2R 0RL, England
First published by Hudson Street Press, a member of Penguin Group (USA) Inc.
First Printing, October 2011

10 9 8 7 6 5 4 3 2 1

LIBRARY OF CONGRESS CATALOGING-IN-PUBLICATION DATA

Campbell, Don G., 1946–
Healing at the speed of sound : how what we hear transforms our brains and our lives / Don Campbell and Alex Doman.
p. cm.
Includes bibliographical references and index.
ISBN 978-1-59463-082-8 (alk. paper)
1. Music—Physiological aspects. 2. Music—Psychological aspects. 3. Sound—Physiological aspects. I. Doman, Alex. II. Title.
ML3920.C16 2011
781'.11—dc22 2011015664

Printed in the United States of America
Set in Goudy Old Style

PUBLISHER'S NOTE
While the author has made every effort to provide accurate telephone numbers and Internet addresses at the time of publication, neither the publisher nor the author assumes any responsibility for errors, or for changes that occur after publication. Further, the publisher does not have any control over and does not assume any responsibility for author or third-party Web sites or their content.

This book is dedicated to the memory of Richard Lawrence and William Horwedel III, who brought music's message to millions through their talents in production and their artistry.

Contents

Preface

When we speak of being of "sound mind and body," we seldom realize that sound itself is the root of being. That sound itself is the route to acquire those things we want so much, a sound mind and body. Most of us spend our lives largely unaware of the sounds that surround us. Sound acts on our psyche and we ignore its impact. This can make us constant victims of our sound environment as the blast of a horn, the screech of a tire, the relentless pounding of a jackhammer all carry us into distraction. Even when we do take note of the sound pollutants in our environment, we often feel powerless to do anything about them. We assume that they're the price of progress.

That doesn't need to be the case. We can consciously and creatively add sound nutrients to combat those ill effects.

Sound nutrition is the core value of the book you hold in your hand. Read it. Listen to it. View it. Think about it. There has never been a book on music and sound with so many multisensorial possibilities. These suggestions will revolutionize your life. Each individual can create his or her own "sound diet" to match personal needs and tastes, to get the sound mind and body he or she desires.

Don Campbell and Alex Doman offer guidelines that can literally turn on our ears and eyes, that can teach us to compose a sonically nutritious day by raising our awareness of the sound effects that tune up our lives. Here, they teach us how to maximize our good moods by using music to stimulate our optimism and increase our day's creative output, as well as how to turn down the sounds that distract and deter us. As these two distinguished experts combine their up-to-the-minute knowledge, vision, and creativity, you are in capable hands as a reader and listener, creating a truly "sound day" from the waking moment through the working day and into the evening.

Designed to enhance creativity, this book coaxes us all to listen outside the box, to create a unique sound landscape suited to our lives and families. Written with simplicity, fine research, and clarity, this book is perfect for the neophyte, the expert, and all of us in between.

Maximize your creativity and productivity with this gold standard course in personal awareness.

Listen, listen, listen.

—Julia Cameron
Author of *The Artist's Way*

Acknowledgments

Many thanks to Caroline Sutton, Meghan Stevenson, and the team at Hudson Street Press in New York, who have brought to the public a feast of facts, ideas, and creative insight.

Appreciation to Gail Ross and the Ross Yoon Literary Agency for seeing the need for this work in today's stressful world.

We must acknowledge Dr. Alfred A. Tomatis (1920–2001) and the many generations he influenced with skill and creativity to help us understand the essential role of the ear in health, communication, and education.

I am indebted to my mentor and coauthor, Don Campbell, who has inspired this essential message about the transformative power of music and sound through his teaching and writing.

Deep gratitude to my grandfather, Robert J. Doman, M.D., who stimulated my fascination with the brain; to my father, Robert J. Doman Jr., who provided the opportunity to clinically investigate the applications of music to help people realize their fullest potential; and to the committed parents of the National Association for Child Development.

Special thanks to Brad Boyajian, my business partner, without whom this work would not have been possible.

I must acknowledge the amazing staff at Advanced Brain Technologies, in Ogden, Utah, who make the mission of sound and music for health happen every day. The faculty, providers, international representatives, and the countless families around the world are the core of energy that creates the positive outcome of my life's work.

I am grateful to the musicians of the Arcangelos Chamber Ensemble and Spring Hill Music for making so many of our audio samples of such high quality.

Thanks to Vera Brandes for her guidance and for organizing Mozart and Science 2006, where she brought Don and me together one evening in Vienna. Appreciation is also extended to Roland Haas, Ph.D., president of International Music and Art Research Association Austria.

Special thanks to Sheila Allen, Gayle Moyers, Joshua Leeds, Billie Thompson, Ph.D., Dorinne Davis, Judy Belk, Ph.D., and the dozens of colleagues who have helped me see the vast importance of sound and its place in our world. Dorothy Lockhart Lawrence and Greg Lawrence have been ever present in their research, recording skills, and friendship.

Muchas gracias to Marival Gutierrez, her family, her staff, and the students and parents of Centro Regiomontano de Educacion Especial, A.C., in Monterrey, Mexico, for making music integral to our work in special education.

I especially thank my wife, Mandy, for her love, patience, encouragement, and support. I simply do not know how I would do this without you at my side.

My son Brendan, whose light shines so bright he has illuminated my path and inspired me to blaze new trails. Zane and Ethan, my stepsons, whose curiosity and laughter bring so much to each day. And my godson, Jake, and brother, Laird, who help make my life so rich. Deep appreciation goes to my mother, Ginger Kenney, for her unwavering support.

Thank you all.

—Alex Doman

My appreciation goes to two generations of music educators, performers, and clinicians who have encouraged me to move forward in communicating music's powerful role in society. Grace Nash, Alfred Tomatis, Norman Goldberg, Annette Dieudonné, Bill Horwedel, Mary Mayotte, and Bess Hieronymus kept me creatively searching for new ways to teach and write about music and musicians.

The Ross Yoon Literary Agency embraced my ideas for a book that would serve a new, emerging world of electronic readers. Without Gail Ross's energy and persistence, these words would not have reached this new level of readership.

I thank Helena Wald, Kerry Doutrich, Annette Ridenour, Christine Stevens, RMT, Amitra Cottrell, Sacha Millstone, Tim Shove, Nina Berger, Catherine Viel, Marc Shulgold, Shaina Harris, and Wendy Young for their research, writing, editing, and music-production contributions.

The many colleagues and friends who have pushed their work from the fringe to the frontier of musical performance, education, social justice, and spiritual depth include Ruth Cunningham, Ana Hernandez, Pat Moffit Cook, Ph.D., Carla Hannaford, Ph.D., Barbara Crowe, RMT, Barbara Reuer, RMT, Arthur Harvey, Ph.D., Dr. Susan Andrews, Chloe Goodchild, James D'Angelo, Paul Madaule, Ysaye Barnwell, Ph.D., Chris Brewer, Daniel Kobialka, Michael Hoppé, Christina Tourin, RMT, Sue Levine, Louise Montello, Ph.D., David Darling, Paul Winter, Jean Houston, Ph.D., Susan Osborn, Jill Purse, Jonathan Goldman, Joy Gardner, Russill Paul, Molly Scott, Ph.D., Silvia Nakkach, Susan Hale, Zacciah Blackburn, Shyla Nelson, Don Grusin, and Marie Carmichael.

I owe much gratitude for the profound knowledge of Marc Rynearson, Heather Anderson, and Janica Quach, at DMX, who have helped me realize that thousands of musical selections are ever available for our wellness and creativity.

For their brilliant efforts to keep music alive and healthy in this world, I must acknowledge MusiCares, the Grammy Foundation, Remo drums, and the National Association of Music Merchants, who cross all boundaries for supporting the arts.

And I must add my profound gratitude to our visionary editors, Caroline Sutton and Meghan Stevenson, at Hudson Street Press.

—Don Campbell

Introduction

Hear Here!

If you stop right now and close your eyes, the first thing you'll notice is that you suddenly hear more things. Where are you? In your office? At home in bed or on your couch? What soundscape surrounds you right now? In my office, with the window open on a summer day, I can hear traffic on the street, two different kinds of birds from the tree outside my window, a horn honking, conversation from neighbors, my fingers on the computer keyboard. I can hear myself taking a deep breath. A Haydn piano sonata plays quietly from my stereo.

Before I closed my eyes, I might have been aware of the sonata and the car horn honking, but not much else. What about you? How many of the sounds that you heard are there by choice (Haydn) or because of the environment you happen to be in (street traffic)? Do you actively provide yourself with nurturing sounds and block or filter noise—or do you just let the sounds of your world wash over you without paying much attention to what's there?

Sound is everywhere—it is as much a part of our lives as the air we breathe and the food we eat. But until now, we haven't properly considered the health values of sound. We may choose organic food at the supermarket and avoid inhaling others' cigarette smoke, yet we rarely pay attention to the equally positive or negative health impacts of sound, the other thing we put in our bodies.

Think about this: How did each sound you heard make you feel? The answer is not always as self-evident as we might think. Each individual has his or her own taste in music, tolerance level for noise and for silence, and habits in terms of allowing sounds into the environment. Some people find absolute silence refreshing; others find it boring. Some work better with the "wallpaper" sound of a radio talk show in the background; others lose concentration with the intrusion of any conversation or noise. Some find meaning and a sense of fulfillment in the clatter of family life, or the sounds of a busy city outside the window, or the workaday noises of an open-plan office space; others long for the aural serenity of a private room or a home surrounded by the sounds of nature.

This book is not about encouraging everyone to live in the same aural world—to wake up to a Vivaldi concerto, for example, then work to a brisk pop background, and fall asleep to a soothing Diana Krall tune. It's about helping you identify which kinds of sounds enhance your own life most effectively at different times of the day and in different circumstances—and which sounds negatively affect your own and others' moods, mental activity, and health. Once you have really listened to, identified, and analyzed the sounds in your daily life, you can begin to reshape what you hear to correct your own and your loved ones' problems of attention, perception, and concentration; decrease your stress level and improve your emotional state; communicate more effectively at home and in the workplace; and create a better sense of community in your neighborhood and in the world.

Why and how does sound have such a profound impact on our daily experience? Many people fail to consider the fact that sound is a physical force. Since the original big bang (which no one heard, but whose effects we all experience), it has existed as a powerful part of the universe, resonating through space, through physical matter, and through all living things. Its basic components—vibration, pitch, and rhythm—can form planets, destroy cities, shatter glass, and bring disparate entities into harmony. On a smaller scale, it interacts with and affects the physical, neurological, and spiritual state of each human being in much the same way that heat can alter the chemistry of physical objects. Think of how the mere act of singing nearly always lifts your spirits, how listening to certain types of classical music clarifies your mind, how playing music with others creates a warm sense of community, and how music with a steady beat that you enjoy makes exercise more productive—and you will realize that sound shapes your life profoundly in myriad ways, whether or not you are aware of it. The trick lies in directing this powerful force—much as you might direct the flow of water from a garden hose—to heal, to enhance, and to engage your life in a wide variety of ways.

When my book *The Mozart Effect* was first published in 1997, much of our knowledge of sound's effects on the human mind, body, and spirit remained in the realm of the anecdotal and even the intuitive. We knew that college students who listened to Mozart's music did better on temporal/spatial tests taken shortly after the listening experience. We had heard from numerous health-care professionals that listening to music appeared to increase patients' tolerance for pain and sped up their surgical recovery times, and that it even seemed to enhance premature infants' growth rates in pediatric ICUs. We had seen how, in certain special programs in schools, drumming circles had a remarkable impact on troubled youth. Few thorough studies had been conducted to scientifically validate these reports or to explain how the results were achieved. Scientists had not yet traced the ways in which rhythm and sound have facilitated connection, communication, and community.

Now, in the twenty-first century, that situation has changed. As a recognized authority on the transformational power of music and the author of more than twenty books about music's benefits in health and education, I have been both privileged and enormously gratified to witness a wave of new research in the areas of music and the brain, and the effects of the sound environment on health. An explosion of new data produced by hundreds of new studies, surveys, and research programs conducted in the wake of *The Mozart Effect* have launched this area of knowledge from the Sputnik of intuition to the Hubble's clear definition of the nature of sound and its organizing energy in our universe. As a better understanding of sound's properties and potential spurred scientists to ask better questions, more sophisticated research methods and equipment have shown that sound does in fact affect our health and healing on a cellular level, and that music can reduce stress and stimulate cognitive processing and memory in measurable, substantive, and lasting ways. Throughout this book, I will point to the recent research behind each of my recommendations for using sound's power to create positive change in your life.

In 2006, I had the pleasure of meeting Alex Doman, the founder and CEO of Advanced Brain Technologies, a brain health and education company whose therapeutic programs harness the properties of sound to improve individuals' listening, learning, and communication skills. Alex's fascination with neurological development is no surprise: His family has been developing methods to help improve brain function for more than seventy years. While serving as vice president of the National Association for Child Development, an international organization founded by his father, Robert J. Doman Jr., Alex began researching the ways in which sound affects brain performance. By the time we met, he had developed sound-based methods—most notably the Listening Program®, discussed later in this book—to address such conditions in children as autism, ADHD, Down syndrome, and brain damage, and to enhance learning and sharpen mental acuity in adults. These programs are most commonly delivered via headphones using sound methods such as a bone-conduction audio system, which carries sound's vibratory benefits throughout the body, and Spatial Surround® technology to stimulate the brain via a full 360-degree listening experience as it exists in the natural world.

Having trained thousands of health-care, education, and music professionals around the world in the application of music-based listening therapies, Alex brought with him hands-on experience using recent developments in music effects research and neuroscience to profoundly improve people's lives. Through subsequent conversations, we found that we share a passion to communicate to others our personal and professional knowledge of sound's benefits. This book, presented in my voice, nevertheless represents Alex's and my combined vision and draws on our experience and research—along with the distilled results of more than three thousand new scientific studies, surveys, and other investigations into the sound-mind-body connection—to show you, the reader, how an improved sound environment can lead to a healthier, happier, more fulfilling life.

To do this, we will take you through a typical day, demonstrating ways to put sound and silence to work enhancing your waking routine, morning commute, work experience, family time, social activities, and sleep. Along the way, we'll demonstrate what types of music can improve your performance in exercise and physical activity; how sound can be used at home and in public to create a private space or to bring others in; how music can decrease stress, improve productivity, and create a collegial environment at the workplace; how sound-related therapies and practices can improve your child's social, physical, and academic functioning; how music is being used in medical settings to reduce pre-operative stress, speed up recovery times, and enhance many different forms of physical therapy; and how music can improve the lives of the elderly, including those with Alzheimer's disease or other forms of dementia. Throughout, you will find not just theoretical information or general advice, but concrete suggestions for altering your sound routine; specific exercises for more effectively accessing the power of pitch, rhythm, and vibration; playlists for use when exercising, working, meditating, and performing chores; and suggestions on how to create a sound environment best suited to your individual tastes and needs.

For those who are reading this book on an electronic reading device with active Internet browser capability, we are particularly excited to be able to add a wealth of audio, visual, and textual enhancements via a simple click on an icon. Throughout the following chapters, ear icons ( ) will take e-readers to sound recordings and informative audio podcasts; eye icons ( ) will link to video lectures, exercise demonstrations, and documentary excerpts; and "idea" icons ( ) will connect you to organizational Web sites, newsletters, and other resources that will help you implement the suggestions we provide. In its print version, *Healing at the Speed of Sound* provides URLs for each of these sources, allowing you to access the same materials via your home computer. This multisensorial approach, using images and sound as well as text, makes especially good sense as we encourage you to open all of your senses to the rich potential for pleasure in your lives, workplaces, and homes.

So often in today's world, we are encouraged to buy our way out of life's inevitable periods of unhappiness or trouble. Sound's great advantage lies in its absolute pervasiveness, its free availability for use in improving and

HEALING AT THE SPEED OF SOUND™

CHAPTER ONE

Awake and Energize

Starting Your Day with Sound

For a few moments music makes us larger than we really are, and the world more orderly than it really is. . . . That is cause enough for ecstasy.

—Robert Jourdain, author and composer

"I had the most wonderful morning," a friend wrote in an e-mail to me last spring. "I borrowed a friend's cabin for a week's vacation in the mountains, but I needed to wake up early to take a phone meeting. There's no alarm clock here, so I decided to try the alarm function on my iPod. I set it to wake me up with a randomly selected tune, thinking I'd get going the next day with Joan Osborne or maybe Elvis Costello. Instead, the first song I heard was my own teenage daughter, Jocelyn, singing a bluesy version of 'Summertime' with her high school jazz combo—a recording we'd made at her recital the year before. I can't tell you how happy it made me to wake up to her voice, now that she's away at college. I lay there in bed for the entire three minutes, looking out the window at the beautiful view while listening to the way Jocelyn phrased each line, remembering how happy she was performing and how proud of her we were, and also letting the song's lyrics take me back to memories of our summers together as a family. When it ended, I turned off the music and just listened for a minute to the birds singing and the wind rustling in the leaves. I can't tell you what a good mood it put me in, Don. I may start doing this every day!"

I had to laugh, reading her words—knowing how much this type A friend of mine, a big-city reporter, depends on her morning routine of competing high-volume radio and TV news and traffic reports, ringing telephones, multiple cups of coffee, a hasty conversation with her husband as he loads the dishwasher and switches it on, and five minutes' play with her yapping fox terrier before she even gets out the door and off to work. For the first time in years—perhaps for the first time since she had left college and started her first full-time job—she had experienced an entirely different kind of "sound overture," and a floodgate of joyful emotions had briefly opened for her as a result. If only she would pause and consider how she might redesign her entire sound environment, I reflected, her fleeting good mood might deepen into a more lasting condition of decreased stress, increased optimism, and better overall health.

What are the first sounds you hear in the morning, before you open your eyes? The loud, insistent beep of an alarm clock? The voice of a news announcer or loud rock music on your radio? The "noise alarm" of a crying baby or honking horns and other traffic noise outside your window? Or are you one of the lucky ones who awakens to just the simple sounds of nature—wind rustling in the trees, a rushing brook, the singing of birds tuning up like an orchestra before the great symphony of your day?

The first moment of awakening is brief, but it's important. What you hear influences your mood, alertness, energy level, and thus your behavior more directly and more profoundly than you may realize. Not only does each particular sound element create an impact, but the ratio of noise to organized sound, the layering of multiple sound sources, and the combined decibel level of all the sounds that greet you can all have a dramatically positive or negative effect. This effect can linger. As with a bell struck by its clapper, the effects of these sounds can resonate throughout your day.

Sound is vibration. It has the power to affect us literally from the atoms up. Certain sounds, provided in the right context and combinations, can organize our neural activity, stimulate our bodies, retune our emotions, and thus allow us to begin our day in a calmer, more productive emotional state.

www.HealingAtTheSpeedOfSound.com/Link2

For centuries, the organizing effects of sound and vibration on matter have fascinated scientists, from Galileo Galilei in the 1600s to the twentieth-century Swiss physician Hans Jenny, who dubbed the phenomenon "cymatics." Here, you can see for yourself sound's power to organize grains of sand scattered randomly across a flat surface. If sound has this effect on the material world around you, imagine how it can affect your body and brain.

Your brain responds to this vibration in extraordinarily rich, complex ways. Once the sound travels through your ear, where it is translated into nerve impulses that then pass to the hearing center of your brain, different neural regions respond to different properties of the sound, just as numerous instruments in an orchestra interpret different parts of a symphony.[1] The right side of your auditory cortex perceives the sound's pitch and certain aspects of melody, harmony, timbre, and rhythm.[2] The left side responds to rapid changes in the frequency and intensity.[3] The surface of the cortex responds to low frequencies, while higher frequencies move deeper inside, close to the center of the brain.[4] The association cortex compares the sound with past memories, looking for a match, while your brain's language centers—Broca's and Wernicke's areas—process any words the sound contains.

The brain then mirrors what it has perceived. Researchers at the Neurosciences Institute, in La Jolla, California, have observed in real time the way brain-wave patterns change to match changing pitches of tone sequences. When the tone sequence grows more coherent—sounding more like a real melody—different parts of the brain interact in a more intense and consistent, or coherent, manner.[5] Scientists at Stanford University have recorded a similar mirroring response to the moments of musical transition in symphonies as one melodic theme evolves into another.

This mirroring phenomenon may be the reason why you don't just perceive, but actively *experience* sound in so many ways. As you listen to music with a strong beat, the region in the brain that controls movement sends sympathetic impulses through your entire body—you want to move. The association cortex not only compares the sound with similar patterns, but actively sparks emotional associations and ideas. Confronted with disorganized sound—traffic noise, a baby crying—your brain creates a stress response that can include a rise in blood pressure and shallow breathing. Pleasant sounds, such as a favorite song or the voice of a loved one, lead to an increase in the level of dopamine in the brain—a response similar to that stimulated by food or sex. Sad songs, such as ABBA's "The Winner Takes It All," can make us feel good in a different way, as the brain responds with a dose of the comfort hormone prolactin—the same hormone that's released when mothers nurse their babies.[6]

Your responses to certain sounds may well be visceral and profound, but they will not always be the same. The effects will depend on your level of attention, the sound's volume, how many other sounds are competing with it within the environment, as well as a phenomenon called habituation—the tendency for a sound's effects on an individual to decrease over time. Habituation can be a good thing, as when you cease to consciously hear the airplanes that fly over your office building many times per day. It can be a bad thing when you stop "hearing" the alternative rock music you were enjoying for the past hour and then can't figure out why it's so hard to understand someone who's talking to you over the phone. Throughout this and later chapters, you will learn how to consider all of these variables when creating your own daily symphony of healthy sound.

Design Your Own "Sound Breakfast"

Sound's personal connection to each human being, as it occurs in particular environments and stimulates unique memories and mental, physiological, and emotional responses, means that no one-size-fits-all prescription exists for a healthy and effective wake-up call. The choice is as varied as the number of individuals on earth. Many people love to wake up to the real or recorded sounds of nature, for example—yet one well-known New York wit has been known to complain that he can't sleep when he's in the country because, to him, a babbling brook "sounds like a subway train entering the station."[7] A friend of mine in Colorado swears by her Zen alarm clock, which brings her into consciousness with a quiet, repeated *ping*; another friend from Texas rises each morning to the sonic challenge of the Aggie fight song that fills him with happy memories of his alma mater and the rush of adrenaline that goes with them.

Whatever works best for you *is* best. The important thing is to choose your sonic nutrition consciously, with your own and your family's best interests in mind. Earlier, I asked you to consider the first sounds you hear in the morning, before you open your eyes. Now ask yourself how well those sounds serve you as you begin your day. Do the clock-radio news reports of auto accidents and terrorist threats depress you even before you climb out of bed and fumble for your robe? If so, perhaps a morning dose of upbeat pop music would improve your mood. Does the loud buzz of an alarm clock frequently jolt you out of a deep, restful sleep, putting you on edge for the rest of the day? Perhaps you'd do better with a soft, gradually increasing chime alarm, or a clock radio with multiple snooze buttons. Are your infant's morning cries about to make you tear your hair out? Waking up to lullabies might soothe your own nerves and then lull your baby back to sleep as you start to comfort her. If you are a morning person or a light sleeper who wakens easily, recorded nature sounds—birdsong, rushing streams, thunderstorms, and so on—may be all you need to recharge you for the day ahead.

Those who need something a little more insistent to lure them out from under the covers might try some stronger, highly structured music, such as Rachmaninoff's lively "Rhapsody on a Theme of Paganini," the Andrews Sisters' "Boogie Woogie Bugle Boy," some lively Brazilian bossa nova, or even the lively beat of drum corps music. If it makes your feet want to move, you'll know you've found the right sound.

www.HealingAtTheSpeedOfSound.com/Link3
(Free Download No. 1)

For the reluctant riser, this bright, uplifting version of a Bach badinerie, performed by the Arcangelos Chamber Ensemble under the music direction of Richard Lawrence, may provide the perfect dose of sonic caffeine.

www.HealingAtTheSpeedOfSound.com/Link4
(Free Download No. 2)

If Bach provides too strong a charge for a weekend wakening, let Christina Tourin's artistry bring you to awareness with this fine recording of "Morning Has Broken" on the Irish harp.

Classical or baroque music makes for a great start to the day for anyone in the creative, academic, or other intellectually oriented fields who likes the idea of supercharging his or her brain even while getting out of bed in the morning, as Johann Sebastian Bach demonstrated with his "Coffee Cantata" more than two centuries ago. Whatever your feelings about the music of Mozart, Bach, and Telemann in other contexts, the fact is that the brain loves its complex structure and symmetrical architecture, which have a demonstrable positive effect on brain activity, cognition, and behavior. In follow-up studies to the groundbreaking Mozart Effect work of Fran Rauscher and other neuroscientists at the University of Wisconsin, Oshkosh, and the University of California, Irvine, researchers at the Osaka University Graduate School of Medicine have found that exposure to Mozart's sonatas improves performance on intelligence tests via an apparent priming effect of the brain.[8] Rauscher herself, collaborating with Stanford University geneticist Hong Hua Li, has found what she believes is a molecular basis of this priming effect: the expression of higher levels of several genes involved in stimulating and changing the connections between brain cells, which in turn leads to improved performance on learning and memory tests.[9]

All music—rock, folk, country, hip-hop, heavy metal, and every other form—has its place in our lives and its appropriate function. But it's important to understand that one reason why classical music has survived through the ages is because, often, its structure helps prime our brains.

Sound Break: Prescription for a Perfect Wake-Up

If You Are	*Try Waking To*
A light sleeper	Recorded nature sounds
A heavy sleeper	Marches, drum corps music, or Strauss waltzes
A new parent	Lullabies to ease both you and baby into the day
A sleepy student	Any selection from the Buena Vista Social Club
A city resident	Bossa nova, Latin jazz
Looking forward to a relaxed morning	American Indian flute music
Looking forward to a busy day	Any selection from Harry Connick Jr.
An information lover	National Public Radio

In the end, the choice of how to begin your day lies in thinking honestly about what makes you happier, more alert, and better prepared to meet the challenges ahead, and then making the simple changes in your soundscape necessary to achieve that goal. Starting your day consciously is a skill, an art. It's not something you do just once, but a habit that you must form for the rest of your life. By changing the way you start your day, you change all your days.

Once you have accomplished this change for yourself, consider how your other family members might do the same. Remember, each individual has his or her own sound requirements and preferences that may not resemble yours. Respect your spouse's or partner's need for a gentler entry into the day by resetting the alarm to a classical music station and leaving the door closed when you leave the bedroom. Keep in mind, however, that even if you use and love a quiet Zen alarm, and your toddler does well with a quiet early session with a children's book or music selection, your teenager may need a rock station broadcast loudly from across the room if he wants to get to school on time. Your and your family members' needs are likely to change with the seasons, too. Darker mornings in the winter may require a higher-volume wake-up call, or more sessions with the snooze button.

Move to the Beat

Now that you're up and out of bed, it's time to get the blood circulating through body and brain. A morning exercise routine is a great way to lift your mood and increase your productivity throughout the day—and as we've already seen, music makes the body want to move. Aside from songbirds, humans are the only creatures that automatically feel the beat of a song, according to Nina Kraus, a professor of neurobiology at Northwestern University.[10] Music entrains our bodies—physically by activating the muscle-control centers of our brains that get us moving to the rhythm, and emotionally by guiding our moods into synchronicity with its own tone.

www.HealingAtTheSpeedOfSound.com/Link5

If you've ever doubted music's ability to entrain the body, bringing it into the beat, watch how Snowball the cockatoo responds to the music of the Backstreet Boys.

Music entrains not just the larger muscles in your body—studies have shown that it affects your heartbeat and breathing rate as well, resulting in lower blood pressure, more efficient oxygen consumption, and a healthier, more productive workout session at the gym. Researchers have demonstrated that the hearts of people exercising on a treadmill work less hard when music is played than when exercising in silence, and that cyclists riding stationary bicycles use seven percent less oxygen when pedaling to music than when not working out to the beat.[11] As a result of this greater efficiency, they are able to prolong their exercise sessions and improve endurance.

Besides setting the pace, your favorite workout tunes engage your attention, distracting you from the strenuous effort of the workout. Music occupies the mind, freeing the body to do its work, as was proven in a 2009 study in which basketball players prone to performing poorly under pressure improved their free-throw scores significantly when they first redirected their attention to the upbeat music and amusing lyrics of Monty Python's "Always Look on the Bright Side of Life."[12] At the same time, music you love releases pleasure-giving endorphins, which, combined with other biochemical reactions caused by your increased heart rate and breathing, drive you to work harder and to prolong your routine.

Classical, rock, country—any style of music you enjoy is fine for a workout, as long as its underlying characteristics suit the form of exercise in which you are engaged. An aerobic workout functions best when accompanied by music with a stimulating tempo, such as techno, rap, hard rock, or even punk. (College students recommend, for example, the music of Disturbed, Limp Bizkit, Fort Minor and its deep bass beat, and Panic! at the Disco's first album *A Fever You Can't Sweat Out*.) A tempo of 120 to 140 beats per minute is ideal during the warm-up phase, as it will bring your heart rate up to that target pace and get you revved up for what's to come.[13]

In the workout phase, upbeat music to stimulate adrenaline flow and songs with lyrics to distract your mind from the effort of your muscles will lead to longer, more intense sessions. During the cooldown phase, switch to "mellow, chill music" to bring down your heart rate and calm you for the day ahead.[14] Many people choose a song or two whose mood or lyrics will set the tone, they hope, for the rest of the day.

Sound Break: Pump Up Your Pulse, Not the Volume!

♫ It's a proven fact that you'll get better results from your aerobic routine if you listen to upbeat music with a strong, rhythmic beat. Keep in mind, though, that when you oxygenate the body your ears become more sensitive. It's fine to start your routine with the music turned up, but lower the volume after a few minutes and focus on the rhythm instead. Eventually, you may be able to put the power of habituation to use in protecting your hearing. After a month of exercising to the same music playlist, you may find that you have internalized the music and can exercise to silence, with the music running through your head.

Bicyclists and runners find music with a brisk tempo—whether it's aggressive with strong lyrics or mellower in mood—ideal for their workouts as well. (Queen, Madonna, and the Red Hot Chili Peppers are popular among treadmill runners, while hard-core cyclists like to pedal double-time to Salt-n-Pepa and Run-DMC.[15]) The importance of a fast tempo was demonstrated in a 2009 British study in which college students were asked to ride stationary bicycles for three thirty-minute sessions while listening to popular music of their choosing. Although the college students were unaware that the researchers had slowed down the tempo of their recorded music by ten percent in one session, sped it up ten percent in another, and kept it at the normal tempo in the third, their performance decreased significantly when the music was slowed. When the tempo was increased their heart rates rose, they covered more miles, produced more power with each pedal stroke, increased their cycling pace, and reported enjoying the music much more. They knew the workout had been harder, they reported later—the music hadn't masked the pain—but the increased pace had increased their motivation, making them more willing to push themselves.[16]

This effect is strongest during the first part of your routine, as you're getting up to speed. According to a 2009 review of research conducted by music-and-exercise experts Costas Karageorghis and David-Lee Priest, once your run reaches an intense level—say, ninety percent of your maximal oxygen uptake—your fatigue and other physical perceptions start to override music's ability to distract you, and your heart rate and pace level out.[17] Still, one recent study conducted by Karageorghis found that listening to music enhanced treadmill runners' overall endurance by fifteen percent—results sufficiently persuasive to convince the directors of London's 2008 Sony Ericsson Run to the Beat half marathon to allow the researcher to set up seventeen live bands, playing music he had selected, to push the runners to the limit all along the marathon's route. Aside from the endurance issue, many runners tell researchers that they simply like listening to music because it "sounds nice."[18]

Sound Profile: Trevor Hoffman

♫ If I were to choose one man as a symbol of music's power to motivate the athlete, it would have to be Trevor Hoffman, former pitcher for the San Diego Padres and Major League Baseball's all-time leader in saves. Hoffman became so well known for psyching himself up for a game by listening to the AC/DC song "Hell's Bells" that the song became a kind of calling card for him, its "death-march bells" played over stadium loudspeakers "at about a gazillion decibels," according to a report in the *San Diego Union-Tribune*, as he walked out onto a field.[19] That kind of entrance may have seemed "more suited to the World Wrestling Federation than the national pastime," as a *San Diego Union-Tribune* reporter wrote in 1998.[20] Still, the pounding, heavy-metal melody, with lyrics screaming about sending victims down below, invariably brings the fans to their feet, convincing them along with Hoffman that they're there to bury the other side. As one observer put it recently, this kind of music-generated euphoria "is what Trevor Time is all about."[21] Thanks to Hoffman's example, other closers in baseball, including Mariano Rivera and Billy Wagner, have adopted their own rousing theme songs as well.

For strength-training routines at the gym or at home, hard rock or other upbeat music with a strong beat is best. Weight lifters are probably right to insist that hard-driving music such as heavy metal[22] works best for them as a motivator, particularly since slow, sedative tunes have been shown to actually decrease individuals' muscular fitness potential over time.[23] But caution—if it is too loud, it may also decrease the effectiveness of your workout, since prolonged exposure to loud sounds has also been shown to weaken the muscles.

www.HealingAtTheSpeedOfSound.com/Link6
(Free Download No. 3)

With "Up to Stay," from the album *One Heart Wild*, courtesy of Silver Wave Records, Danny Heines's marvelous jazz guitar gets us up and moving for three and a half minutes, without overpowering us.

There is, of course, a place for gentler music in the realm of exercise. Stretching or yoga routines work best with soft, contemplative music (try your favorite New Age music or selections by Enya) or recorded nature sounds, which set the stage for the appropriate meditative mood and flow.

www.HealingAtTheSpeedOfSound.com/Link7
www.HealingAtTheSpeedOfSound.com/Link8
www.HealingAtTheSpeedOfSound.com/Link9

The Beat of Your Own Drummer

When choosing the best music for an exercise routine, the number of beats per minute in a song you select is more important than its genre or style, since your heart rate will speed up or slow down to match the music's pulse. Some online music stores, such as Power Music (link 7, above) and Yes! Fitness Music (link 8), offer preassembled playlists of songs suitably paced for aerobics, step classes, cycling, yoga, and other types of fitness routines—or allow you to create your own custom mix of selections at the tempo you need. But you probably don't need to buy new music to create an excellent playlist. Dj BPM Studio (link 9) provides an extensive list of popular songs organized by beats-per-minute, free of charge. By consulting the list, you can assemble your own exercise music from selections you already own, at precisely the pace you need.

If you are unaccustomed to or simply not interested at this time in initiating a full-out morning exercise routine, consider this enjoyable alternative for getting the pulse racing and the adrenaline flowing for the day: Put on some music by Beethoven or John Philip Sousa and actively "conduct" it, using your whole body to actively shape, sculpt, and blend the music. If you prefer rock 'n' roll, you can benefit from much the same body-mind aerobic action with thirty minutes of *Guitar Hero*, *Rock Band*, or air guitar played along with your favorite band.

Sound Mind, Sound Body, Sound Home

Awake and fully energized, you can now begin your day with new awareness—hearing sounds, perhaps, that you haven't been conscious of for years. As you shower and dress, prepare breakfast, feed the pets, and gather with your loved ones around the breakfast table, pay attention to the quality of sound vibrations reaching your ears in each room of your home. In the bathroom, does the faucet drip or do the pipes run, creating an annoying dissonance that interrupts your thoughts? Does an electric toothbrush or shaver send low-pitched sonic vibrations through your bones? Are your ears assaulted by the noise of a hair dryer? In the living room, is a radiator hissing or a humidifier emitting a low rumble or hum? Is the television on? In the laundry room, is the low thrum of the washer or dryer tugging your spirits down? What about the kitchen? Do you hear the high-pitched grinding of the dishwasher? The refrigerator condenser clicking on and off? Does the coffee grinder offend your ears as you make your morning beverage, and the coffeemaker grumble and moan?

As the household begins to stir, how often does the telephone ring? Is loud rap music emanating from your teenager's room? Do the kids shout to each other from room to room, or do they make the effort to talk face-to-face? How much noise is coming in through the windows? Do you hear the neighbor's lawnmower, or dogs barking, or a garbage truck, or airplanes passing overhead?

So many of these aural influences affect our mood without our realizing it. When sounds are layered one over the other, their decibels combining and their sound waves colliding, we can start to grind our teeth, snap at our partners, and lose our tempers without even knowing why. I recall one friend's story of a week when his young child was ill and he had to stay home with him, trying to fit in some work on his laptop at the dining table whenever he had a chance. "I tried to concentrate on the proposal I was writing, but I kept getting more and more irritated, even angry, and unable to concentrate," he said. "At one point, just when I was trying to tune up a particularly troublesome paragraph, Davey called out from his room that he thought he was going to throw up. I slammed down the materials I was going through and ran into the bedroom, only to find him vomiting all over his blankets and pajamas. I'm ashamed to say it, but I completely lost control. I yelled at him for something he obviously couldn't help, and jerked the covers off his bed and pushed him into some clean clothes. Afterward, horrified and ashamed, I apologized to him and went back into the dining room. I stood there for a second and really listened. There was an incredible level of noise in that room: the banging of the dryer from down the hall, the screeching dishwasher in the kitchen, a motorcyclist revving his engine over and over, and a dog that had been barking down the street for what seemed like hours without my consciously noticing it. I'm not excusing my behavior, but the thought did cross my mind: No wonder I blew up! We already have a smoke alarm and a carbon-dioxide warning device in this house, but what I really think we need is a noise alarm."

My friend hit the nail on the head with that last remark. It is astonishing how much noise most of us tolerate in today's world, when the very definition of the word *noise*, according to K. D. Kryter, author of *The Handbook of Hearing and the Effects of Noise*, is "acoustic signals which can negatively affect the physiological or psychological well-being of an individual."[24] Described as the most pervasive pollutant in America, noise presents a significant threat to human health. Not only can it affect your hearing, but at certain levels it can increase blood pressure, change the way your heart beats, increase your breathing rate, disturb your digestion, contribute to the development of ulcers, interfere with sleep even after the noise stops, intensify the effects of drugs and alcohol, speed up the appearance of signs of aging, and affect the fetuses of pregnant women, possibly even contributing to premature birth.[25]

It is no wonder, as George Prochnik points out in his book *In Pursuit of Silence*, that police officers such as John Spencer, of Washington, D.C., claim that the majority of domestic disputes they encounter are actually noise complaints. "You go into these houses where the couple, or the roommate, or the whole family is fighting and yelling and you've got the television blaring so you can't think, and a radio on top of that. . . . They're fighting about the noise. They don't know it, but that's the problem."[26]

In general, the louder and more prolonged the noise, the more harmful it is to your ears—the sound waves damage the tiny, delicate hair cells, or cilia, in the inner ear—not to mention your sense of well-being. Most people know that noise levels are measured in decibels (dB), and that the higher the decibel level, the louder the noise. What you may not know is that decibel numbers increase *logarithmically*—that is, a noise level of sixty decibels (the loudness level of laughter) is ten times as loud as fifty (the sound of rainfall or of normal conversation). As a result, decibel readings indicate an unsafe level of noise much more quickly than most people realize.

The cilia in the inner ear can be damaged by a brief, intense, very loud impulse, such as an explosion. Continuous and/or repeated exposure to noise above eighty-five decibels can also cause gradual hearing loss—and regular exposure of more than *one minute* of noise above 110 decibels risks permanent damage.[27] Some people assume that once they adapt or are habituated to dangerously loud noise it will no longer harm them. It's easy to believe this, as noise-induced hearing loss is usually gradual and painless. But your assumption that you have adapted to the earsplitting noise of the coffee grinder in your kitchen is more likely an indication that your hearing has already diminished.

Below, I have provided a list of decibel levels for sounds to which we are often exposed in and around our homes. However, since we can't all carry around decibel readers and unfortunately we don't have those noise alarms wished for by my friend, keep in mind the general rule that a particular noise level is potentially hazardous if you must raise your voice to be heard, if you can't hear someone two feet away from you, if the speech of people around you sounds muffled or dull, or if you have pain or ringing in your ears after you leave the noisy area.

HOW LOUD IS IT?

This noise chart gives an idea of average decibel levels for everyday sounds in your home environment.[28]

Decibel Level	*What We Hear*
10 dB	Normal breathing
40 dB	Refrigerator humming
50–60 dB	Moderate rainfall
60–65 dB	Laughter
65–75 dB	Dishwasher
70 dB	Vacuum cleaner, hair dryer
78 dB	Washing machine
70–80 dB	Busy traffic
80 dB	Garbage disposal, alarm clock
85–90 dB	Lawnmower, motorcycle
98 dB	Farm tractor
100 dB	Train, garbage truck
103 dB	Jet flyover at 100 feet
110 dB	Jackhammer, power saw
120 dB	Jet plane take-off, band practice
145 dB	Boom cars

I hope I have increased your awareness of the deleterious effects of unwanted noise. The next step is to use this information to consciously reshape your sound environment, beginning inside your home. I have asked that you listen to the many sounds within each room in your house or apartment. Now take a moment to rate the sound condition of each of your rooms in terms of how noisy it seems to you. Since noise is defined as any sound that negatively affects the physiological or psychological well-being of an individual, I want you to think a little less in terms of volume this time and more in terms of "annoyance factor." The satellite radio jazz channel playing in the living room may be turned up too loud, for example, but it's probably less irritating than the sound of your two kids arguing in the bathroom over who used all the hair gel.

There's a reason why your ears perceive the sound of people arguing as "empty" and disruptive, while a classical sonata sounds clear and serene. Empty sound—the noise of a coffee grinder or of traffic outside—consists of a chaotic pattern of sound waves that, when interacting with your auditory system, cause your brain and body to respond in chaotic ways. Empty sounds are like empty calories: They just do not nourish. Uncluttered sound, on the other hand—such as slow classical music or a calm, quiet human voice—forms a regular and coherent sound-wave pattern, which your brain also reflects. Of course, no matter how coherent sound waves are when they are emitted, they can collide with others when combined in a contained space, creating a new, chaotic pattern that increases our stress level even when we are consciously unaware that it is there.

Decreasing empty sound, or noise, can often be a simple, commonsensical process once the sounds' sources have been identified. Turn off the television. Wait to start the dishwasher until you are about to leave the house, or at least the kitchen. Fix the dripping faucet in the bathroom. When you are blow-drying your hair, hold the dryer farther away and aim at the back of your head, *not* toward your ear. Consider using earplugs to protect your hearing. When buying a new hair dryer or electric shaver, choose one with a low noise decibel level, or use it at a lower setting.

FIRST STEP TO A SOUND LIFE

How noisy is your daily life? Moving through your home, estimate and circle the sound levels in each area: 1—very quiet; 2—aware of sounds; 3—filled with moderate sounds that include music you have chosen; 4—loud; 5—very loud and annoying. How many 4s and 5s did you discover? Once you know where your sound challenges lie, you can begin to work on getting the "noise numbers" in your life as low as possible.

Area or Sound Source	*Loudness Rating*
Your bedroom	1 2 3 4 5
Other bedrooms	1 2 3 4 5
Bathroom	1 2 3 4 5
Kitchen	1 2 3 4 5
Living room	1 2 3 4 5
Dining room	1 2 3 4 5
Den or recreation room	1 2 3 4 5
Laundry room	1 2 3 4 5
Home office	1 2 3 4 5
Workshop	1 2 3 4 5
Garage	1 2 3 4 5
Plumbing	1 2 3 4 5
Heating/air conditioning	1 2 3 4 5
Outside	1 2 3 4 5
Other	1 2 3 4 5

Once you have decreased the aural chaos, you can begin to create a healthy sound environment by deliberately adding meaningful, coherent sounds throughout your home—sounds that nourish your mind and heart, regulate your body, and bring your family together—much as a composer might create a symphony or a designer might choose color accents for each room.

How can sound help you create a more serene, healthy ambience? Consider these four sonic tools for changing your environment in positive ways:

- Entrainment: The process of modifying brainwaves, breath, movement, emotions, or thoughts by matching the rhythm of an external stimulus, such as music. (Slow music entrains your pulse to a slower rate; chaotic sounds entrain your emotions to a higher state of tension.)

- Iso-Principle: The process of moving gradually from one tempo or level of intensity to another, either within a single musical selection in just a few minutes' time or over the course of an hour or so as one listens to a playlist. By matching a physical rhythm or emotional state and then slowing down or speeding up, music provides a comfortable bridge to a modified state. (The song "Happy Birthday to You" slows down at the end, broadening the sense of general goodwill. "Bolero" gradually intensifies over time, keying up the emotional state of the listener.)

- Masking: The process of using sound to cover up other sounds that are disturbing. (You may not be able to abolish the traffic noise outside your window, but you can mask it with a sprightly Bach concerto.)

- Diversion: Using music to get the mind onto a completely different track. (Instead of sulking because your partner went off to work and left you to do the dishes, put on some lively pop music and dance your way through that unpleasant chore.)

Consider the ways you can use each of these tools to improve your own and your loved ones' lives at home. In the living room, you might *mask* the dispiriting clank of the radiator with some tinkling chimes positioned in the opposite corner of the room. In the bathroom, you could *divert* attention from the everyday sounds of splashing and brushing by opening the window to the breeze and the birds. As your overly energized partner bounds through the house, smartphone in hand, you could employ the *iso-principle* to calm him down a bit with a playlist beginning with Duke Ellington's "Take the 'A' Train" and ending with Miles Davis's "Kind of Blue." And as the family gathers around the breakfast table, put the power of *entrainment* to use by playing some soft, energetic music—a little Herbie Hancock, perhaps, if you're a jazz fan—to stimulate conversation, lift moods, and reinforce family connections before you all disperse for the day.

Even if you are the only human occupying your home, entrainment might come in handy for other living beings around you. It's useful to know that according to some animal experts, pets' moods lift just like humans' when listening to happy, upbeat songs. (Just be sure the lyrics don't include a clearly voiced "no," one expert tells us, or your pet will just shut down!)[29]

www.HealingAtTheSpeedOfSound.com/Link10

In this TED talk, sound consultant Julian Treasure explores ways to turn down the volume and restore your relationship with sound.

The Harmony of the Hemispheres

It can be quite enjoyable to tweak the sound cues and rearrange the sonic cushions throughout your home, observing the impact of these changes on yourself and others. But it's important to remember the need for sound privacy as well as conviviality within the domestic sphere. If you share your home with others—family members, roommates, or anyone else—try to make room for thirty minutes of quiet time before you leave the house for the day, and encourage others to do the same.

If you're lucky, you can retreat to a room of your own, shut the door, and put on some quietly invigorating instrumental music while you check your e-mail or read the paper. If that's not possible, you can still create your own private sound environment by investing in a pair of high-quality headphones for use at your computer or in a quiet corner armchair. Think about the activities ahead of you that day and choose a private playlist that will charge you up for whatever challenges you face. If you didn't sleep well but are facing an important meeting this morning, fast-tempo, high-frequency music (Chuck Berry or Aretha Franklin, anyone?) will provide you with a dose of sonic caffeine. If you need to draw on your creative skills today, spend this time with classical music, such as Handel's Oboe Concerto no. 3 in G Minor, and let its beautiful architecture "organize" your brain. Baroque music, such as the first movement of Bach's Brandenburg Concerto no. 3 in G Major, can energize you both physically and mentally, its faster tempo activating the most alert (beta wave) brain state, its bright tonal qualities enabling you to work, study, think, and maintain a positive, productive attitude. If you anticipate a stressful encounter today—with an angry boss, an ex-spouse, a financial auditor—put on the headphones, close your eyes, and listen to some soothing, reassuring folk music, Brahms, or a round of early Beatles tunes.

I find the music from Trent Reznor and Atticus Ross's 2011 Academy Award–winning soundtrack of *The Social Network* most interesting for this purpose. Each piece presents a different mood—great calm, peace of mind, frenetic, geeky, high energy, and so on. You can sample each of the tracks on the soundtrack album's page on Amazon.com. Sense the different moods and tension immediately through the dichotomy of electronic, yet organic, music.

Whatever your need, there is an appropriate sound to meet it. If you like, you can amplify and enhance its effects by listening on bone-conducting headphones. These headphones, designed for use with personal music devices and now easily available in electronics stores and via the Internet, deliver the sound's healing vibrations directly through the bones of the skull, adding subtle vibration to the skin and skeletal system and engaging the whole body with the sound. (The speed of sound varies with temperature, humidity, and altitude. The higher the temperature, the faster the sound waves propagate.)

www.HealingAtTheSpeedOfSound.com/Link11

Hum Your Way to Harmony

Even without bone-conducting headphones, you can give yourself some bone-conduction stimulation by humming a little every day. As I demonstrate in this video, humming in the proper position causes your whole body to resonate, especially the bones of your skull and spine. As you hum, the vibration through your skeletal system combines with your slow, deep intake and outflow of breath to revitalize you. By performing this exercise just five to ten minutes at the start of each day, you will not only find that you experience increased energy, but the quality of your voice will improve as well, becoming richer and more resonant as more of your body participates in vocal expression.

An advantage of headphones is that you are still available to your family or housemates, if necessary, while you are using them. You might take advantage of this situation to end your private time with a brief period of silence. With all the talk about the healing power of sound, it's important to remember that silent periods are equally necessary—that they fortify, soothe, and recharge the mind and body in their own way as well. A five-minute time-out allows you to organize your thoughts, review and process recent conversations and events, and meditate briefly on what's really important for you to pay attention to today, rather than focusing only on what others demand of you. Experiencing silence also reawakens your awareness of the noise around you at other times. This is why the Center for Hearing and Communication has instituted a minute of silence—a Quiet Diet—from 2:15 to 2:16 on the afternoon of their annual International Noise Awareness Day.[30]

With a Song in Your Heart

Wake-up call, moving to music, a soundscaped home, a private moment with or without sound—by the time you go out the door, you will have created a morning prelude to your day, perfectly suited to your own tastes and needs. Raising your awareness of the sound around you, and redesigning your sound experience as you begin your morning, will not just enhance those hours as you are experiencing them, but will extend through the day as you go off to work with a clear mind, tempered body, and a mood improved by more pleasant interactions with your loved ones.

As you continue your new sound routine each morning through the weeks to come—as the "habit of beauty" becomes a part of your routine—you are likely to find that your overall attitude and your life are improving as a whole. The British newspaper columnist Simon Jenkins put it best when he described the part of the brain that recognizes sound as a field of neurons arranged like rows of growing stalks of corn. "The music drifts across it in a breeze, leaving its indent on the corn," he wrote. "The deeper the indent the easier it is for the same breeze to follow it a second time, while the deeper the indent, the closer it is to the soil where it agitates the pleasurable endorphins."[31] With repetition, your morning ritual of sound and music, contemplation and exercise, song and conversation, will become an integral part of your sense of self, adding depth, meaning, and precious memories to your mornings, and bringing you to a healthier life.

CHAPTER TWO

Out in the World

Sound in Public and in the Workplace

There is music in the air, music all around us; the world is full of it, and you simply take as much as you require.

—Sir Edward Elgar

"SILENCE, SILENCE: in a thousand senses I proclaim the indispensable worth of Silence,"[1] scribbled the Scottish historian Thomas Carlyle in frustration 170 years ago. Carlyle had been pleased to join a new wave of Victorian-era professionals choosing to work at home, but as a writer with a high sensitivity to noise, he found it impossible to concentrate with the cacophony of clattering carriages and chattering pedestrians outside his study in London. A plague of street musicians caused particular distress as they roved the residential lanes, grinding organs outside the windows of chosen victims until they were paid to wander elsewhere. The last straw came when Carlyle's neighbor chose to acquire a flock of fashionable Cochin China chickens,[2] whose clucking and crowing drove the writer nearly mad. "All summer I have been more or less annoyed with *noises*," he complained to a friend.[3] In such a "dizzy, scatterbrain atmosphere,"[4] how could he possibly complete his biography of Frederick the Great?

When threats to assassinate the "vile" organ-grinders and "Demon Fowls"[5] went unheeded, the furious Scot decided to create his own solution by commissioning a special attic workspace—a "SOUNDLESS ROOM!" where "the world, which can do me no good, shall at least not torment me."[6] After spending a fortune soundproofing the study with double walls and sound-muffling air chambers beneath the slate roof—and seething over the clatter of the laborers and craftsmen—Carlyle found the results disappointing. Noise continued to filter in and interrupt his thoughts, yet the room was so tightly sealed that when he closed himself inside for a smoke he soon passed out from lack of air and was only discovered by a housemaid in the nick of time, "senseless upon the floor."[7]

Today, living in a world much noisier than Carlyle's, most of us can sympathize with his longing for total silence—the only condition in which he felt he could fully concentrate. But others are less distracted by ambient sound and may even prefer a little background activity to keep their minds alert. (It's interesting to note that Carlyle's wife, Jane Welsh, counted herself among this latter group, writing in surprise about the noisy renovations, "It is amazing how little I care about it. Nay in superintending all these men I begin to find myself in the career open to my particular talents."[8]) Whatever your current feelings about the sonic state of your workplace—a world in which you no doubt spend a large proportion of your time—you will find that the sound-management tools here improve its quality. You may be surprised by how effectively a well-designed soundscape can decrease fatigue, increase productivity, put clients at ease, improve your own and others' morale and workplace communication, and protect your health and hearing.

First, though, let's consider how best to navigate the ocean of sound that, for most of us, separates home and the workplace, in order to end our commute in the same relaxed, invigorated state of mind as when we exited our front door.

A Sound Transition

"I love my drive to and from the city each day," Karen, an associate, tells me. "I spend my days at the office surrounded by people and my mornings and evenings surrounded by my family. I love them all, of course, but so often that hour in the car is the only time I have to myself. After I drop the kids off at school, I flip on the radio, listen to my favorite jazz programs, mull over the issues that have come up in the family, review what

I want to accomplish at work, and kind of take stock of where I am in my life and where I want to go. The car becomes my oasis. When traffic is stalled, that's a bonus as far as I'm concerned—it means more time for me. I just sing along with the radio until traffic starts again. Those private singing sessions are some of the best times I've ever spent alone."

Not all of us are able to put up with the chaos and delays of commuting with Karen's degree of equanimity. But many, if pressed, would admit that we sometimes enjoy the period of transition, when nothing is expected of us but to get from one place to another and we can amuse ourselves however we see fit. Far from a tiresome chore to be accomplished every day, your commute, like Karen's, can become a welcome opportunity to relax your mind, consider the big picture, and recharge before you face the workplace or return home. The sound tools you learned to use in chapter one—masking, diversion, entrainment, and iso-principle—can help to facilitate this process.

Sound Break: Earbook

♫ Although much of the discussion in this chapter concerns music and how it can be used to counter the effects of noise, audiobooks are certainly worth considering for your commute as well. Many of us, lacking the time we would like to settle down with a good narrative at home, have come to treasure our literary intervals on the daily commute. Whether you prefer motivational treatises, historical or scientific ventures into the unknown, a suspenseful mystery, or a literary novel, an audiobook can stimulate your imagination and provide insight into your work world even before you walk through the door.

Your first commuting concern is likely to be protection from noise—an unwelcome intrusion that can so easily disrupt the sense of well-being you established at home. Noise can range from the annoying (a wailing baby on the bus) to the outright damaging (the 90-decibel screech of an approaching subway train) or, even worse, the 145-decibel "boom car" sitting next to you at a traffic light. When not driving, your best defense is to cancel out the chaos reaching your ears with noise-reduction headphones, earplugs (available in drugstores and sporting goods stores, or custom made through your audiologist), or even earmuffs in cold weather. Absent these, you can mask the noise by playing low, soothing music on your car stereo or on a personal music device with earphones.

www.HealingAtTheSpeedOfSound.com/Link12

How Do the Sounds Around Us Impact Our Lives?
Let me introduce you to the effect of noise on the body and spirit, in this television special originally broadcast on ERBU-TV.

Personal music devices, such as iPods and smartphones, equipped with custom-designed music services such as the iTunes Genius Mix and Pandora, have in fact hugely empowered commuters in creating their own aural universe. No longer is it necessary to play "random radio roulette," flipping from station to station on the radio, hungry for something but not knowing what, in a hunt as frustrating and soul sucking as a late-night search for nutritious food at a gas-station convenience store. Now, with personal music devices, we can prepare our own nutritious "audio snacks."

A first step in this process is to ask yourself which sounds or other irritants on your commute trigger your anxiety or anger, or actually cause physical pain. Horns honking on the highway? The sound of drills and hammering at a construction site? Children shouting on the way to school? Take a moment to list your top ten commuting triggers. Then look at the audio selections on your personal music device and ask yourself, "Is there something here that will divert me from the triggering element so that I can maintain my healthy state of mind?" A highly organized Bach cantata might provide just the counterbalance to a traffic snarl in the city. Simple folk tunes or lullabies, or a children's audiobook, can divert you and a wailing toddler in the backseat at the same time. Some upbeat rock 'n' roll can be just the ticket for riding out a period of stopped traffic on the highway or passing time in the airport until your flight begins boarding.

No matter how frustrating your commuting experience, with headphones or your car stereo, you can entrain yourself to the positive mood of the music you choose, or gradually move yourself, using the iso-principle, from high-speed enervation toward a calmer, more creative mental and emotional state. You can even name each list according to its purpose—"Traffic Jam Jazz," "Summertime, and the Living Is Easy," or "Chill Out."

Again, as with the music you chose to wake and exercise to at home, the musical genres you select are less important than their underlying sonic qualities. Essentially, you want to create music playlists that provide the best "sound mileage" for the energy you expend in listening to them. To this end, it helps to think of different kinds of music as falling into three different gears, like those on a car. Within each gear's range, the music's effects vary depending on the tempo and the volume at which it is played.

- First gear consists of low sounds with a low frequency—like the low rumble of a hot rod. First-gear sounds require a great deal of energy to transmit, and so create huge sound waves. They therefore pack an enormous punch in terms of energy and can travel great distances—think of whales communicating in the ocean. When first-gear sounds are pulsing at high volume—subwoofers in boom cars, for instance—this energy can cause actual pain and can damage the ears. But when played at low volume and slow tempo, under sixty beats per minute—like the music you typically hear during a massage or the low-frequency vibration of the aboriginal didgeridoo—they can soothe, deepen the breath, and calm the mind.

www.HealingAtTheSpeedOfSound.com/Link13

It's no coincidence that didgeridoo music was selected for this meditation video. These first-gear sounds can go a long way toward easing stress and anger during a tense commute.

- Second gear includes mid- and high-frequency sounds with a moderate tempo of fifty to ninety beats per minute. The baroque music of Bach and Vivaldi falls into this category, useful for focusing the mind by entraining the brain waves to an alpha state for optimal attention and learning.

www.HealingAtTheSpeedOfSound.com/Link14

There's something about the "Spring" movement of Vivaldi's *Four Seasons* that invites us into the world of human interaction in a delightful, upbeat, inspiring way.

• Third gear features sounds with a wide frequency range and faster tempos—above ninety beats per minute. Music in this category increases your heart rate and energy level as you listen, and includes the kinds of music you chose to motivate and energize you when exercising.

www.HealingAtTheSpeedOfSound.com/Link15

The fast, rhythmic acoustic guitar of "Juan Loco," by the Mexican duo Rodrigo y Gabriela, will shift you straight into third!

Music of each gear has good and bad applications; each can be useful in the right context. Low-frequency sounds tend to be grounding, for example, while high-frequency sounds energize. Slow tempos calm us, while fast tempos invigorate. Since virtually all musical genres, composers, and bands make use of each of the three gears—and even many single selections, such as George Gershwin's "Rhapsody in Blue" and Led Zeppelin's "Stairway to Heaven," move from one gear to another with ease—all gears are no doubt fully represented in your personal music library. What's important is to use each gear for the appropriate occasion. By choosing your music with an awareness of its frequency, tempo, and volume, you can turn each commute into an opportunity for mental, emotional, and physiological enrichment.

Another word of caution, though, about volume: Keep the music on the moderate or soft side to avoid damaging your hearing. If you are listening to amplified music in a confined space, such as a car, turn down the volume so that the sound waves do not batter your ears.[9] Avoid using cell phones more than necessary: Studies have shown that talking on these phones for more than an hour each day can damage users' hearing thresholds, and that long-term cell phone use may cause inner ear damage that could lead to loss of hearing in the higher frequencies.[10] Personal music devices, listened to through headphones or earbuds, can also easily damage your hearing when the sound is turned up too loud. Experts suggest that, as a good rule of thumb, the volume is too loud if someone three feet away can hear the music from your headphones. If this is the case, turn it down—and don't be afraid to caution others to turn down their devices as well. You're doing them a favor today *and* tomorrow. Music transmitted to the brain via earbuds may be one of the main reasons, as such organizations as the National Institutes of Health report, that hearing loss in our society is appearing much earlier in life than it did just thirty years ago.[11]

Sound Break: Sonic Refuge

♫ Sometimes, the best gift we can give our ears is, simply, silence. If your most treasured time alone occurs on your daily commute, turn off the music or the news for at least five minutes to clear your thoughts and settle your emotions before you arrive at work or at home. If you are on a bus, train, or plane, give your ears a rest and use earplugs for ten minutes. These intervals of silence can become an oasis in your busy schedule—and may even motivate you to make time for two or three more such sessions throughout the day.

Music While You Work

If you are an American factory worker, construction worker, soldier, firefighter, disc jockey, or any one of the nine million people who, according to the United States Environmental Protection Agency, are regularly exposed to hazardous noise levels in the workplace,[12] protecting your ears is a most serious matter. Excessive noise on the job leads to fatigue, stress, and hearing impairment. By increasing blood pressure and levels of adrenaline and cortisol in the bloodstream, it can even lead to death. Chronic exposure to noise above approximately sixty decibels, for example, has been associated with increased heart attacks in men. At work sites where the average noise level is above eighty-five decibels over an eight-hour period, federal Occupational Safety and Health Administration (OSHA) regulations require employers to establish a program protecting employees' hearing. If you suspect that the noise level where you work is above that threshold, and nothing is being done to protect workers' health, you can and should take legal action to redress the situation.[13]

www.HealingAtTheSpeedOfSound.com/Link16

Here, you will find information on OSHA's five-phase hearing protection program and other government regulations protecting workers' sound-related health.

Even outside these work environments where sound's damaging effects are formally recognized and combated, however, noise can become a disruptive element that decreases productivity and threatens your health. Eileen, a former client of mine, once confided to me that it was the noise in her former employer's offices that prompted her to leave and start her own business at home.

"You know the way fluorescent lights sound?" she asked me. "That high whine, combined with the noise of the computers and the sudden clatter of the printer going into action every few minutes, was enough to make me want to leave. I used to get so exhausted, trying to make myself heard over the phone with people chatting by the coffee machine ten feet away—I could never focus, never concentrate. By the end of the day, my vocal cords were shot, and I almost always went home in a bad mood. It's not perfect at home—I still have to put up with traffic and barking dogs—but at least I can control the noise level, most of the time. I just couldn't stand it at that other place."

We aren't all as lucky as Eileen, able to leave an environment we don't like and retreat to the quiet of a home office. Still, considering the negative effects of noise on employee morale, health, and productivity, it's crucial to take what steps we can to improve our sound environment, wherever we work. Putting the printers and copiers in a separate room with a door can make all the difference in a noisy office. Carpets, sound-muffling cubicles, simple sound baffles, or even electronic sound-masking technology can cut the clatter, chatter, and din of the people working around you to a minimum.

Recently, in my work with Aesthetic Audio Systems, I completed an acoustic and environmental sound assessment for a new hospital in California. For the sake of convenience, an ice machine had been placed in every nurse's station in the hospital, creating a horrible hum at all times and an even worse rumbling commotion when it made ice. Only with the removal of the ice machines could the nurses truly relax and focus. The right music wasn't needed in this case—just the absence of those sounds.

Talk with your employer about ways to decrease the noise of equipment or machinery, amplified sound, and other irritants in your workplace. If you own or manage the business yourself, perform a "sound audit" to identify any distracting or harmful noise at the work site. Ask other workers for ideas on altering the soundscape at work to make the environment less stressful and more productive. If your office manager or coworkers prefer the business to sound "busy" (and some do), at the very least you can shield your own ears from noise's harmful effects with noise-reducing headphones or earplugs, just as you do at home and on your commute.

The Cruelest Profession

♫ Ironically, one of the most hazardous professions in terms of hearing loss is that of a musician in a band or orchestra. Rock musician Pete Townshend, of the Who, has frequently pointed out that after years spent standing in front of a giant stack of speakers, "I have terrible hearing trouble. I have unwittingly helped to invent and refine a type of music that makes its principal proponents deaf."[14]

Recently, attempts have been made to address this problem. In 1990, California rock musician Kathy Peck founded Hearing Education and Awareness for Rockers (H.E.A.R.), with a ten thousand–dollar contribution from Townshend, to serve as a clearinghouse for information on the dangers of excessive noise and as a way to provide adequate hearing protection to musicians and music lovers.[15] Meanwhile, the European Union has issued a directive limiting the loudness of symphony orchestras,[16] and a number of orchestra conductors have taken to wearing earplugs during rehearsals and performances, where sounds can exceed government standards by as much as four hundred percent.[17] Transparent plastic barriers are now sometimes used to protect musicians seated in front of the brass and percussion sections, whose explosive sounds can be especially harmful. Yet studies continue to show that too few musicians regularly use hearing protectors, and that a majority suffer from hearing losses of fifteen dB or more.[18]

Productive Sound

Once you have decreased the level of noise at work to the greatest extent possible, it's time to consider the productive ways sound can be used. Throughout history, music has played an important part in helping to get work done—from the sailors' shanties sung in the nineteenth century to improve teamwork aboard ship, to the call-and-response songs African American slaves used to make time pass more quickly, to the BBC Radio's twice-daily *Music While You Work* broadcasts, which greatly increased factory productivity during wartime,[19] to the piped-in pop music that keeps many white- and blue-collar workers moving today.

If you work alone, or with people who are open to the idea and have compatible tastes in music, consider providing a musical soundtrack to increase your own productivity, improve morale, and mask low-level noise. A number of companies now produce such music, professionally designed to suit a variety of company needs. By using your knowledge of sound gears and their effects, you can create your own working soundtracks suited to your own and your fellow workers' tastes and needs.

In an office setting, for example, second-gear music can be used to increase alertness. The tempo should be lively, but not so fast that it demands your attention. Bach's highly organized music would fall into this category, providing a light, invigorating, and not overly emotional sound palette that delights the ears while allowing workers to focus on the task at hand. Keep in mind the danger of habituation: Vary music styles at least every thirty minutes or so, mixing in some light piano jazz and even silence now and then. And keep the volume low. Indoors, music should operate at a nearly subliminal level—loud enough to be heard, but rarely noticed.

Certain genres, which may be fine for private listening, are better avoided in shared environments. Music with a deep pulse or sense of pushing forward, such as heavy metal, punk, or hip-hop, with their pulsing beat and rapid tempo, may irritate even some younger workers and hinder performance. (It's interesting to note one experiment in which mice exposed to ten hours per day of Mozart's music cut the time it took to run a maze by fifteen percent, while mice exposed to ten hours daily of hard rock not only slowed their maze-running time by three hundred percent, but in one case even had to be separated after they began attacking one another in their cage!)[20] Still, there are always exceptions to the assumption that classical is best. Just ask Earl Lucas, chief designer of the 2010 Ford Taurus. While they were working on the project, Lucas's senior designer, Dean Carbus, sketched away to the sounds of trance music and R&B. Instead of ordering him to shut it down, the entire team began to listen to the music, and as a result experienced a newfound freedom in their creative work. "When you've got good music, it's amazing how many shapes come out," Lucas said. "You lose track of time."[21]

Chances are probably better that in your workplace, if one employee likes New Age music, another loathes it with equal passion. You may be able to negotiate such differences in a democratic way by subscribing to such music services as Pandora, the Hype Machine, or Fuzz, which allow listeners to signal their likes and dislikes within a series of songs, thus "teaching" the service to offer more selections in that vein. If this proves impossible, or if you share a workspace with too many employees to find common ground, you may find that worker satisfaction rises when each individual is allowed to listen to music privately.

www.HealingAtTheSpeedOfSound.com/Link17

Read our in-depth discussion of "Music in the Workplace," an overview of the latest research on the topic, to learn more about the ways in which sound can improve employee mood and increase productivity on the job.

Music to Your Ears

Personal music devices have in fact become a common sight in offices, allowing employees to work to their favorite tunes without disturbing coworkers. Recent surveys in the United States and Britain reveal that as many as eighty percent of workers now listen to music[22] for twenty to thirty-six percent of their workday.[23] If some employers regret the use of such devices ("They're pretty much wired into these kids' heads," one Chicago advertising executive lamented),[24] employees themselves claim that music via earphones helps them focus, increases their productivity,[25] improves their mood, and stimulates creativity. A survey of nearly three hundred individuals conducted by researchers at the University of Sheffield's Department of Music, in Great Britain, found this to be true across a wide range of occupations, from administrative assistants to researchers to professional athletes, working in environments ranging from open-plan offices to shared living areas at home.[26]

Listening to music "lets me think, allows me to chill and unwind," reported one administrative assistant. If it's a punk song, "I can imagine all my stresses being screamed out with the song." A project manager claimed that his own choices of music gave him spiritual strength. "It connects me with my creative forces and fulfills a need for deeper experience." A purchasing coordinator said that her music "takes my mind off the things that are really stressing me out—calms me down and clears my mind." And a secretary observed that workday music "makes me more relaxed and puts me in a good mood, which means I am nicer to people, especially on the telephone."[27]

The majority of experiments bear out these observations: One study of fifty-six software designers who claimed that listening to music improved their mood and enhanced their perception while working, for example, showed that without their music they took longer to complete their work and their work quality declined.[28] Personal music devices allow individuals to choose the music that works best for them, no matter how divergent. Some depend on them as a tool for keeping their minds off non–work related events going on in their lives. For example, Peter Hubert, a twenty-eight-year-old draftsman for Bigelow Homes in Aurora, Illinois, listens privately to heavy metal music while drawing his intricate building designs, dismissing the notion that the pulsating rhythm of hard rock intrudes on his work. "It puts my head somewhere else so I can concentrate on what I'm doing," he claims.[29]

Of course, there is a downside to the use of these devices, just as there are positive and negative aspects to nearly every use of sound. In a group setting, personal music players can have an isolating effect. Others in the office may resent having to wave their arms or tap you on the shoulder to get your attention. ("It can infuriate some work colleagues, if they are non-listeners," admits one computer programmer.)[30] The tendency of earphones to "leak" can also irritate colleagues working nearby. ("Overhearing part of someone's music . . . seems to be far more annoying than hearing the whole thing," music psychologist John Sloboda observes.)[31] More profoundly, earphones or headphones can prevent users from being able to participate in work-related discussions and cause them to miss out on opportunities for informal learning. "Often at work, you learn a lot just from the buzz in the office," notes researcher Anneli Haake. "If you close yourself off from it, you can't take part. Being qualified isn't just about having the right education; it's also about communicating within groups and learning from others."[32] One of the workers whom Haake queried in her research, a technical infrastructure specialist, agreed that "I have to be selective about listening to music at work, because I find that I miss out on a lot."[33]

One way to avoid some of these problems is to use the devices no more than about fifteen minutes per hour, and to remove your headphones immediately for conversations and meetings with coworkers. Such precautions are advisable in any case when concentrating on work, and by avoiding habituation you can fully benefit from music's strengths. Many experts, including Illinois-based behavioral psychologist Russell Riendeau, consider music a vital part of most workplaces. Without music, he claims, "you'd probably have an extremely depressed, desensitized, unmotivated, less healthy human being," simply because it helps us feel better.[34]

Sound Break: Earworms

♫ We've all experienced them—those songs that get stuck in our heads, playing over and over and over, refusing to leave. Scientists call these tunes "earworms," and attribute their power to their typically simple verse-chorus structure and their constant repetition in public spaces, in the workplace, or at home. We start to sing along, perhaps not consciously. Our bodies begin to move to the beat—if only to a slight degree. Before we know it, we're hooked—still humming the song hours later in bed while turning out the light.

Despite their unappealing name and high irritation quotient, however, earworms can occasionally come to your rescue on the job. If you're stuck with performing a boring task, humming "We Will Rock You" under your breath a few dozen times may make the time pass more pleasurably. If "Papageno, the Bird Catcher's Aria" from Mozart's *Magic Flute* is on your mind, softly sing a few bars and see if anyone at work responds. The act of giving in to the constantly cycling "You Are My Sunshine" in your head may actually brighten your day. In other words, earworms are not always our enemies; sometimes we can learn to use them as our truly personal, inner music device.

Take Five

By now, we're all aware of how devastating cigarettes are to our health. Yet several people have confessed to me over the years that one reason they found it so hard to stop smoking was that they missed the fifteen-minute cigarette breaks they took at work several times each day. A self-mandated break allowed them to step back from the flow of work and the office politics—to relax, consider their job activities from a broader perspective, and sometimes come up with new, creative solutions to seemingly intractable problems.

Music provides a way to enjoy the benefits of the fifteen-minute break in an immeasurably healthier way. Instead of timing the breaks to satisfy a cigarette addiction, you can keep your playlists ready for those times when your "higher self" most needs to get away. Just as you listed the ten most common negative triggers on your daily commute, you can identify your most stressful periods at work and prepare a "music massage" to precede them or to relax you afterward—to move yourself toward a better emotional, mental, and physical state and perform more effectively on the job.

If you feel overwhelmed by deadlines or by all the items on your to-do list, or if the prospect of an upcoming meeting is making you tense, calm and clarify your mind by retreating briefly with some relaxing second-gear musical selections with a tempo of around sixty to sixty-eight beats per minute. Many tunes sung by Frank Sinatra, Andrea Bocelli, Bette Midler, and Diana Krall would fit the bill. Alternating with slower, transitional pieces of instrumental music (slow jazz, easy baroque, or a quiet guitar piece) will help slow your heart rate and breathing, soothe your emotions, and allow you to organize your thoughts.

 **www.HealingAtTheSpeedOfSound.com/Link18**

Calm and Clarify

Listen to this short sample of Native American flute music by the musician Golaná. You'll find it's the perfect antidote to a frazzled mind.

Has an incident at work made you angry or upset, or do encounters with a particular coworker make you want to scream? If so, close the door for a moment and plug into some second-gear music performed at a slow tempo, such as Ralph Vaughan Williams's "The Lark Ascending," Gabriel Fauré's "Pavane," or the beautiful, reflective second movement of Mozart's Piano Concerto no. 21 in C Major, known as the theme from *Elvira Madigan*. As the music flows through you, close your eyes, let its serenity fill your mind and body, slowly exhale the tension away, and then slowly inhale peace and harmony. You will be amazed by how effectively this activity can take you to another place emotionally, and restore your sense that all is right with the world.

When lack of sleep has left you feeling sluggish and unable to focus at work, third-gear music at a faster tempo—a little faster than your heartbeat—can reboot your brain and recharge your body. Dial up some Latin dance music on your personal music player, close your eyes, and imagine you're performing with your favorite partner on *Dancing with the Stars*. Let the inner movement give you a workout, and you'll be able to return to work with energy, enthusiasm, and a much better mood.

Sometimes we need music to motivate us, to get us marching forward to conquer the world. A prime example of this kind of music is the song "Fired Up, Ready to Go!" which created so much momentum and energy during the 2008 political campaign season. Rhythm and blues, rap, and upbeat rock with a strong beat all work well for this purpose, using the power of diversion to get you up on your feet and moving. Whether you listen to this motivational music alone or with your coworkers—say, to rev yourselves up for a sales presentation—it will get your heart pumping and your energy high.

If you feel the need for some inspiration and want to activate your creative mind, try this exercise: Make yourself comfortable—leaning back in a chair with your feet up, or lying down on a couch if you can—and set your personal music device to the "shuffle" feature. As the first music selection begins, close your eyes, imagine that the music is the soundtrack to a film, and watch the film's "images" projected onto the screen of your mind. Put yourself in the film—watch the action from the perspective of you, the star. Perhaps you see yourself walking down the street where you live. Notice what the houses look like, how fast you're moving, and who else is out and about in the neighborhood. Do you stop and interact with someone? Do you suddenly develop a superpower and fly over the rooftops? Exercises like this, using music and imagery, serve as powerful stimulants to the imagination and can help you break out of the box of habitual thinking.

Sometimes, in order to recharge, it's necessary to put a little more distance between yourself and the workplace. If you've tried listening to music and still feel uninspired, put the personal music device away and go out for a short walk around the neighborhood, letting the sounds of the larger environment massage your ears. Do you work near a public park or near a fountain, river, or waterfall? Stroll in that direction, nourishing your brain and your spirit on the sounds of children playing, water splashing, dogs playing fetch with their owners. Savor each sound—its texture, its tone, the way its quality changes as you near open spaces or water. Let your senses linger on the murmur of conversation as others pass you, the sound of a barge's warning bell, or a train's whistle, or your own footsteps on the sidewalk, the grass, the rustling autumn leaves. Don't think about these sounds—just immerse yourself in the ocean of sound.

Now, walking back to work, focus less on the sounds around you and more on sounds you can create inside your head, without the help of a music-playing device. Note the rhythm of your stride, and imagine a marching band accompanying you down the street. Hear the drums, the beat, and the energy; let the music move you. Pick up the beat, slow down the beat. Continue experimenting, expanding your repertoire to other types of music that you prefer. By the time you reach the office, you will have created your own "inner iPod"—a selection of melodies you can call to mind whenever you need refreshment.

www.HealingAtTheSpeedOfSound.com/Link19

The city of Stockholm, Sweden, has found a way to encourage citizens' creativity while they prompt them to get a little exercise. Imagine coming across these "piano stairs" on your own break from the office!

When Music Manipulates

Just as employers have long used music to motivate their workers, and just as you have learned to use music to shape your own experience on the job, today's audio architects have developed sophisticated ways to manipulate consumers through sound. Your walk away from the office may have exposed you to many examples of this type of manipulation, from the high-frequency melodies of an ice cream truck, which have such a Pavlovian effect on children (and many adults), to the music piped into shops to help create brand identity, strengthen store loyalty, and increase sales.

Music can target consumers in remarkably specific ways: One study showed, for example, that when French music was played in a British supermarket, French wines outsold German ones by a three-to-one margin.[35] It can strongly influence customers' behavior: Merchants have found that faster music encourages them to finish their shopping quickly, while slower tunes tend to lengthen the shopping experience so that shoppers buy more.[36] Restaurant owners can also move customers through quickly by piping in faster, up-tempo music, or encourage them to linger and savor their meals by playing slower, more relaxing tunes in the background.[37] Research has shown that the choice of piped-in music influences hotel guests' perceptions of the hotel brand and their opinion of its decor, and that certain types of music encourage guests to spend more time and money in the hotel and improve their moods while waiting for service.[38] The volume of music can also affect customer behavior: Researchers have found, for example, that male bar patrons tend to drink more when the music is louder.[39]

Sound Profile: Chris Babb

♫ In the Detroit Metropolitan Airport, Delta Air Lines followed the path of most air carriers by piping music into the cabins in order to alleviate some of the stress of traveling. It didn't take long for flight attendants to notice that certain relaxing music selections also seemed to encourage passengers to find their seats and get settled significantly faster when boarding. "Once we started down that path," says Chris Babb, the airline's manager of in-flight entertainment, "we put more research into it. It's made quite a difference for our passengers and flight attendants."[40] Babb now deliberately assembles playlists with this and other purposes in mind. Aware that fliers have divergent tastes in music, he focuses on upbeat songs such as "Got It Good," "So Sublime," "A Good Start," and "Today Is a Good Day" to create an upbeat, positive, friendly sound environment. "It's a balancing act to find the right groove for boarding/disembarkation that is contemporary while appealing on some level to a massive global audience," he admits. "Also, the music can't be too intrusive, as flights depart and arrive at all hours." But his choices work. Flight attendant Mimi Rawlinson reports, "You definitely notice a mood change when the music's on. Passengers are more upbeat. They get settled in faster."[41]

It's somewhat unsettling to think that our choices about how much time we spend eating or how much merchandise we buy may be determined partly by a "sound expert" we've never met. There's not much we can do about it, but awareness of its purpose and effects can at least help us defend ourselves against undesired forms of sonic manipulation. We might also consider how music affects clients or customers, as well as employees, at our own place of employment.

Setting the Tone—Music for Clients and Customers

The reception area, the "hold" function of your telephone system, and the company Web site's home page represent most businesses' first chance to make a good impression on a client or customer—and sound can greatly influence the positive nature of that impression. What do you yourself hear as you enter your own company's world through one of these portals?

Is music piped into the waiting room or on the telephone, or added to the Web site? If so, does the style of music suit your company's personality and its products? Is the selection of songs or instrumental pieces thoughtful and varied? Is the volume low enough to avoid irritation or distraction?

Another question to ask yourself is whom the music choice most benefits—your employees or your clients. On a recent visit to my dentist's office, for example, the rock and pop music was so loud and disturbing that it seemed to amplify the stress of the procedure I was undergoing. When I asked the dental assistant about it, she said, "Oh, this keeps us active and in a cheerful mood all day." While that is a laudable goal, one would hope that in a medical setting the patients' comfort would come first. As we will see in chapter five, pain and anxiety can be measurably decreased when patients listen to soothing, low-volume, slower-tempo music. The quite different music at my dentist's office delivered the message that employees' desires trumped patients' needs—not a message that is likely to encourage clients to return. Take a moment to consider this issue where you work, and adjust volume, music choice, and noise levels to make your customers feel as comfortable as possible.

Of course, music is only one form of sound that can be used to create an atmosphere that visitors will find pleasant and welcoming. A British professor writes that he keeps a recording of birds singing by a stream running continuously in his office. Not only do the sounds mask the noise of traffic and "bring up images of the Yorkshire dales" for the professor, but they're very soothing for student-teacher conferences, too. "My students say it makes my office feel very relaxed," he writes.[42] In that serene environment, better communication is likely to take place.

It's important to keep in mind that some people, including some who visit your workplace, can barely tolerate any kind of piped-in sound. Pay attention to your clients' responses to the sound environment during their visits to your workplace. Do they appear irritated or unnecessarily stressed? Do they have trouble hearing or making themselves heard? When you speak to them on the telephone after they have been on hold, listening to recorded music or announcements, do they complain about the wait, or do they comment on how much they enjoyed the swinging jazz and almost wish you hadn't answered? Check for any e-mailed comments on the music that accompanies your Web site. If you feel it's appropriate, ask clients what they think about the sounds that greet them while they are meeting with you on the job. Sound is just one part of a comprehensive effort to please customers that every business must make, but it's a surprisingly important element. Improve the sound environment in your workplace, and clients and workers both are likely to generate more business.

Symphonic Production

Both literally, with music, and metaphorically, with our managing style, "orchestrating" employee morale, productivity, and customer satisfaction is really what business is all about. Roger Nierenberg, the former music director of the Stamford Symphony, in Connecticut, and author of the book *Maestro*, has made a career out of providing corporate CEOs and managers with a musical experience that allows them to explore this process—by handing them a baton and allowing them to conduct a professional orchestra. In these hands-on seminars provided through Nierenberg's company, the Music Paradigm, business leaders viscerally experience the moment-by-moment feedback loop between workers and leader that results in great art—and great business as well. "The orchestra is an ideal laboratory for doing simulations of organizational dynamics," Nierenberg explains. "Communications are so fast you can experiment with one behavior and immediately see results. It invites people to question their assumptions about organizational issues in a nonconfrontational way."[43]

Lyn Ravert, a senior manager with Cubic Transportation Systems, of San Diego, calls it "a golden experience." She enthuses, "I felt so drenched in the music, so willing to throw myself into the moment." She felt, also, a tremendous sense of responsibility as she led the team of orchestra members, seeing how the moves of her baton determined how well they functioned. When Nierenberg, demonstrating, barely moved the baton, one of the musicians complained, "You're stifling the music," and the associate concertmaster remarked, "It certainly is not inspiring." When he focused only on the work of a few lead musicians, micromanaging their performances, a violist with a small part said afterward, "I had the feeling you didn't know we existed." Nierenberg also demonstrated the employees' responsibility in symphonic production by asking the violinists to relax and let their minds wander as they played. Discordant music and a snickering audience were the result.[44]

If you own or manage a business, you can orchestrate your own "symphonic" organization even if you don't literally take lessons in wielding a baton. Simply pause to consider all the ways in which you can improve morale, communication, creativity, and customer satisfaction at your workplace so that the parts of your company combine to create an even greater whole. Sound can play a major role in instituting these changes, beginning in the parking lot, suggests Russ Riendeau, where some employers mount speakers to create a musical ambiance from the very first and last moments on-site. Inside the workplace, consider creating a "jam room" with a few drums and other musical instruments, where employees can bond, blow off steam, and spark their own and others' creativity. Further enhance the quality of your employees' work life, and strengthen ties to your community, by inviting a local music group or high school jazz band to perform at a company event, or asking a musician to give a talk to employees about the creative process.[45] Welcome employees' suggestions of music to add to your company's Web site. Ask for their ideas for ways to use sound to speed up production or decrease stress on the job. Remember, you are all members of this orchestra, each with an important part to play in your company's symphonic score. It takes a masterful conductor to bring a business to prominence, but even the humblest piccolo player can make a game-changing contribution now and then.

Sound Profile: Barbara McAfee

♫ Barbara McAfee always loved music. But as a young woman beginning a jazz-singing career in the Midwest, she could hardly control her stage fright enough to perform. It was not until she looked to the music itself for guidance that she learned how to move beyond her shaking hands and quavering voice to the power residing within the music. "Music is a core metaphor for how I see the world," she says now. "It expresses things that are too big for words."[46]

Today, McAfee puts her talent to use in passing on the lessons she has learned from music to employees and managers in such businesses as Blue Cross Blue Shield, Wells Fargo, and Best Buy. As a "keynote singer," she uses songs with pointed lyrics to open employees' minds and hearts, to forge connections and create a sense of community at the workplace. Her song "Brain Rats," for example, pokes fun at the negative messages we tell ourselves that so often inhibit our productivity. "Who You Gonna Be When You Do What You Do?" invites listeners to bring more of themselves to their work. Songs like this, she says, "bring more levity into the conversation." Employees are able to "use that language" to talk about the workplace dynamics. "Music opens up places you can't get to in any other way," McAfee concludes. Just as music helped her find her voice years ago, so, with music, she now helps others find theirs.[47]

Can You Hear What I Say?

One last sound consideration regarding the workplace has to do with communication between members of the workforce. Good communication is obviously of prime importance on the job—yet many people are unaware what their tone of voice communicates to others, while others often fail to fully perceive what is being said to them. We will explore this topic in more detail in the following chapter, as we trace the development of hearing and speaking skills from fetal development through early childhood. But for now, take a moment to consider whether you are helping or hindering the exchange of information at work. Do you mumble, or speak too fast? Is your voice unusually high- or low-pitched? What does your tone of voice convey—openness and excitement, or criticism and negativity? Ask a coworker, friend, or even your spouse or partner to give you feedback about your voice and communication style. Better yet, record a meeting, interview, or workplace conversation and analyze it yourself. Keep in mind that it's not just the words that are important—your voice pitch, speaking pace, emotional expression, and emphasis combine to send all kinds of messages to listeners about your attitudes toward them, toward the topic under discussion, and about yourself.

If you feel that subpar communication skills are getting in the way of work production, camaraderie, or morale, consider hiring a professional listening therapist or media coach to help you make improvements. Even in difficult economic times, this kind of support may turn out to be worthwhile, with a dramatic impact on your career. Researchers have found, after all, that the deciding factor for many patients when deciding whether to sue their surgeons for unsatisfactory outcomes was the quality of the surgeons' tone of voice—that is, the subtextual messages it conveyed—when communicating with them![48]

www.HealingAtTheSpeedOfSound.com/Link20

Roxy's Journey

Sometimes workplace communication problems lie not with the speaker but with the listener. Roxy Cross, a single mother of nine in Santa Cruz, California, had long struggled with depression, insomnia, and difficulty focusing in busy settings like her cubicle-office at work. Finally, when the stress of miscommunication grew too great, she sought help through the Listening Program, a listening-therapy method produced by Advanced Brain Technologies. Listening to specially modified music on bone-conducting headphones served to calm her autonomic nervous system, training her brain to block out noise. To her relief, it greatly reduced her level of stress as well, allowing her to improve her sleep patterns and her moods, and to become a better listener. Read her blog, Roxy's Journey, to learn more about her experience.

CHAPTER THREE

Music of Life

How Our Earliest Development of Hearing and Speech Leads to a Lifetime of Sound

Before we make music, music makes us.

—Joachim-Ernst Berendt, *The Third Ear*

Now that you have begun to replace the noise in your environment with more nourishing sounds, let's pause to take a closer look at the ways in which your physical, emotional, and intellectual development have been profoundly affected by sound's physical properties—rhythm, pitch, and frequency or vibration—from your earliest days of life. Your manner of speaking, of walking, of interacting with others socially and emotionally—your ability to really hear what others are saying to you, to focus on tasks, and to stick to your goals until you have achieved them—all of these aspects of your personality and demeanor have been shaped to some degree by your interactions with sound. In a very real sense, throughout childhood, adolescence, and adulthood, sound has made you what you are today.

In recent years, a wave of new research, powered by new technology and diagnostic techniques, has provided us with fascinating glimpses of the specific ways in which this process works. Studies conducted around the world have demonstrated how sound's energy shapes the brain's development before birth; how its rhythms regulate our physical movements; how pitch, tone, and musical structure can fine-tune the mind and sharpen listening skills; how music making improves students' test scores and communication skills; and how professional musicians' brains actually differ in structure from the brains of nonmusicians. The conclusion reached by British and American scientists at the "Musical Brain" conference at London's Royal Institution in 2001—a gathering marking the culmination of the 1990s' "Decade of the Brain"—was that, far more than just a cultural phenomenon, music is "a biological fact of human life" intimately involved in our physiological functions.[1] In this chapter, we will examine that research and consider how these findings can improve your life and the growth and development of those around you.

Overture

The music of your life began with a heartbeat. From the moment you acquired the ability to process sound in your mother's womb—sometime during the second trimester of your development—the steady thump of her beating heart permeated your developing body and brain, imprinting its rhythm over and over, millions of times before your birth.[2] Other sounds washed around you too—the loud, constant rush of blood flowing through the placenta, the gurgling sounds of digestion, the comforting vibration of your mother's voice resonating through her body and yours. From outside, the novel sound patterns of human laughter, conversation, traffic, machinery, and music permeated the wall of the womb and were transmitted to your ears through the amniotic fluid, though their frequencies were filtered and you, immersed in liquid, heard only muffled sounds.[3] Penn State neuroscientist Rick Gilmore suggests that, as a result, the voices of your family members probably sounded like "the squawk of the muted brass instrument that depicts grown-ups talking in the animated *Peanuts* cartoons." Nevertheless, "there is a lot of information in that filtered and muted sound stream."[4]

As parents have long known, the fetus responds easily and frequently to sound in the environment, particularly during the final trimester. Pregnant musicians have reported feeling their unborn children kick in time to the music they play—sometimes even stopping and starting as the music stops and resumes.[5] Writer and radio host Al Letson tells of the nights in bed when he and his unborn daughter exchanged kicks and gentle pokes through the wall of her sleeping mother's stomach—a rhythmic communication that laid the groundwork for an intense connection between them once his daughter was born.[6] For decades, scientists have routinely documented such fetal responses to loud sounds, in the form of startled responses and increased heart rate.[7] The fact that babies can hear outside sounds is indisputable. The more interesting question is whether the fetus *understands* these sounds in any sense. When you heard music or your mother's voice, did you actively *listen*, and did those sounds carry meaning for you? Did they affect the development of your brain and body? And following birth were you able to remember them?

In fact, the depth and range of the fetus's sensation is far greater than most of us realize. The developing brain perceives through contrast. A sudden change in sensory stimulation—the sound of laughter, say, mixing with the background sounds of your mother's body—told your fetal brain that something new had happened. When this stimulation entered your auditory cortex, your brain responded with a sharp "What's that?"—and went to work trying to connect the sound with past experiences and fit it into a developing pattern of understanding. Your brain was not simply registering sound, in other words, but was actively trying to make sense of it.[8] And as it fit together the pieces of the sound puzzle of the world outside, these patterns were mirrored in its own development. With each new sound pattern, new neurological pathways were carved, like grooves in a vinyl record.

Researchers have traced this process in a number of ways. Their studies show that the fetus not only senses sound from outside the mother's body, but it differentiates between novel and familiar sounds, responding physically to new sounds while growing indifferent or habituated to those that are repeated consistently.[9] This recognition of the familiar, in which the fetal brain stops responding to an often-repeated sound with "What's that?" represents the first form of learning.[10]

The fetus is capable of remembering what it has learned as well. In one well-known study, researchers directed a quiet vibratory sound toward the mother's abdomen, followed by a loud sound. The first time this was done, the fetus did not respond to the gentle stimulus, but did respond to the succeeding jarring sound. When the sequence was repeated, however, the fetus responded to the quiet sound, as though remembering the sound pattern and anticipating the loud stimulus to follow.[11]

Your brain's search for patterns and its sensitivity to sound contrasts allowed you to learn and remember the cadence and inflections of your mother's voice before you ever left the womb. While still in utero, you could distinguish between her language and a foreign tongue, probably due to the differences in rhythm. The downbeat in spoken language is "like an edge finder, or the boundary of rhythm" for the fetus, explains Ann Senghas, a psychologist at Barnard College, in New York.[12] At the same time, as studies have shown, your neurons learned to prioritize some sounds. When a sound became important—when your mother's singing to you during pregnancy, for instance, increased the levels of positive hormones in her blood, which in turn nourished you—your cells' response to that tone increased. Your brain learned to respond strongly to her singing as a source of pleasure[13]—the beginning of the lovely mother-infant bonding process that continued after birth, and one reason why your mother's lullabies could so effectively soothe you and help you drift toward sleep.

Developing human brains seem particularly attuned to music—even more than to language—no doubt due to its structural complexity and interesting patterns. A song does not have to be beautiful, or even directed at the fetus, to be remembered after the baby is born. Infants often recognize and respond to the theme songs of television shows their mothers watched most while pregnant, for example. Just as certain foods are more nourishing than others, however, even if all types provide calories, high-quality classical, world, and other complex instrumental and vocal selections provide broader and more varied stimulation to the fetus than the typical theme song or simple pop tune.

A Parent's View

Having grown up in a family of prominent pioneers in the area of neurological development, having researched brain development himself as an adult, and having spent two years researching and coproducing a series of neurologically stimulating recordings called Music for Babies, Alex

Doman considered himself well informed on the relationship between infants and sound. Only this year, however, did Alex himself become a parent. Not surprisingly, the experience of witnessing his baby's development and birth gave him an entirely new perspective on the role music can play in helping an infant thrive.

"This was my first child," Alex explains. "I was eager to use the music I had worked so hard to produce, and my wife, Mandy, who had had two children before this, looked forward to comparing her previous experiences to this new pregnancy, immersed in healthy sound." Early in the first trimester—weeks before their son, Brendan, had developed the ability to perceive sound—Mandy began listening to her favorite upbeat music on bone-conducting headphones. Studies have shown that regular listening to recorded nature sounds, or music with positive lyrics and pleasing rhythms, such as traditional children's songs, increases the levels of serotonin and other positive hormones in the bloodstream.[14] By adding these music sessions to a stress-reducing routine that also included cutting down on work hours, reducing noise, exercising regularly, and eating organic foods, Mandy was able to provide Brendan with a highly nourishing bath of positive hormones every single day. The bone-conducting headphones, which caused the music's vibrations to resonate through her body, provided extra stimulation for development. By moving to the music's rhythms, Mandy entrained Brendan to the beat. As Mandy grew more comfortable with her listening routine, Alex encouraged her to expand her listening to other musical genres—world music, rock, hip-hop, jazz, classical—in order to introduce Brendan to the richness of the musical world that awaited him.

Listen to This

♫ As news of music's beneficial effects on fetal development has spread, numerous music-delivery devices designed to be placed directly on the belly have been marketed to pregnant women. Since such devices rarely come with reliable guidance regarding volume levels, users run the risk of playing the music too loudly and causing fetal stress. Mothers can more safely provide their developing babies with nourishing sounds and stimulating vibration by listening to low-volume music through bone-conducting headphones placed on the ears.

In the second trimester, as baby Brendan developed the ability to perceive sound, the Domans began to sing daily, and grew more specific and directed in their music selections. They began to create playlists limited to certain gears, or frequency ranges, in order to address specific developmental aims. Low-frequency, first-gear music most effectively stimulated the vestibular system—the ground zero of sensory organization, as it controls balance, equilibrium, visual organization, our sense of body in space, and muscle control.

Next, they moved to the second-gear, middle range of frequencies—the range in which language is heard, processed, and expressed. These sounds stimulated the auditory pathways necessary for optimal listening, speaking, and communicating with others, as well as for perceiving and processing such aspects of music as pitch and dissonance. Finally, they focused on the third-gear, high range of frequencies, with its more refined levels of communication affecting neuronal development.

After spending several weeks listening to music in this high-frequency range, Mandy returned to the midrange, and finally reviewed the low range. To ensure exposure to the full range of high-quality sound frequencies that humans are capable of hearing, she also listened to a full fifty-hour course of listening-therapy recordings of Mozart, Haydn, and Vivaldi through the second and third trimesters. In this way, she ensured full stimulation of the auditory system—the only system to reach adult size in utero and fundamental in the organization of the brain.

As the third trimester approached, the Domans used music to prepare Brendan for his post-birth environment as well. "We began playing the music that we would play for him after the birth," Alex explains. Selections included favorite recordings of lullabies and folk music as well as instrumental pieces from the Music for Babies collection. Meanwhile, Alex's two stepsons—Zane, then fourteen years old, and ten-year-old

Ethan—grew interested in the idea that they could communicate with their younger brother before he was born. Ethan began singing to Brendan, while Zane played lullabies softly on his electric guitar—just one way in which music helped the blended family grow closer as the pregnancy progressed.

Listen to This

We have seen the ways in which music can be used to stimulate or soothe the fetus in beneficial ways. Music provides benefits to the mother as well:

- Music makes pregnancy a more natural and enjoyable process.
- Music has been proven to reduce psychological as well as physiological pain.
- In the birthing room, music blocks out unpleasant or distracting noise, wrapping the mother in a "sound blanket" of comfort and safety.
- During labor, music distracts from pain, stimulates pleasure responses, and helps focus attention and breathing.
- Music can enhance and support the spiritual process of the laboring mother.
- During childbirth, music can reduce the need for anesthesia.
- Following the birth, music can reduce pain with no negative side effects.
- Music facilitates bonding between the mother and her new baby.[15]

By the time the pregnancy drew to a close, music had become an integral part of both parents' relationship with their unborn baby. Driving to the hospital the day of the birth, they listened to a playlist preselected for the occasion: soft melodies performed by Robert Linton, the guitarist who had played at their wedding. The beautiful, gentle sounds, so deeply meaningful to the couple, set the mood for the birthing experience that followed.

Arriving at the hospital, Alex set up a Bose docking station and a pair of headphones in the birthing room, each with a personal music device loaded with calming, soothing music for labor, for the birthing process, and for baby Brendan's entry into the world. "We were surprised that the staff at the hospital—one of the top one hundred birthing hospitals in the U.S.—were unfamiliar with the use of music during birth," he reports. "Hardly anyone had done it before." Nevertheless, the staff respected their wishes, and in fact enjoyed the peaceful, inviting atmosphere the Domans created with their soft music, dimmed lights, and aromatherapy so much that staff members dropped in for visits whenever they could through the hours that ensued. What a contrast their still, peaceful oasis made to the family snack station down the hall, where family members chatted loudly and fathers made frantic calls on their cell phones at all hours.

 **www.HealingAtTheSpeedOfSound.com/Link21**

The Green Doula, a blog for pregnant women, provides suggestions for building a childbirth soundtrack to take with you to the hospital. Music can help relax you as labor begins, support and encourage you as you move through active labor, and soothe you and your baby once the birth is completed.

Finally, the moment came for baby Brendan's arrival. As the doctor entered the room and the newborn started to emerge, Alex put on the music they'd chosen for this moment—the *Peaceful Baby* album, from his Music for Babies recordings. "Quite quickly and easily, after only six very gentle pushes, Brendan eased into the world—perfect in every sense, and calm," his father says. "He was greeted and comforted by sound he knew—his mother's voice, his father's voice, and the gentle, low-volume sounds of the music to which he'd been listening in utero." Delighted as his parents were, it came as just an added bonus—and surely had nothing to do with their music regimen—that Brendan was born on Mozart's birthday!

Listen Up

Surprisingly, about thirty percent of U.S. hospitals do not perform hearing screenings for newborns. Undiagnosed hearing loss in newborns is a serious issue, since a great deal of brain development takes place aurally in the earliest months, and diagnosis before age one generally leads to a much better prognosis for auditory health in later years. If testing isn't done at birth, problems usually aren't noticed until the child exhibits language problems at age two or three—so be sure to have your newborn tested by the pediatrician or an audiologist if a test is not performed at the hospital.

"Of course, the experience was completely different from what I had imagined in many ways," Alex admits. Like many new fathers, he found that events involving babies do not always proceed exactly as planned. In particular, he began using the selections in his own series of recordings for babies in different, more creative ways. "I found more specialized uses for them," he explains, "playing certain music from *Cheerful Baby* when we fed him, some *Peaceful Baby* music when we changed him, still other music when we put him to bed." In other words, just as it is important for each adult to create a sound environment best suited to his or her needs and tastes in music, so too can parents experiment with ways to design the most nourishing, supportive environment for their child.

Meanwhile, the entire family continued to sing, talk, and read to Brendan, giving him the kinds of auditory input that he was capable of processing. "While breast-feeding, my wife continues to listen to all kinds of beautiful music," Alex reports, "knowing that low stress levels will make for better breast milk." One album—*American Lullaby*, a collection of folk, country, gospel, and traditional bedtime songs produced by Ellipsis Arts—became not only Brendan's favorite, as evidenced by his responses, but his parents' as well.

Throughout his journey toward toddlerhood, Brendan has remained consistently ahead of his developmental milestones. Sound continues to play a big part in his life. His favorite toys are a collection of drums that are scattered around the house, which he carries with him to play with from one room to the next. Even without the drums, he constantly claps and dances in time to the music he hears, sensitized to rhythm and melody through constant exposure from before his birth. It's hardly surprising that so much musical input has influenced not only his motor and aural skills, but his personality and intellect as well. "Everyone remarks on how alert, engaged, and connected he seems," his father says. "From the beginning, he was a very easy baby—never sick, fussing, or complaining. Of course, every parent believes their baby is the best who ever lived. I admit I'm one of them—and I believe sound has much to do with who Brendan is."

Sound and the Newborn

It should be clear to you now that by the time you were born, you were already on remarkably familiar terms with many aspects of your sound environment, from your parents' voices to the music and other sounds you had heard regularly while inside the womb. As an infant, when you heard a familiar voice—particularly that of your mother—your head would turn toward the sound source.[16] You had so successfully integrated the pulse of her heartbeat that in infancy you instantly noticed a dropped beat or a change in rhythm in a song.[17] Your brain, always responding to novelty and trying to fit it into learned patterns, also reacted to differences in pitch within a new environment. Your musical sophistication was so great, in fact, that at birth you already had your own musical preferences, and would soon start to express them by responding to a favorite lullaby with full-body wiggles and even coos,[18] and to displeasing sounds by squirming, turning away, or even crying.

From your earliest weeks of life, your understanding of the emotional components of music was also very strong. By age five months, you began responding differently to bright and cheery melodies than to sad and gloomy ones, even if you couldn't comprehend that some were "happy" while others were "sad."[19] Your deep familiarity with the songs your mother sang, or the recorded music you heard while in the womb, provided you with a sense of comfort and continuity, allowing you to bond with your mother and to relax into an expanded sense of security, which the rhythms and melodies provided. Perhaps that's why mothers have always sung such songs to their newborns from the first moments they hold them in their arms, muses Norman Weinberger, a neurobiologist and auditory neuroscientist at the University of California, Irvine. They do so "because babies *understand* it."[20]

www.HealingAtTheSpeedOfSound.com/Link22
(Free Download No. 4)

Sleep, Baby, Sleep

This performance of Gabriel Fauré's Berceuse, from *Dolly Suite*, performed by the Arcangelos Chamber Ensemble, will help calm you as well as your little one. Here you will also find links to a number of providers of music for babies, including Rockabye Baby, with its lullaby adaptations of rock tunes, Advanced Brain Technologies' Music for Babies collection, the Children's Group's Mozart Effect: Music for Babies series, and even *Jersey Babys*, an album of adaptations for infants of songs from the Broadway hit *Jersey Boys*.

Your Mother's Voice

There is no question that a profound form of communication takes place when a mother holds her child in her arms and sings. Studies have shown that babies are born with a strong preference for their own mother's voice, no matter how tuneless, over any other form of music.[21] Of course, as an infant you were drawn to the familiar and reassuring—the voice that had guided your development inside the womb. But beyond that, as researchers have discovered, mothers tend to instinctively choose songs based on their baby's particular mood,[22] and by expressing that mood in song, succeed in "synchronizing" their infant's emotional state. This process of emotional communion enhances and extends the relationship established before birth, creating a sense of security, which is required for optimal infant development.[23] But it also brings the baby to a state of attention, allowing him or her to take in an enormous amount of information while listening.

Dr. Alfred A. Tomatis, an otolaryngologist specializing in voice and hearing disorders who practiced in Paris beginning in the late 1940s, wrote and lectured extensively on the topic of the central role of the mother's voice in awakening communication within the newborn—that is, in providing the pace, the pattern, and the pulse her child would need to connect to the outside world. Like birds, he pointed out, babies learn to use their voices by listening to their parents, or others close to them, within a certain critical period of development. As their loved ones sing, read, and talk to them, babies have the opportunity to study the adults' faces and expressions, to see and hear how they form sounds and words. They attend not only to the words themselves but also to the pitch, vibration, rhythm, tone, emphasis, emotion, and context in which these messages are delivered. This unique pattern of vocal properties is as unique to the speaker as his or her fingerprints or face.[24] The information conveyed causes neurons to fire in the brain of the listening child, creating new neuronal connections, expanding neural networks, and thus moving the child forward in his or her mental, physiological, and emotional development.

Tomatis understood, more than any other clinician at the time, the immense influence the mother's voice has in this way on her child's own ability to focus, to learn, to comprehend emotion, to be in sync with his or her own body and movement, and to communicate—that is, to develop his or her own unique "voice," or identity. But Tomatis went further than this. "The voice can only produce what the ear can hear," he famously wrote and frequently repeated. The child can only experience and express the information that he or she has received and internalized from others with whom he or she has an emotional bond. If something interferes with that close communion with the mother's voice, auditory processing disorders can result—developmental problems in the areas of learning, attention, communication, and physical and social skills.

Sound Break: Hear Yourself

♫ Take a moment to record your own voice, both talking and singing. Now play it back and listen. Aside from the words or lyrics, what does your voice tell you? Pay attention to its tone, its rhythm, its melody. Does it sound happy? Is there energy? Hesitancy? Aggressiveness? What messages about your past experiences, your current state of being, your hopes and dreams does it carry? Do you hear vestiges of your mother's or father's voice in yours? What messages would your voice communicate to a newborn who knows nothing of life outside your own voice?

It is an amazing insight into the power of early education and speech development to realize how the mother's voice can pattern not only the brain and the style of communication but also the physical body's sense of itself in the world. But for those whose patterning had been insufficient in one way or another, what can be done? To address this issue, Tomatis developed the Tomatis Method—specific forms of listening training that would help remedy these developmental deficits and restore and maintain an individual's true "voice." Essentially, Tomatis provided to the patient the sounds with which he or she had failed to connect the first time around.

A patient would begin by listening through specially designed bone-conducting headphones to recordings of his or her mother's voice, filtered to sound as it did inside the womb. This most primal of sounds, listened to in daily sessions, would instill in young patients a sense of safety, release their stress, and allow them to rebuild and strengthen the connections between their inner and outer worlds. Tomatis added other sounds to provide additional benefits to the brain. He found, for example, that listening to recordings of Gregorian chant increased some children's sense of physical and emotional balance, and that recordings of Mozart's music, filtered to a particular, narrower range of frequencies, trained the brain to discriminate those frequencies—thus restoring listening deficits and improving speaking and attention skills.

Tomatis helped his patients exercise their new skills by enabling them to reexperience the gradual evolution of their own speech development. Stimulating their emotional pleasure centers through play therapy using toys, pets, and art materials, he moved the patients from baby talk—"ooo" and "coo"—into more meaningful expressions. As they played, children were able to reconnect the sounds of their speech with their own sense of joy, and speech and emotion became better integrated. Their voices began to better communicate their inner state.

Finally, Tomatis designed a cybernetic loop that allowed patients to hear their own voices through ears and bones simultaneously. The child's brain, having patterned itself on the mother's voice, on Gregorian chant, on the highly organized music of Mozart, and on the experience of pleasurable activity, could now create a patterning feedback loop with his or her own voice. This step stood as a final stage of auditory integration. Children with speech and communication disorders who completed the program—typically involving sixty hours of listening in two-hour blocks over the course of several months[25]—demonstrated marked improvement in a striking number of instances.

Tomatis, working in the mid-twentieth century, progressed in his work largely through intuition, experimentation, and observation, constantly trying new methods and techniques, retaining only what worked. Scientific research in recent decades has confirmed many of his findings. We know now, for instance, that music does, in fact, improve brain function by activating neural circuits in many different areas of the brain and by providing crossover activity between the right and left hemispheres. The resulting dendritic growth and strengthened connections provide a priming effect, improving our ability to listen well and thus helping the brain work better.

Research has also demonstrated that listening programs such as the Tomatis Method affect the central nervous system via the vagus nerve, which travels throughout the body, sending messages to and from many organs so our bodies can function optimally. In the process, the vagus nerve acts as a regulatory device, helping us respond to stressful situations and then return to a calm state, for example. The vibration provided by modified music delivered through headphones with bone conduction improves vagal regulation in the head, neck, and chest areas, improving our physical and emotional integration so that we can more successfully engage socially.

As scientific studies have continued to bear out Tomatis's findings, a second and third generation of experts have expanded on the original components of the Tomatis Method. Several have developed listening therapy courses of their own, using bone-conducting headphones and other listening devices. More information on these programs can be found in appendix two at the end of this book.

www.HearingAtTheSpeedOfSound.com/Link23

Sheila Allen, occupational therapist and codirector of Pediatric Therapeutics, in Chatham, New Jersey, who has conducted extensive research into the use of bone-conducted sound in treating children with developmental disabilities, has found convincing evidence that this type of music-based listening therapy helps speed up the integration of the auditory and vestibular systems when included in a comprehensive pediatric therapy program.

This animated video, illustrating how air- and bone-conducted music reaches the brain, demonstrates the ways in which music listening therapy can sync mind and body in powerful, effective ways.

Listening, Speaking, Thinking

Nurtured by rhythm, vibration, and sound in the womb, stimulated by language and song in the arms of your mother and other close caregivers, you were welcomed to a wonderful world of sensory perception. Music's varied rhythms, pitches, melodic risings and fallings, and conveyance of emotional states opened your ears to new kinds of neural patterning, serving as a kind of pre-language for you. As you grew, your ability to hear these tonal and rhythmic elements equipped you to begin to recognize individual words. In this way, language entered your life.

Evolutionary scientists have long studied the link between music and speech in the human brain. Charles Darwin suggested that in the darker reaches of our prehistory, an intermediate state of human evolution existed, characterized by "a communication system that resembled music more closely than language, but was identical to neither."[26] In his book *The Singing Neanderthals*, Steven Mithen, a professor of archaeology at the University of Reading, in England, echoed this suggestion, positing that humans once employed a kind of "protolanguage" that may have served as a precursor for both modern speech and song[27] and that served as both a method of communication and "a sort of social glue."[28]

There's no doubt about the close relationship between music and spoken language. Because they share a number of elements—rhythm, melody, and pitch—music and speech are processed by the brain in similar ways.[29] Many areas in the brain that respond to music are also crucial in our use and understanding of language—such as Broca's area, which deals with both musical sight reading and with language processing and organization. Studies have shown that symphony orchestra musicians exhibit larger volumes of gray matter in this area depending on the number of years they have been playing an instrument.[30] Broca's area is also associated with memory, which no doubt explains the findings that, while the region's size typically decreases as people age, musicians continue to average fifteen percent more gray matter here even when well into their sixties.[31]

A small area known as Heschl's gyrus—part of the auditory cortex in the temporal lobe, where sound first reaches the brain—plays a similar dual role. A study comparing the size of this region in musicians and nonmusicians observed startling differences, with the gray matter in the auditory cortex of professional musicians found to be 130 percent higher than that of nonmusicians. Even among amateur musicians this region was measurably larger.[32] As Heschl's gyrus has been found to be essential in the learning of a foreign language, it is no surprise to learn that musicians demonstrate a higher ability than nonmusicians to pick up the rudiments of a made-up tonal language.[33]

www.HealingAtTheSpeedOfSound.com/Link24

This little girl is not just dancing. By responding wholeheartedly to music's rhythm, pitch, and energy, she's learning to speak clearly, to express herself fully, and eventually to read!

The upshot of these connections is that musical activity has stimulated your music, language, and communication abilities simultaneously throughout your life, and will continue to do so through all the years to come. As your family members sang nursery songs and bounced you rhythmically on their knees, you learned to savor the musical qualities of words, to speak, and, eventually, to read with ease. From the beginning, you focused on the vowels and consonants produced by your caregivers, and sometime in the first half year of life you began trying to produce them. These vocal experiments, researchers have come to understand, are an essential precursor to speech and a key predictor of a child's cognitive and social development.

As researchers have noted, babies all over the world babble in similar ways, creating repetitive syllables, playing around with elements of speech they have picked up from their sound environment. At first, your *ooh* and *aah* sounds sounded nothing like words, and your parents probably didn't think of them as serious attempts at language. Still, if they responded with smiles and cries of delight, you were encouraged, and by the second half of your first year, you began to produce syllables combining both vowels and consonants that sounded like they might be words. "Parents recognize the syllables as negotiable," observes D. Kimbrough Oller, a professor of audiology and speech-language pathology at the University of Memphis. When you said "ba ba ba," your father may have assumed you were trying to say "bottle" and offered you a bottle in response. Again, these kinds of interactions encouraged you to continue practicing sounds and syllables, developing your mouth muscles, learning to move your tongue properly to mimic your family members' sounds.[34]

Listen to This

♫ "As a pediatrician, I always ask about babble," writes the well-known physician and author Perri Klass. "'Is the baby making sounds?' I ask the parent of a 4-month-old, a 6-month-old, and a 9-month-old. The answer is rarely no. But if it is, it's important to try to find out what's going on. If a baby isn't babbling normally, something may be interrupting what should be a critical chain: not enough words being said to the baby, a problem preventing the baby from hearing what's said, or from processing those words. Something is wrong in the home, in the hearing or perhaps in the brain."[35]

Obviously, the more these loved ones spoke with you and sang to you, the more stimulation the language centers of your brain received. Babies have to hear real language from real people to learn these skills—television doesn't do it; nor do educational videos. As pointed out earlier, the emotional connection between speaker and infant creates the environment for optimal learning. Researchers, including Michael H. Goldstein, an assistant professor of psychology at Cornell University, have shown that optimal learning occurs during those moments when parent and child are actively communicating—that is, when you babbled and your parents responded in specific ways, perhaps replying to your "ba ba" with "Bottle?" and handing it to you. "We think that babies tend to emit babbles when they're in a state where they're ready to learn new information, they're aroused, they're interested," Professor Goldstein explains. Your parents' frequency and quality of response went a long way toward determining how verbal you would become. "It's about creating a social interaction where now you can learn new things."[36]

During your second year of life, you began to shape the sounds you had heard and practiced into the words of your native tongue. To observers, it might seem that your first words and phrases appeared spontaneously, almost effortlessly. You now know, however, how much rhythmic, tonal, emotional, and social stimulation goes into the creation of any baby's first words.

It's important to understand, too, that the use of words goes much deeper than the ability to speak effectively. Some scientists have suggested that until we have language, we don't really begin to think—that words make our first thoughts, rather than thoughts making words. If this is true, and if we take into account scientists' claim that we can reproduce only the sounds we hear, then it pays to reconsider the German philosopher Martin Heidegger's definition of listening as the most elementary gesture of thought.[37] All the more reason to pay attention to the kinds of sounds with which we surround ourselves, and to strive for the highest-quality sound stimulation we can possibly achieve for our families and friends.

Growing the Brain with Sound

As we have seen, active engagement with music—throwing mind, body, and emotions into the experience—greatly enhances its benefits. Research has shown that while holding a child and singing to him is a good thing, dancing with him or bouncing him on your knee while singing can more effectively stimulate his neural development, while expanding his understanding of music.[38] Babies learn early to provide themselves with some of this full-body neural stimulation by shaking a rattle or clapping their hands in response to music. A little later, they teach themselves to "sing"—that is, to emit random spontaneous song fragments—at about the same time that they are practicing speech, so their singing and babbling reinforce each other. In early childhood, rhythmic movement in games and exercise leads to improved speech and reading skills, while stimulating neural organization as well.

In fact, music researchers have found correlations between music making and some of the brain's deepest functions. If you studied and performed music as a child, the activity not only provided you with pleasure, but it most certainly strengthened your neural synapses, enhanced your sensory and perceptual systems, and improved your memory. Making music with others enhanced your ability to work well in groups, to harmonize with others, and to assess and correct your own performance. The act of decoding musical notation exercised your reading skills, while performing music improved your breathing, posture, and articulation.

A number of studies, including a recent one by E. Glenn Schellenberg, of the University of Toronto, have demonstrated that the IQ scores of children who take weekly piano or voice lessons tend to rise more quickly than those of their untrained peers.[39] This happens, Schellenberg tells us, because the study and performance of music—"memorizing, expressing emotion, learning about musical interval and chords"—engages nearly all sectors of the brain, including those used in mathematics, language, and other intellectual pursuits.

 **www.HealingAtTheSpeedOfSound.com/Link25**

In this excerpt from the Library of Congress's Music and the Brain series, Dr. Gottfried Schlaug, director of the Music and Neuroimaging Laboratory and the Stroke Recovery Laboratory, at Beth Israel Deaconess Medical Center and Harvard Medical School, talks with host Steve Mencher about the notable differences between the brain of a musician and that of a non-musician.

Music: Your Bridge to Adulthood

Music's positive effects on your development did not stop in early childhood, but continued through your high school years and beyond. In fact, looking back on your adolescence, you may agree that music served as such an effective transition tool between childhood and adulthood that it would have been almost impossible to survive your teenage years without it—and that the songs you loved during that period continue to move you even today.

By the time you were in high school, if you were lucky, years of engagement with music had so sharpened your listening skills that you were able to converse effectively with teachers and other adults, easily handle the give-and-take of conversation with friends, and actually hear what your girlfriend or boyfriend was trying to say to you. Music's rhythms had instilled in you the ability to regulate your body, your emotions, and your own choices, and the understanding that few things can be learned in "several easy lessons," which you got from practicing, helped you stick to a task until you got it right. These successes increased your self-confidence and feelings of self-sufficiency.

Participating in musical activities continued to develop your intellectual skills, too, just as it did through early childhood. Compared with nonmusicians, you were better able to focus your attention, take good notes in class, and write with grace, eloquence, and a strong sense of narrative structure. It's no wonder that teenagers who play a musical instrument score significantly higher on the SAT than nonmusicians, as many tests have shown,[40] and that the more years a teenager has studied an instrument the higher his or her likely achievement in math, science, and the language arts.[41]

Even a neighborhood rock band provides a teenager with the invaluable experience of working creatively with others, including showing up on time, communicating successfully, and taking responsibility to prepare and perform as expected—all skills that carry over into our adult lives. Writing or selecting songs to perform allows us to test our parents' and society's boundaries in a safe way, while helping us learn who we are and what we have to say. If we're lucky, playing together in a band also introduces us to that mysterious sense of musical communion—when everything comes together, a sense of trust and belonging takes hold, and self-consciousness and feelings of insecurity and unworthiness melt away beneath the invigorating, all-encompassing rhythm of the song. For some of us, those kinds of musical experiences were once incredibly healing, with effects that have lasted a lifetime.

Sound Break: Do You Remember?

♫ Many of us can look back on one or more songs that had a profound impact on us in our teenage years. List five songs that you sang as a teenager. What was it about each one that moved you back then? Which musical elements—the lyrics, the rhythm, the melody—had the strongest effect? How have your musical tastes changed in the years since then? Do you feel more connected to music now, or less?

The Band Plays On

All of this information relating to sound and human development carries enormous implications in terms of educating our children, enhancing their emotional and creative lives, and treating mental and developmental disabilities—all topics that I will discuss in the next chapter. For now, though, I would like you to take a moment to reflect on what you have learned here in terms of your own childhood and later development.

How did music facilitate your relationships with family members? Would more music in your lives have improved communication, led to greater scholastic success, or otherwise enhanced your time together? As you have seen, sound and the brain, emotions, communication, and movement have been inextricably bound together from the very beginning of your life. Knowing this now, you can use the power of sound to empower your brain, your emotions, your personal expression, your physical health, your relationships with others, and the social climate of your community. In the chapters that follow, I hope to show you how.

www.HealingAtTheSpeedOfSound.com/Link26

This iconic photograph, by Lynne Sladky for the Associated Press, of New Orleans Saints' Drew Brees swinging his young son up into the air after the Saints' 2010 Super Bowl victory—with the toddler wearing noise-canceling earmuffs to protect his ears from the roar of the crowd—led to a rash of child-size earmuffs and headphones purchases and a wave of praise for the proud father, who showed such healthy concern for his son's ability to hear.

CHAPTER FOUR

Rhythms of the Mind

Sound and Music in Education

I would teach children music, physics, and philosophy: but most importantly music, for in the patterns of music and all the arts are the keys of learning.

—Plato

Now that you understand the profound ways in which sound has shaped your own life from your earliest days, it is clear how important music is in tuning up the bodies and minds of children. As more and more music programs are cut from our nation's schools, we must consciously consider how to integrate music and a healthy sound environment into children's lives, to shape their growth and health in positive ways. Even if you have no children or grandchildren at this stage of your life, you may be able to use your new awareness of music's role in mental and physical development to improve the lives of your young relatives, neighbors, and children in your community.

Ideally, by the preschool years, children have already benefited from pre-birth exposure to music's soothing sounds and reassuring rhythms, which enriched the hormonal balance in their bloodstream and laid the groundwork for healthy neuronal and physiological development. They entered the world to the familiar sounds of family members' voices and lullabies heard while in the womb. If they were born ill[1] or premature,[2] music may have helped decrease stress, encourage nursing, and distract from the pain of medical procedures, thus allowing for faster weight gain and a shorter stay in the hospital. Full-term babies could rely on familiar lullabies to settle into a regular sleep routine, and could then go on to feast on the stimulation provided by their family members' voices as adults and older children sang and spoke to them, danced with them, and bounced them rhythmically in their arms and on their knees.

During this same period, as we have seen, sound and music equipped children with nearly all the basic language skills that carry through to adulthood. The window of opportunity for picking up language begins at birth and ends sometime between the ages of eighteen months and three years, after which time the assimilation process becomes increasingly difficult. This is one reason why it's so important to stimulate babies and toddlers with high-quality music and soothing words throughout their early years. These same years are also the critical time for developing a "listening vocabulary" of music—not surprising, considering the fact that human language and music perception are rooted in the same regions of the brain. Giving a child a rich diet of music during this period will help determine the ease with which he later acquires skills in appreciating, performing, and moving to music. As we will see, the more comfortable the child is with music-related activities, the more effectively those pursuits can lead to academic success, physical grace, emotional balance, and creative thought.

Fortunately, music is not a kind of "medicine" to be administered to children, but is an activity we can all enjoy together, no matter what our age. To enhance your own pleasure as well as your child's, select the highest-quality children's songs, folk tunes, and classical music you can find to play at home. "Children deserve only the most worthwhile music," points out Lorna Lutz Heyge, cofounder of Musikgarten, an early childhood music program. "The songs of childhood are remembered for life. They must be worth remembering—songs of musical, textual, and cultural value."[3] The pleasure the child feels in the music will create an optimal "learning" state of mind, much like the intense communication enjoyed by mother and child during the bonding process. Good music will encourage you to participate fully, bringing your child's attention to the different sounds and the changes in sound as they occur,[4] encouraging him to move to the beat, to sing along, and to interpret through dance how the music makes him feel.

www.HealingAtTheSpeedOfSound.com/Link27

One can see joy expressed in every gesture this three-year-old makes as he conducts the fourth movement of Beethoven's Fifth Symphony. Just imagine how the music is stimulating his brain!

As early as possible, suggest ways in which your child can begin using music to express herself. For example, when you read a bedtime story, have her provide a musical soundtrack by singing or tapping on a zither or other instrument. These activities link the vestibular and auditory levels of the listening ear—a vital skill for all kinds of learning. Act out a favorite story with her in song and dance, or make up songs about a favorite picture or activity. Or sing your way through one of your child's *least* favorite activities, such as getting out of bed or getting dressed. It can transform a chore into a fun part of the day. All of these ways of connecting action, imagination, and emotion will help your young child visualize stories, thoughts, and ideas.

Sound Break: Musical Eyes

♫ Select a favorite piece of instrumental music to listen to with your child. While listening, discuss with her what pictures, colors, or stories the music brings to mind for each of you. Then play the selection again, encouraging her to act out these images with her body—impersonating, say, a happy butterfly when listening to one section of the music and a busy little groundhog when listening to another. The more specific you are with your suggestions (an excited, twirling dancing princess rather than just a dancing princess, for example), the more you will stimulate her imagination. Let her suggest some ways for you to act out the music too. Not only will this interlude exercise your child's mind, but it may well create some happy memories for you both in the years to come.

As often as you can, let your little one choose which musical activity you engage in at any particular time. He'll take great satisfaction in taking control, and will benefit more from an experience he especially enjoys.[5] And whether you are listening, singing along, or actively playing music together, relax and have fun. Children love movement, dancing, and rhythm, and these activities provide a joyful, nonthreatening environment for learning. Your participation will encourage his close attention and speed up neuronal development.[6]

Listen Up

♫ From earliest toddlerhood, music's rhythm and rhyme can be used to reassure your child, ease anxieties, curtail tantrums, and teach new skills in simple, pleasurable ways. Next time your child objects to an activity, try musically narrating your actions as you move through them—singing, for example, "We're going in the car, we're going in the car! First we put our coats on! One sleeve, one sleeve. First we put our coats on! Two sleeves, two sleeves . . ." You will be amazed by how easily the rhythm carries your child through the activity, and how effectively adding funny lyrics or sound effects and punctuating your song with a kiss or a hug will distract him from his former sour mood. Before he knows it, he'll be buckled into his car seat and singing along happily as you turn the ignition key. And music's magic will most likely improve your own mood, too.

If you play a musical instrument yourself or enjoy singing along with the radio, be sure to include your child to the extent possible. Even if you don't rank your own musical ability very high, you can bring excellent music activities into a child's life by participating in such parent-child early childhood music programs as Musikgarten or Music Together®, in which trained educators lead families in enjoyable and relaxing music making, song, and dance. If you are unable to attend such a program, you can purchase videos of music classes for home use on the Web sites of these organizations, or perhaps borrow them from your local library. While you're enjoying participating in these musical activities with your toddler, consider taking some music classes of some kind yourself in the future. After all, as music education researcher Donna Brink Fox has pointed out, an adult who has never played an instrument attempting to help children with music lessons can be as difficult as non–English speaking parents trying to help their offspring with English spelling, grammar, and reading lessons. A piano lesson once a week, or participation in a church or community choir, is likely to expand your understanding of music in ways that will eventually benefit a child.[7]

A World of Sound

Starting preschool or kindergarten represents an enormous step for a young child. Whereas life at home centered around him exclusively, to some extent at least, a classroom setting demands that he share adult attention, toys and play equipment, and his personal space with many other children. He must learn to focus on group tasks, express himself clearly, develop his motor skills, master the rhythms of social give-and-take with his peers, manage his emotions, start to assess his own actions, and understand that he can improve his performance with practice. He will continue developing his language skills, along with the fine motor skills he will soon need for writing. He will learn to look at the world, and at the challenges he encounters, from a creative problem-solving point of view. He will expand his knowledge and appreciation of the stories and songs of his culture. Ideally, he will also begin to develop an aesthetic appreciation for music and a positive attitude toward school.

Listening to music, making music alone and with others, moving to rhythmic sounds, and ideally participating in such early childhood music-instruction programs as Orff Schulwerk or Kodály will help guide your child through all of these areas of development. As we've seen, music as an activity engages nearly all sectors of the brain, positively impacting childhood development, cognitive abilities, and brain function. Learning and performing music strengthens the synapses between brain cells, positively impacting the sensory and perceptual systems, cognitive abilities, fine and gross muscle action and coordination, the motivational or pleasure system, and learning memory. Group music activities encourage social awareness, and learning and remembering a song's nuances or memorizing a piece for performance engages memory. Furthermore, as Dr. Rosanna Wong Yick-ming, executive director of the Hong Kong Federation of Youth Groups, points out, music performs all of these tasks in an atmosphere of enjoyment, enthusiasm, creativity, and participation—the four essential elements for optimal early educational development.[8]

Both the Kodály Method, developed by Hungarian composer and educator Zoltán Kodály in the mid-twentieth century, and the Orff Approach, created in the 1920s by the German composer Carl Orff and his colleague Gunild Keetman, link their enjoyable, enriching music activities to the stages of young children's development—and both have long demonstrated their effectiveness in promoting growth in all of the areas described previously. Studies have shown that as little as thirty minutes of Kodály music instruction per week can help get children "in sync" with themselves and others, improve their behavior and self-esteem,[9] encourage creativity and visualization, and strengthen the rhythm, articulation, breathing, posture, and expressive skills they will need to become good readers.

Meg de Mougin, an Orff-certified music instructor and codirector of the Midwest Institute Academy of the Arts, points to the ways in which Orff-type rhythmic movement and singing also prepare children for reading. Good pitch discrimination has long been shown to help children learn to read, as it helps with the critical process of sounding out words. Orff's special music develops this listening skill by exposing children to new and varied sounds, directing them to listen and hear in new ways and guiding their voices toward greater variety and expression. Singing games, play parties, and folk dances strengthen children's sequential learning abilities, also necessary for learning to read.[10]

Sound Break: Hum Along, Invent a Song

♫ The link between music and language becomes especially clear as we see the way preschoolers and kindergartners unconsciously *sing* their thoughts out loud. Usually, the song consists of a familiar melody—or bits of several different melodies—with the child's own "lyrics" slipped in. If you notice your child experimenting in this way, reward her for her creative effort by asking her to repeat the song and then singing it along with her. Write the song out in musical notation, if you are able. If you don't know how to write music, just draw a short line for each note, higher or lower on the page to indicate the relative pitch. Then write the lyrics underneath, as with this example, sung to the tune of "Ring Around the Rosy":

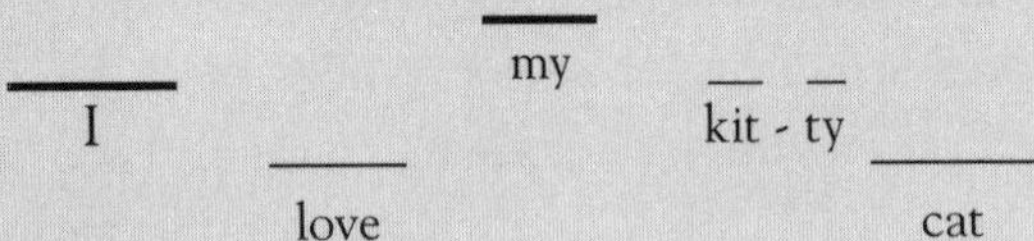

You can further reinforce the experience by illustrating the song with a little drawing, as in a children's songbook; singing the song again and perhaps clapping along to show your child how much you enjoy it; and singing it to other family members later. Outside of your child's hearing, encourage family members to casually hum or sing the song to themselves in her presence, so she can have the experience of watching her creation become a part of the family culture. Watching something she created become a work of real value is a powerful experience for a very young child, contributing to her self-image as a smart and inventive individual.

Another essential task addressed through the use of music and musical games involves the development of "midline crossing" skills—that is, the child's ability to cross the midline of the body with ease. In order to read well, our eyes must travel easily from left to right and back. It is hard to train the eyes to do this, but whole-body crossover activities, such as waving streamers in a figure-eight pattern for a Chinese ribbon dance, or playing a rhythmic rock-passing game, teach the body to orient itself in this way and lead naturally to the fluid, fine motor eye movements needed for reading. Perhaps this is why researchers report that children taught with games and songs at the preschool level tend to test higher in reading all the way up to age fifteen, and that an IQ advantage of ten to twenty points has frequently been observed.[11]

www.HealingAtTheSpeedOfSound.com/Link28

Here, you will find video demonstrations of more musical exercises that can help advance young children's language, reading, and writing skills. Join me for a quick lesson on rhythmic speech and tonal speech that will work for parents and children alike.

A third music program open to preschoolers—the Suzuki Method, developed by the Japanese violinist Shinichi Suzuki after the Second World War—focuses on learning to play such musical instruments as piano, violin, and cello. Suzuki is sometimes called the "mother-tongue method" of music instruction, because its teaching methods are modeled on the natural way in which children learn to speak. First, parents are encouraged to create an environment in which children are immersed in a musical culture—by listening to and experiencing music at home, attending concerts, befriending other music students, and so on—just as babies are immersed in an environment rich in language. Next, like babies learning sounds and syllables, young music students are prompted to imitate on their instruments the music they hear. For example, parents may play a recording of "Twinkle Twinkle Little Star" performed on violin over and over in the home. Then, after a period of listening, they will encourage their child to begin imitating one phrase of the song, then another, on a child-size violin, moving at their own pace just as they progress in speaking words and sentences. As with language, daily parent-child interaction is emphasized, along with other kinds of practice such as collaborating (playing music) with peers, communicating (performing) frequently, and learning to read and write music only later, after the imitative and integration steps have been mastered.

Given that the Suzuki Method so closely resembles the language-acquisition process, it's no surprise that learning to play an instrument in this way encourages greater expressiveness in verbal as well as musical communication. The fine motor movements developed in playing piano or violin will come in handy when your child starts to write, while the process of decoding musical notes will make learning to read words easier. Equally important, the Suzuki learning process itself—the methodical progression of listening, imitating, assimilating, and expressing oneself musically—creates excellent learning habits for all kinds of experiences in later life. It's no surprise, then, that children who play an instrument generally perform better in school.

On the neuronal level, playing an instrument also improves auditory discrimination and spatial and temporal reasoning skills[12]—higher-brain functions needed for learning math and science. Studies have shown, in fact, that playing an instrument as a child literally makes the brain grow, with certain neural regions expanding through frequent use just as muscles develop through exercise. By adulthood, the brain area used to analyze musical pitch is an average of twenty-five percent larger in musicians than in those who don't play an instrument. More significantly, the corpus callosum, a trunk-like bundle of neurons connecting the two brain hemispheres, is significantly larger in musicians—particularly among those who began music studies before age seven.[13] An enlarged corpus callosum allows for more efficient communication between the two sides of the prefrontal cortex, where intellectual planning and foresight are generated, and of the premotor cortex, the site of action planning.[14] The interhemispheric link also allows access to the sources of our emotional and cognitive qualities, which have been shown to be isolated from each other. Christine Beckett, a professor in the music department at Concordia University, in Montreal, noted that "with music, the brain lights up like a Christmas tree on both sides."[15]

Parents often worry that starting music lessons at such a young age constitutes "pushing" the preschooler. But researchers including Dr. Gottfried

Schlaug have found that the younger the age at which musicians began training, and the more years of instruction they receive, the greater the growth of certain areas of the brain.[16] This may be because, as researchers have discovered, very young children tend to participate more fully in music programs than older students, without self-consciousness or self-doubt. Their willingness to learn and grow, making the mistakes that naturally go with the process, helps them maintain enthusiasm and a healthy practice routine. Young children also believe that they can improve with practice, whereas adolescents may give up too easily, erroneously concluding that if they can't play well right away they have no "talent" and will never be good enough to perform.[17] By starting your child on the road to mastery at an early age, in a program like the Suzuki Method, which allows for easy, natural progression at the child's own pace, you are helping him develop skills of persistence that will see him through many academic and other challenges in the years ahead. For these reasons, in addition to the real pleasure most children experience in mastering a musical instrument, it's well worth seeking out a music-instruction program as early as the preschool or kindergarten years.

It's undeniable, as we've seen, that music is a crucial element in the lives of preschoolers and kindergartners. But it's also important to consider what other kinds and quality of sound surround them throughout their school day. When you drop off or pick up your child from the classroom, or when you visit on parents' days, pay attention to the volume, pitch, and frequencies of the sounds that reach your child's ears every day. Does the teacher tend to shout over the din of the children's activity, or does she take a moment to quiet the children before speaking in a calm, nourishing voice? Do floor mats or carpets, curtains, and sound-absorbing ceiling tiles soak up some of the noise? At nap time, do the adults in charge create an atmosphere of restful silence, or softly play recordings of classical music or folk tunes to soothe restless preschoolers' spirits?

www.HealingAtTheSpeedOfSound.com/Link29

Take a look at Noisy Planet, a Web site designed for children age eight to twelve by the National Institute on Deafness and Other Communication Disorders. Noisy Planet can provide you with facts you can use in advocating for hearing protection for your children, and can clue your children in on the need to be aware of the levels of sound in their world.

Pay special attention to the toys supplied to the children—not just at school, but in your own home as well. It is hard to believe, but some toys sold in stores, such as walkie-talkies, cap guns, vehicles with sirens or horns, talking dolls, and even musical instruments, emit sounds so loud they can cause not only pain but also permanent hearing damage in children. A toy siren or electronic toy may emit sounds of ninety decibels—the level at which workers are required to wear ear protection on the job. When children hold the toys directly to the ear, as they often do, the noise level striking their ears can rise as high as 120 decibels, the noise equivalent of a jet plane taking off.

If you are reluctant to discard overly noisy toys you already have at home, at least cover the speakers with duct tape, or remove the batteries and let your child play with the object without the noise. Strongly encourage your child's teachers to do the same, or insist that the toys be removed altogether. Don't hesitate to step forward and make your case. Many adults are simply not aware of the potential dangers posed by noise. By educating the caregivers at your child's school, you will perform a great service not only for your own child, but for all of his or her peers as well.

Sound Academics

A generation ago, children without access to music instruction in preschool or kindergarten could be sure of encountering such programs in elementary school—and we continue to like it that way. According to a nationwide Gallup survey, ninety-five percent of Americans consider music a key component in a child's education, and more than seventy-five percent feel schools should mandate music education.[18] Today, however, budget cuts and pressure to meet testing goals and other prescribed academic benchmarks have pushed arts instruction out of the school curriculum to an ever-greater degree. I count myself among the many, many educators who consider this a tragic turn of events, particularly in elementary school as children's brains continue to develop, as their social interactions expand, and as they face the demands of academic schoolwork and homework for the first time. As Nina Kraus, director of Northwestern's Auditory Neuroscience Laboratory, has noted, "Eliminating music classes is a mistake. We've found that by playing music—an action thought of as a function of the neocortex—a person may actually be tuning the brain stem." This is a finding with important implications in both educational and clinical areas.[19]

Listen Up

- First-graders with developed rhythm skills have been shown to perform better academically than those with lower rhythmic test scores.[20]
- Second- and third-graders who were taught the relationships between eighth, quarter, half, and whole notes scored one hundred percent higher on fractions tests than their peers who were taught fractions in the traditional way.[21]
- Students who take piano or singing lessons for at least one year gain more IQ points over the course of that year than those who take drama lessons or no lessons at all.[22]

Consider the joy with which children participate in music-related activities. Dancing, singing, making music alone or with others, or simply listening quietly to recordings or live performances rekindles in students the state of openness and joy they experienced when bonding with family members who sang to them as infants, and with caregivers who played musically with them in their earliest years. You, too, may feel liberated by the musical explorations you undertake with children, particularly if you endured negative musical experiences—such as being asked to be a "silent singer" in chorus—in your own childhood.

Music encourages the flow of serotonin and other positive hormones through the listener's circulatory system, and stimulates the euphoric centers of the brain.[23] It stimulates the limbic system—the seat of emotions—along with another area connected to emotions called the rostromedial prefrontal cortex. Both of these regions are also responsible for certain kinds of memory. This may be why particular songs call up such vivid emotional memories, giving us the sense that we are almost reliving romantic, joyful, or tragic moments from the past. Certainly, as brain-based learning expert Eric Jensen tells us, the most significant learning occurs when the emotions are engaged.[24]

Clearly, music—particularly music with lyrics or rhythmic speech—provides a kind of "hook" for the brain's memory centers that allows us to retain information. Rhythmic songs and chants have long been useful in helping young children learn the alphabet: Remember how to spell *Mississippi* ("M-I-crooked-letter-crooked-letter-I . . ."), and "I before E except after C." Songs cling to our brains in less helpful ways too. We have all suffered from earworms—those songs that get stuck in our minds and repeat over and over until we think we'll go mad. Brain imaging shows that this phenomenon may occur because after a song ends, the brain continues exactly the same activity it was involved in while the song was playing. When songs have lyrics, the brain keeps the melody playing with even fewer neural regions involved.[25] This may be the reason why we remember a tune all the way through more often than the lyrics.

Involving the body in the music-making process seems to make learning even more effective. One well-known study showed that in a traditional passive-listening classroom setting students gained short-term memory, but when active musical methods such as singing, clapping, and moving were used, the students used more parts of their brain *and retained the information for a longer time.* "Whether the better memory is due to the greater involvement of the brain is not yet known," writes the head of the research team, Norman Weinberger, of the University of California, Irvine, "but it seems clear that the active music-making regimen was definitely better at producing stronger long-term memory."[26]

 **www.HealingAtTheSpeedOfSound.com/Link30**
(Free Download No. 5)

Uno, Dos, Tres

Listen to this excerpt of a Spanish language lesson in which the teacher speaks to the beat of specially composed rhythmic background music. This "musical" technique can increase attention, focus, and enjoyment when learning any of a number of subjects. Try it yourself by downloading the background music via this link and letting its beat guide you as you read aloud to your child or practice foreign-language vocabulary or grammar.

Music's links to memory probably have much to do with its ability to improve reading skills, as many studies have demonstrated. I pointed out earlier that language and music skills share many regions of the brain. Most of the strengths that music develops—pitch discrimination, rhythm, articulation, breathing, good posture, expressiveness, visualization, creativity, the ability to cross the body's midline and to decode written symbols—work directly to enhance literacy skills as well. After conducting a meta-analysis of thirty studies on music's effectiveness in this area, Jayne M. Standley, of Florida State University, concluded that when the music activities incorporated the specific reading skills the children needed, the benefits were significant. She also pointed out that the promise of music-related rewards, such as getting to join a singing group or attend a children's-music performance, worked effectively to encourage students to work on their skills.[27]

Just as a good rhythmic sense has enabled many children to easily assimilate the speech patterns they need to become strong readers, so an inability to detect the beat has been identified as a common trait among dyslexic children. Recently, scientists have made encouraging strides forward in using remedial rhythmic training to successfully address this disability. Certain scientifically designed games, for example, in which dyslexic children must respond very fast to patterns of tone, have been shown to encourage a sense of rhythm and thus improve reading abilities.[28] Regular singing or instrumental sessions have been found to have a similar positive effect. One study conducted at Northwestern University showed that the number of years a person practices music strongly correlates with progress in the kind of sound encoding needed for speech[29]—implying that young people with reading disorders can improve their skills through music-based approaches. Listening sessions through bone-conducting headphones, using acoustically modified classical music, can be effective as well.

We appreciate music's ability to lure our children out of increasingly sedentary lives—to help them develop coordination and a level of comfort with their bodies, along with the confidence that goes with physical mastery. We are excited by the creativity music fosters in children, the experience of working with a team, and the self-esteem that is not always as easy to gain through the so-called core curriculum.

Of course, the real reason most of us hope that our young children will experience music is because music is fun and rewarding. What more could we wish for our children than the chance to experience the satisfaction of revising a performance with a teacher until it sounds right, the thrill of performing it for families and friends, and the experience of expressing oneself while joining creatively with others? Participation in creative arts experiences is valuable for every child, regardless of his or her level of talent. If your elementary school child can spend only fifteen minutes a day working and playing with music, that's sufficient. Starting there, any child can build a relationship with music over time. Before you know it, you'll be the proud parent of a teenager able to impress his friends with ten favorite tunes played on a piano or guitar, and in the process create social bonds and build self-esteem to last a lifetime.

Sound Profile: Drum 2 Change

♫ Drum 2 Change, a yearlong drumming program instituted for third- through sixth-graders in the Elkhart Community Schools, in Elkhart, Indiana, makes use of music's "fun factor" to encourage children to work harder at school. After the first four weeks of drumming sessions, students who wish to continue are required to sign a contract promising to keep their grades up while in the group. About twenty percent of the original group choose to continue with the program. From that group, thirteen students are chosen to participate in an "elite" drumming group called Roots of Rhythm, which tours the state performing for music educators and student assemblies.

Students acknowledge that staying in the group can be difficult. "You have to get your grades up and you can't miss a lot of days," says fifth-grader Uriel Chairez. The program, which emphasizes such values as teamwork, focus, and respect, has been shown to increase participants' self-confidence, create greater community feeling, and generate higher test scores. As sixth-grader Monica Campos says, drumming "helps you think better on tests."

Still, the drumming group's leader, Dawn Ashton, insists that she is more interested in her student drummers' "life skills" than test scores or music performance. She has been pleased to observe a significant increase in students' confidence and willingness to help one another. The drumming experiment has been so successful, in fact, that more groups have been planned for nearby schools.[30]

When Children Miss the Beat

As powerful an influence as coherent sound can be, if you can't make sense of the sounds around you, the effect can be devastating. "Inconsistent" is how Chris's mom describes him. This smart, charming, but often frustrating fourth-grader brings home report cards with both A's and F's. "In the morning before school I can tell him to put on his coat and backpack to get ready for the bus, only to find him on the floor playing with his favorite action figure," she says. "When I ask him why he isn't getting ready, he says, 'I didn't hear you.' His teacher says he seems constantly distracted by the noise around him in the classroom, and when she calls on him he almost always has to ask someone what page they're on. He doesn't seem to understand how to get along with other kids. It breaks my heart to see how much time he spends alone. The psychologist tells me he has a high IQ and doesn't have ADHD.

His hearing is normal, but there is some disconnection. I wish someone could tell me what's wrong so I could help my son. I worry so much about his future."[31]

Millions of individuals have shared Chris's experience. An extreme sensitivity to noise and difficulty understanding spoken language make it hard for them to read, spell, learn, and comprehend successfully—and often lead to difficulties at school, with friends, and when interacting with adults. When tested, they are often found to have normal hearing and intelligence. Declared "healthy"—or, worse, misdiagnosed as being hyperactive or having ADHD—they continue to struggle, and those around them come to think of them as underachievers. As a result, their self-esteem declines, leading to more failure in a frustrating and debilitating downward spiral.

Fortunately, audiologists and other medical professionals have begun to recognize this "invisible" condition as a *listening* disability—that is, the individual hears normally but the brain can't understand what it hears. An estimated two[32] to twenty percent of children may suffer from this inability to fully recognize and interpret sounds—usually referred to as an "auditory processing disorder" (APD).[33] But, as in Chris's case, the condition can be difficult to identify, particularly since children who suffer from it don't usually understand that they process sound differently than others—that not everyone can "hear their eyelashes blink," as one child put it, or that others don't feel overwhelmed by the sound of their own breathing and heartbeat—and so they don't report problems to adults. Some children learn to cover up perceived weakness—getting up in the middle of the night to do their homework when the house is quiet, for example—and in doing so make their problems harder to detect.

Sound Profile: Rosie O'Donnell

♫ In an interview for the *New York Times*, talk-show host Rosie O'Donnell recalled the day she first realized that her son Blake, then a first-grader, needed serious help with his problems in communicating. She had taken Blake to get a haircut and, told by her son that he wanted a "little haircut," she told the barber to give him short hair like his brother's. Afterward, in the car, Blake burst into tears—and only then, after questioning, did O'Donnell understand that by "little haircut" he had meant that only a little hair should be cut—that he wanted only a trim. Mortified, she pulled off the freeway and gave her son a hug. "Blakey, I'm really sorry," she said. "I didn't understand you. I'll do better."[34]

O'Donnell had already been sufficiently concerned about Blake's vague expression and other difficulties that she'd engaged a speech therapist to help him. Now, however, she sought out Lois Kam Heymann, a speech pathologist and auditory therapist, who determined that Blake's speech and listening difficulties were the result of an auditory processing disorder. His difficulty distinguishing between sounds—mistaking *bed* for *dead*, for example—slowed down his comprehension until he fell so far behind in a conversation that he couldn't make sense of what was being said. Difficulties retaining words he had heard led to a limited vocabulary and reading and spelling problems. Jokes and metaphors were frequently beyond his ability to comprehend.

Thanks to Heymann's auditory training methods, detailed in her book, *The Sound of Hope*, and O'Donnell's tireless efforts on her son's behalf, Blake is now taking accelerated classes in high school and applying to top colleges. "I remember I used to dream of the day he would be able to wake up in the morning and just say, 'Mommy,'" O'Donnell confesses. "To see the difference in who he is today versus who he was . . . and then to contemplate what would have happened had we not been able to catch it—I think he would have been lost."

Her experience with Blake's disorder inspired her to become an advocate for the cause, putting her celebrity status to work in bringing attention to the condition so that other children might fare equally well.[35]

Of course, not all language and learning problems indicate APD by any means, just as all cases of APD don't lead to language and learning problems. The checklist below suggests the kinds of behaviors that should alert you to the possibility of APD in your child, but an accurate diagnosis can be made only through careful and accurate diagnostics conducted by a multidisciplinary team,[36] ideally including a teacher or educational diagnostician, a psychologist, and a speech-language pathologist. If these experts consider APD a possible cause of your child's issues, they may refer him to an audiologist—the only type of medical professional equipped to make such a diagnosis. The audiologist will administer a series of tests to measure the auditory system's physiological responses to sound. Because brain function is so variable in very young children, these tests can usually be accurately administered only to children age seven or older.[37]

Sound Break: Symptoms of Auditory Processing Disorder

♫ Signs that the brain may have a problem understanding what it hears include:

- Misunderstanding spoken instructions
- Frequent requests for repetition and clarification
- Difficulty hearing conversation with background noise present
- Poor auditory memory—especially working memory and sequencing
- Easily distracted by sound
- Difficulty telling speech sounds apart
- Hypersensitivity to certain sounds
- Distractibility
- Low academic or career performance
- Reading difficulties
- Language problems
- Behavior changes in certain environments
- Challenges in relationships

Of course, all children experience one or more of these symptoms at one time or another. If your child consistently exhibits many of them, however, or if the symptoms persist, it's important to have his listening abilities professionally assessed.

Once APD has been diagnosed, much can be done to mitigate and even resolve a child's issues. Rosie O'Donnell describes the ways in which she diminished distracting noise in her home by installing carpets, cushioning furniture legs with strips of felt, and cutting back on large, noisy gatherings. Parents and other adults can learn to simplify their conversation with the child, avoiding confusing metaphors and abstract references. Teachers can be of great help inside the classroom, perhaps even agreeing to wear a small microphone to direct their voice to the child's ears via headphones.[38] Meanwhile, the condition itself can be treated through the type of music-listening training program discussed in chapter three. The act of listening to specially modified music helps to "retune the ear," directing focus to certain frequencies, helping the listener attune to single sounds within a sea of background noise, and improving her sense of balance, movement, and timing through the use of Spatial Surround technology, in which the music seems to move around the listener in three-dimensional space. Therapy of this kind has been proven effective, generally leading to more significant improvement in children's functioning and test scores when coupled with high-quality therapy services as compared with the standard therapy alone.[39]

At the far end of the continuum of sound hypersensitivity and attention difficulties is the broad range of symptoms called autism spectrum disorders. For autistic children, sound can be distracting to a debilitating degree. In chapter three, we pointed to the ways in which listening programs with bone conduction have been shown to help these children as well, complementing other forms of treatment.

www.HealingAtTheSpeedOfSound.com/Link31

Peter Jennings discusses autism treatment at the Spectrum Center, and Valerie Dejean describes how the Tomatis Method is used to treat autism.

Music making has also been shown to be quite effective as part of the treatment regimen for autistic children. Rhythmic activities, such as drumming, singing, or playing the piano or another instrument, help children with autism gain a greater sense of control. Music's structure supports them, yet at the same time it provides a path toward spontaneity, which can help them let go and become more playful, observes Ann Lehmann, of the Australian Music Therapy Association.[40] As they master rhythm patterns, tunes, and chords, these children's self-esteem rises. Studies at Aalborg University, in Denmark,[41] and at the University of Pavia, in Italy,[42] among other institutions, have shown that these activities improve autistic children's communicative behavior, emotional responsiveness, attention span, and behavioral control.

www.HealingAtTheSpeedOfSound.com/Link32

Autistic Piano Express, founded by Alex Citron, a music teacher experienced in teaching children with autism, provides autistic students with a fun, effective, and flexible curriculum for learning to play the piano by ear. In this way, students may choose their own songs and play them in their own unique style. The results have been impressive. As one student's mother testifies, "[Alex's] 'Piano by Ear' technique has given our son the opportunity to learn the piano in a way that makes sense for him at his own pace. Not only does Nick enjoy playing the piano; it seems to have a way of calming him and holding his interest for long periods of time." Occasionally, a student even succeeds in rising above the level of beginner. Alex Ritter, a teenager from San Antonio, sheds all of his nervous tics as he begins to play complex pieces by Bach and Brahms.

Bach and Brahms melodies aren't the only therapeutic tool in our musical toolkit. Across the country, drumming groups have begun to form to help children with autism and other developmental disorders lead more integrated, richer lives. Drums and Disabilities, the nation's largest nonprofit community outreach organization helping children with autism, travels to high schools, malls, sporting events, and parents' and teachers' organizations to demonstrate the physical and cognitive benefits of joining in the beat.[43] Since the 1990s, the Strong Institute, founded by Jeff Strong and Beth

Kaplan after more than a decade of research into the traditional uses of musical rhythm techniques around the world, has provided recorded hand-drumming rhythms to individuals with neurodevelopmental disabilities, including autism, ADHD, and learning disabilities.[44] And Beat the Odds, a collaborative program of the nonprofit Arts and Healing Initiative and the UCLA Collaborative Centers for Integrative Medicine, combines contemporary drum circles and group counseling to help students cope with such challenges as ADHD, depression, anxiety, and post-traumatic stress.

Drumming programs, economically feasible and thus sustainable, can serve as a culturally relevant way for at-risk teenagers to manage anger, depression, and stress, to regulate the emotions, stimulate the mind, and provide other forms of therapy without the cost and stigma of more traditional types of counseling. The programs can easily be extended to benefit the entire school community as well. "Think of the heart. The heart connects all of us," says Simone LaDrumma, leader of drumming circles in a number of Seattle schools.[45] A fifth-grade member of another such group attests that through drumming he has learned that "you have to care about each other" and take responsibility for your own actions, and that "sticking together we can accomplish even more."[46]

www.HealingAtTheSpeedOfSound.com/Link33

When drumming, adolescents join with others in healthy, joyful, creative communion. The rhythms help regulate their emotions and spirit. Particularly for teenagers who feel outside the mainstream, drumming together can be a healing experience. If your school doesn't provide a drumming program, look for a drumming circle or workshop in your community—or start one yourself. Here, watch drumming expert Christine Stevens describe the advantages of community drumming.

A Sound Transition

As their children enter middle school, parents often lament the change they see in them, from curious kids always asking questions about the world to teenagers who seem interested only in video games, the computer, TV, and one another. It's an undeniable fact that the creative life of children often tends to diminish as they move toward the high school years. Po Bronson and Ashley Merryman, coauthors of *NurtureShock: New Thinking About Children*, suggest that many teenagers, as they start to feel overwhelmed by rote schoolwork, become discouraged and bored, losing the sense of motivation and engagement with the world that leads to creative thinking.[47]

In an article for *Newsweek* titled "The Creativity Crisis," the authors pointed to an alarming statistic: While American IQ test scores have risen steadily by about ten points with each generation, reflecting increasingly rich environments that stimulate children's intelligence, their creativity test scores peaked in 1990 and have since been on a significant, steady decline. This is tragic news not just for individual Americans, whose creative scores as children have been shown to predict their success as entrepreneurs, professors, physicians, scientists, inventors, writers, and all types of artists—but also for our society as a whole as we face enormous challenges in the twenty-first century that will require highly creative solutions.

It's no wonder, as the authors point out, that a recent IBM poll of fifteen hundred CEOs identified creativity as the number one "leadership competency" of the future.[48] In recent years, countries including the United Kingdom, members of the European Union, and China have worked hard to replace the rote-drilling elements of their secondary-school curricula with programs designed to encourage students' creative skills. But in the United States, where time allotted to arts education has dropped twenty-two percent since No Child Left Behind was enacted,[49] teachers find themselves so pressured to meet curriculum standards that they find little time or energy to address issues of creativity. "In effect, it's left to the luck of the draw who becomes creative," write Bronson and Merryman. "There's no concerted effort to nurture the creativity of all children."[50]

Much needs to be done in terms of policy to correct this problem in our schools. In the meantime, however, you can address this issue with your own teenager by seeing to it that he continues his music education. It should come as no surprise by now that the music activities that sharpened his listening, speaking, reading, writing, and expressive skills as a younger child will continue to support him in such academic areas as math, science, language arts, and even taking good notes in class. Studies in the United States have shown that music participants receive more academic honors and awards than students who don't study music. In addition to these substantial advantages, music has been shown to be highly effective as a creative "reset" button for adolescent students who might otherwise drop out of academic life.

Listen Up

- Music students score higher on their SATs. In one study, college-bound seniors who'd had school music experience scored fifty-two points higher on the verbal portion of their SATs and thirty-seven points higher in math than those without arts instruction.[51]
- Learning to control tempo and rhythm during group music-making activities has been shown to help students improve their performance of routine activities that adolescents typically neglect.
- Surveys show that secondary students who participate in band or orchestra report lower current and lifetime use of alcohol, tobacco, and illicit drugs.[52]
- Music has a particularly significant positive effect on the achievement of disadvantaged students. A U.S. Department of Justice survey found that arts programs for at-risk youth decrease delinquent behavior, increase academic achievement, and improve self-esteem and attitudes about school and their own futures.[53]
- Schools producing the highest academic achievement in the United States are spending twenty to thirty percent of the day on the arts, with special emphasis on music.[54]
- The foremost technical designers and engineers in Silicon Valley are almost all practicing musicians.[55]
- Medical school graduates who play a musical instrument have been shown to score higher on practical medical tests than those with no musical training.[56]

Creativity can be defined as the ability to assess a problem and respond with an array of original, useful, and productive solutions. To be creative requires two different kinds of thinking: divergent thinking (the generation of many unique ideas) and convergent thinking (combining these ideas to get the best results). Neuroscientists tell us that when confronted with a problem, our brains first perform a largely left-hemisphere search for the basic related facts and familiar solutions. If this doesn't provide a satisfactory solution, the right and left hemispheres work together to scan less directly related memories and associations while looking for "unseen patterns, alternative meanings, and high-level abstractions."[57] When a connection is glimpsed, the brain instantly focuses on the insight and locks it in, binding together all of these disparate impulses into a single idea. "This is the 'aha!' moment of insight," write Bronson and Merryman, "often followed by a spark of pleasure as the brain recognizes the novelty of what it's come up with. Now the brain must evaluate the idea it just generated. Is it worth pursuing?"[58]

Sound Break: Express Yourself

♫ Music can inspire some student musicians' best writing. Encourage teenagers to supplement their musical experiences by maintaining a log of their music-rehearsal sessions, their personal progress in learning to play an instrument, or their responses to the music they listen to. Encourage them to write reviews of professional performances they attend, or to create program notes, requiring research, for an upcoming musical event. In the process of writing, they are likely to discover that they have strong musical views and opinions—and this discovery may prompt them to explore the world of music even further.

All of these skills—the ability to scan for remote associations, to recognize patterns, to switch focus quickly from the big picture to the immediate moment, and to assess whether a solution is "aesthetically" appropriate—are developed through music making. Musical improvisation appears to be an especially effective exercise in developing creative skills, actually changing the brain's neurological pattern over time. In a recent study, neuroscientists Daniel Ansari, of the University of Western Ontario, and Aaron Berkowitz, of Harvard, demonstrated that college music majors use their brains differently than nonmusicians when improvising a piece of music. What they learned was that the musicians could turn off the part of the brain that reads incoming stimuli to see if it's relevant to the task at hand. What this means is that they were able to block out all distraction, hitting "an extra gear of concentration."[59]

Other researchers observed the same phenomenon with professional dancers visualizing an improvised dance. Charles Limb, of Johns Hopkins University, pointed out that the medial prefrontal cortex "lights up" in the brains of jazz musicians as well, as they begin to improvise. Interestingly, Limb adds, this latter region is the same area activated when we're talking about ourselves, about who we are.[60] Limb feels this makes sense, because when musicians are improvising, they're spontaneously composing—in other words, "they really are revealing themselves musically. It's like your own musical autobiography."[61] Or, as Dr. Paul Brewer, jazz educator at Aquinas College, in Grand Rapids, Michigan, said in a recent interview, "Improvising means playing everything you know about music and yourself, as well as every song you've ever heard."[62]

This last finding cuts to the core of why music so strongly benefits adolescents in particular—immersed as they are in the process of learning who they are, what they have to contribute, and how they fit into society. In choosing the music they play, teenagers define their personalities and their place in society. In playing music with others, they interact with peers in a most intimate, creative fashion, expressing themselves artistically and then stepping back to hear what others have to say.

Sound Break: Compose Yourself

♫ In all this talk about the neural effects of listening to and performing music, it's easy to forget the benefits and the pleasure of composing an original piece of music. "Creating music is problem-solving of the most difficult order," wrote Charles B. Fowler, my mentor in music education. "It requires us not only to use our musical skills to create a logical sequence of notes, but to consider who we are and what we have to say."[63]

Writing songs or instrumental pieces should be included as part of every teenager's education. If your teen is not encouraged to compose by her teachers at school, urge her to try expressing herself musically at home on her own. It isn't necessary to learn the rules of musical notation before attempting to compose. The learning is in the doing. In the process of composing, adolescents learn a great deal about themselves. She may be surprised by the ideas, dreams, emotions, and observations that emerge.

Adolescents' tribal tendencies are satisfied as well through the interdependence of a musical ensemble, band, or chorus. An individual member's performance impacts his relations with his fellow musicians and the group's overall success. These "natural consequences" make excellent character builders in the teenage years. Music's demand that adolescents learn to harmonize with others will carry over into their relations with their families, with authority figures, at work, and elsewhere for the rest of their lives.[64]

When we step back and look at all the rewards teenagers can reap from musical education, it's no wonder that such activities frequently serve as a stepping-stone to help students win acceptance to the colleges they choose. As Fred Hargadon, a former dean of Stanford University admissions, said in one interview, "We look for students who have taken part in orchestra, symphonic band, chorus, and drama. It shows a level of energy and an ability to organize time . . . that tell us they can carry a full academic load and learn something else."[65]

We all know that not all teen music is performed or listened to in adult-provided educational settings. Popular music that appeals to teenagers has been a source of consternation for adults, possibly for as long as there have been teenagers. Yet there seems to be little evidence behind the frequent suggestions in the media that "dark" pop-music styles such as goth, grunge, rap, punk, and heavy metal cause depression, violence, promiscuity, drug use, or suicide among teenagers.[66] On the contrary, such music can often prove cathartic for teenagers under stress, helping them manage their emotional distress and return to a relative state of emotional equilibrium. Adolescents frequently depend on music to calm them down when they're angry, to stimulate their creativity, and to help them settle down to work. Believe it or not, some even claim it helps them get better grades in school.[67] A study by Patrick Hunter, a Ph.D. psychology student at the University of Toronto, implied that people listen to sad music because they want to—because they are simply not interested in being happy for the moment, and sad music provides a much-needed emotional release.[68]

So lighten up on teenagers about their music choices. Invite them to play their music in the car or on the family stereo occasionally—but then take the opportunity to ask them about the music and what it means. You may be surprised by what you learn about hip-hop or heavy metal and, even more important, about your teenager.

Turn It Down!

Potentially much more damaging to teenagers than popular song lyrics is the volume of the sounds they're listening to. Often it seems as though adolescents are surgically attached to the earbuds of their personal music players—that is, when they're not talking on their cell phones. Nonstop listening is not only an irritating habit for those who wish to communicate with teens; it also is likely to permanently damage their hearing. Recent surveys reveal that 5.2 million young people between the ages of six and nineteen have experienced hearing loss directly related to exposure to excess noise.[69] More than half of all the hearing-impaired individuals in the United States today are younger than sixty-five.[70] Some seventy percent of young people themselves acknowledged in one survey that at some point they had experienced tinnitus (constant ringing in the ears), while sixteen percent reported that the ringing had appeared more than once a week.[71] One in five can no longer hear rustles or whispers, or make out consonants like T's or K's.[72]

It's little wonder that such a plague of hearing problems has spread across the nation, with personal listening players capable of delivering sound of up to 120 decibels—the equivalent of a gunshot or jet engine.[73] Cell phones have been shown to damage hearing as well: A 2007 study reported at a meeting of the American Academy of Otolaryngology–Head and Neck Surgery Foundation indicated that those who spend more than an hour each day on their phones have a worse hearing threshold than those using cell phones less.[74] Despite efforts by such hearing-damaged rock musicians as Pete Townshend, adolescents continue to attend loud music concerts and clubs, and perform in their own bands and orchestras, without protection for their ears.

It is difficult to get teenagers to change their listening habits. Many depend on their music to self-regulate during these years of hormonal turmoil. Few are willing to risk looking "uncool" by wearing earplugs at a club or concert. Most share the adolescent belief in their own invulnerability. A startlingly large number are unaware that the affliction is permanent, that a drop in hearing will not go away.[75] In a study conducted by audiologists at West Virginia University, nearly half of college students surveyed said they listened to noisy equipment without any ear protection; only about one-seventh of those who worked in noisy environments wore hearing protection devices; and close to half of those who knew that listening to loud music could cause hearing loss nevertheless refused to protect their ears.[76]

Manufacturers have been made aware of the dangers, and a few have made an effort to reduce the maximum output of players. While the Apple iPod's maximum volume remains at 115 decibels—equivalent to a helicopter taking off—software has been added to late-model iPods that allows users to set a maximum volume limit and even allows parents to "assign a combination to prevent the setting from being changed." In the meantime, the European Union has capped the default maximum volume of all MP3 players sold in Europe at eighty-five decibels, with an override option allowing users to increase the level to one hundred decibels—and there is hope that the United States will eventually enact similar regulations.[77]

For now, however, the best way to protect your teenagers' ears is to educate them about the potential for long-term damage. Turning down the music, reducing time spent with personal music devices and cell phones, and replacing earbuds inserted in the ear with generally less damaging headphones that cover the ear are as important for your adolescent as wearing a seat belt in the car or a helmet when bicycling. Insist also that those who fall asleep listening to personal music devices set the sleep timer for thirty minutes, so their ears are not exposed to sound through the entire night. As more teenagers understand the facts, earplugs will become as commonplace as shin guards in soccer. We can only look forward to that day.

Listen Up: Earbuds, Headphones, or None of the Above?

♫ Since 1979, when the Sony Walkman turned walking with headphones into a universal phenomenon, headphones and earbuds have become a ubiquitous accessory with personal music devices, mobile phones, laptops, and tablet computers. As the number of American teenagers with hearing loss has increased by a horrifying thirty-three percent over the past half-dozen years, choosing between earbuds and headphones for one's child has become an issue fraught with anxiety. On the one hand, a 2008 European study determined that listening to music on headphones at high volumes for more than an hour a day risks permanent hearing loss after five years. On the other, researchers tell us that because earbuds don't cancel out as much outside noise as headphones do, earbud users typically turn the volume up higher to drown out exterior sounds, and so the potential damage is even worse.[78]

Of course, teenagers love having the power to listen to their music privately, without sharing it with adults. Truth be told, many adults love the quiet provided when teens plug in the earbuds. But, as the writer Llewellyn Hinkes-Jones recently suggested in the pages of the *Atlantic* magazine, "The shared experience of listening with others is not unlike the cultural rituals of communal editing. Music may not have the primal necessity of food, but it is something people commonly ingest together." Perhaps—not only for the sake of your teenagers' ears but also to enhance a sense of family togetherness and sharing—it might be good to drop both headphones and earbuds frequently and return to good old-fashioned speakers. Listening to and discussing each other's music can be a wonderful way to keep communication open through the teenage years.[79]

Music for Life

Adolescence poses challenges for practically every family—but with music you will find the years passing more pleasurably and the results worth the effort as your teenager becomes a young adult. Through the twenties, thirties, and beyond, music continues to tune up the brain. In an updated study of the Mozart Effect, conducted at Osaka University Graduate School of Medicine, in Japan, the neural activity of ten men and women ages twenty-five to thirty-five was observed as they listened to Mozart's sonata (K. 448) and then took a Japanese version of the Tanaka B-type intelligence test, which includes a spatial-reasoning subtest. Researchers observed dramatic activity in the regions of the brain responsible for spatial-temporal reasoning, suggesting the possibility of a direct priming effect of Mozart's music. In other studies, music majors have been shown to score highest in reading among all majors, including English;[80] to be most likely of all college graduates, including biochemistry majors, to be admitted to medical school; and to be emotionally healthier than their nonmusician counterparts, feeling more confident in test-taking situations and reporting fewer emotional concerns and alcohol-related problems.[81]

Simply listening to music makes college students happier, according to a study conducted recently in Sweden. In the study, college students ages twenty to thirty-one were randomly beeped several times each day over a period of two weeks and were asked if they were listening to music and how it made them feel.[82] It was discovered that thirty-seven percent of the time the students were listening to music when they were beeped, and those who were engaged with listening were "more likely to be experiencing feelings of happiness or elation," while those not listening claimed to be experiencing "anger, irritation, anxiety, fear, boredom, or indifference."[83]

www.HealingAtTheSpeedOfSound.com/Link34

Music helps us remember everything from our ABC's in preschool to complex formulas and foreign languages in our college years. What more pleasurable way can there be for college students to brush up on their French than to sing along with Edith Piaf?

Ideally, as our young people grow into adulthood, they will be moved to not only continue their involvement with music, but to share the great joy they have experienced with others less fortunate than themselves. In 2002, a group of college music majors from a prestigious university spent nine weeks teaching voice and instrumental performance to one hundred at-risk elementary school children in an urban after-school program in Southern California. The program not only provided the children with a safe, structured environment, but it exposed them to the positive influences of enthusiastic young musicians teaching a subject they loved. Both teachers and students pronounced the program very successful as a mutually enriching form of cultural exchange.[84]

Music paves the way for collaboration, cooperation, and an overall spirit of enthusiasm and fun. Children whose journey toward adulthood has been enhanced by the joy of singing, moving, and sharing music with others understand sound's ability to create a sense of community, heal the spirit, and forge bonds between people who would otherwise never join together. What better future can we hope for, for our children and for the generations to come?

CHAPTER FIVE

The Harmony of the Body

Sound's Power to Heal

You can look at disease as a form of disharmony. And there's no organ system in the body that's not affected by sound and music and vibration.

—Mitchell Gaynor, M.D.

Now that we have examined the many ways in which sound shapes the development of our bodies and minds, it is easy to understand how it also influences the state of our health every day of our lives, in good ways or bad. This relationship between an individual's sound environment and his sense of well-being has been intuited for centuries, since the days when Orpheus, the Greek father of song, was believed to have taught humanity the art of medicine, and when Confucius observed music's therapeutic impact on the human mind, spirit, and behavior.[1] For eons, shamans, healers, and religious leaders have attempted to purge illnesses and "retune" body and mind via chants, singing, and the use of drums, sacred gongs, and other instruments.[2] As the musician-philosopher Hazrat Inayat Khan has pointed out, the human body responds to sound like a living resonator. "The whole mechanism, the muscles, the blood circulation, the nerves, all are moved by the power of vibration"—and so it's only logical to conclude that different sounds create different effects.[3]

By the nineteenth century, even Western healers such as Florence Nightingale had begun to take note of sound's potential to distract patients and mitigate pain during operations performed only with local anesthesia,[4] to speed recovery following surgery or illness, and to calm the spirits of those confined to mental institutions. In 1944, as sound's power to heal became more widely recognized and acknowledged in the scientific community, the first music therapy program was created in the United States. Today, the American Music Therapy Association boasts more than thirty-eight hundred members who work at hospitals, clinics, schools, hospices, and elsewhere, using music to help heal, regulate, and improve function in the human body and mind.

In recent decades, many new studies have demonstrated in specific ways how different kinds of sound generate certain measurable physiological changes, whether as a subliminal influence, a focused listening experience, or a physical activity requiring active engagement. Researchers now know, for example, that merely listening to upbeat music in a style one likes causes the blood vessels to expand (thus increasing blood flow), improves breathing patterns, and spurs increased production of endorphins, the brain's "euphoria hormones"—thus decreasing stress and creating an overall feeling of well-being.[5] It also boosts the immune system through increased production of the protein immunoglobulin A (IgA), used by the body to fight disease. Group drumming, playing in a band or orchestra, and singing magnify these effects. One study by scientists at the University of California, Irvine, revealed that when members of California's Pacific Chorale rehearsed Beethoven's demanding, emotionally complex *Missa Solemnis*, their IgA levels increased by 150 percent—and when they performed the piece before an audience the levels increased by a whopping 240 percent.[6] The singers themselves attributed their improved sense of good health and well-being to the sheer euphoria of the experience.[7]

 **www.HealingAtTheSpeedOfSound.com/Link35**

Euphoria is a powerful disease-fighting state, which is something we can intuit, but to have it borne out by scientific evidence is reassuring and encouraging. There's something healing about the very act of singing. Listen to this beautiful song, "This Majestic Land," by Michael Hoppé. How does it make you feel inside? How does it affect your breathing, your heart rate, your thoughts, your mood? Now sing along and notice how much better you feel!

Just as significantly, research tells us that listening to music one doesn't like has the opposite effect, causing the blood vessels to constrict, breathing to quicken, and feelings of stress to increase. When we consider how effectively high-volume music and chaotic sound are used as a torture technique to break down prisoners' defenses, it is easy to see how prolonged exposure to unpleasant music or noise can negatively affect the immune system, speed the aging process, increase levels of anxiety and depression, contribute to infertility and impotence, and increase the risk of heart attack and stroke.[8]

Sound and music, then, make for a two-edged sword that can enhance or detract from our health depending on how, when, and where they are present in our lives. In this chapter, we will explore the ways in which you and your loved ones can use sound in positive ways to relieve pain, to eliminate or manage the symptoms of certain health conditions, to decrease anxiety before surgery and speed recovery afterward, and to enhance physical rehabilitation. We will examine the ways in which rhythm and sound can be used in treating such psychological issues as depression and post-traumatic stress disorder as well, and in helping individuals summon the will and the strength to meet the health-related challenges they face.

 **www.HealingAtTheSpeedOfSound.com/Link36**

As part of the Library of Congress's Music and the Brain series, Steve Mencher talks with Concetta M. Tomaino, executive director of the Institute for Music and Neurologic Function, about music's positive impact on a variety of health conditions.

Music to Manage Pain

Most of us can remember the relief we felt as children, after scraping our knees or elbows, when a parent or other caregiver soothed our pain with a Band-Aid and some loving chatter or song. "Don't worry," your mother may have said in a singsong voice as she applied an antibiotic. "We'll clean this up, dab on some cream, and the hurt will be all gone." Almost magically, her voice helped to make the pain fade away, allowing for a loving embrace and a quick return to playtime.

As it turns out, this instinctive way of banishing pain and distress has nothing to do with magic. Scientists have found that the sound of a loved one's voice, or some favorite music, actually creates physiological responses that can decrease stress and hasten recovery. In the book *Music Therapy and Pediatric Pain*, edited by Joanne V. Loewy, music therapists, physicians, and others explain how a crooned "Now I'm going to put the Band-Aid on" redirects a child's attention from sensations of pain toward the process of recovery. They tell us that holding the child and softly humming, singing, rocking, or simply breathing rhythmically—first at a pace that mirrors the intensity of her distress, then gradually decreasing toward a more normal tempo—allows her to escape her own discomfort and meld with your more stable state of being. One recently published study demonstrated that healthy volunteers who listened to pleasant music while researchers heated a spot on their forearms experienced less pain than subjects given the same treatment in silence.[9] Singing about a painful experience as it happens (improvising a "Needle Song," for instance, while getting a shot) works even more effectively, as it allows a child to "give the pain a voice" and thus assert mastery over the experience. Some scientists believe that the act of singing may even literally prevent pain, not just distract from it, by blocking the neuronal pathways that would otherwise transmit pain-related impulses to the brain.[10]

www.HealingAtTheSpeedOfSound.com/Link37

On the Health segment of ABC's *Good Morning America*, Dr. Michael McKee, a psychologist at the Cleveland Clinic, discusses ways in which low-volume music can be used to manage pain, relax patients, help them access and express emotion, and decrease heart rate, particularly when patients are allowed to select the music that they like best.

Children are not the only ones who can benefit from these techniques. Like younger individuals, you are likely to feel much less anxious when climbing into the dentist's chair after listening to soothing piped-in music for half an hour or, even better, your own calming, low-volume selections via headphones. Studies have shown that listening to soft, percussion-free music[11] in medical waiting rooms lowers heart rate and measurably diminishes other symptoms of distress.[12] Keep the music going during the procedure as well, if you can: Researchers have found that soothing music helps patients of all ages endure stress-inducing or painful medical tests with little or no sedation, in less time and with fewer staff members in attendance.[13] The next time a nurse draws your blood, try humming or singing to literally block the perception of pain. (Don't worry—nurses have seen and heard everything!) Singing softly, humming, chanting a mantra, or even playing a harmonica—all of which encourage deep, rhythmic breathing and improve blood circulation—can help reduce anxiety and decrease pain during periods of longer-term discomfort, too, caused by certain illnesses and medical conditions and procedures. Just as gentle rocking and rhythmic breathing helped soothe us as children, researchers have found that tapping a foot or beating out the rhythm of a song, tilting an ocean drum back and forth, or in some cases simply waving a scarf to music can help reduce the perception of chronic pain in people of any age, thereby lessening the need for pain medications or even hospitalization in some cases.

Listen Up

♫ Few people better understand the two-sided nature of sound better than those who suffer from migraines. For many, certain sound frequencies or types of sound are the cause of their excruciating pain. Yet, others find that certain kinds of sound or vibration provide welcome relief from the same condition. One study published in the *European Journal of Pain* showed that listening to pleasant music diminishes the pain of migraine headaches in many children. A surprising number of adult migraine sufferers testify to having found relief by "self-medicating" with the sonic vibration caused by rock music with a strong bass or drum beat, the lower-range sound vibrations from a Tibetan singing bowl held close to the head, the music of Bach played on a church organ, and even, in one interesting case, the chance sonic vibration of hummingbird wings passing close to the head![14]

The Sound of a Cure

The same properties of sound that help us manage pain can also help prevent or decrease the severity of certain illnesses and medical conditions. The soothing music that temporarily lowers your heart rate in your doctor's waiting room, for example, can help alleviate hypertension when listened to regularly over the long term, perhaps lessening the need for medication. Pleasurable music coaxes the blood vessels to widen and the body to produce chemicals that protect the heart, thus decreasing the risk of heart failure or stroke if listened to for half an hour or more per day.

Sound vibration not only helps relieve the pain of migraines for some, but can actually help diminish the frequency of chronic sinus infections, an affliction that strikes more than thirty-seven million Americans each year.[15] Researchers have discovered that daily humming sessions create vibration in the sinus and nasal cavities, which increases air circulation, blood flow, and the production of nitric oxide, thus inhibiting bacteria growth and infections.[16] Two recent studies conducted in Stockholm, Sweden, confirm the effectiveness of this practice, showing levels of nitric oxide rising in the sinuses to levels fifteen times higher than when individuals simply breathe deeply.[17]

 **www.HealingAtTheSpeedOfSound.com/Link38**

Listen to me demonstrate breathing and humming exercises that can reduce sinus problems for you this winter.

Music's ability to redirect attention has proved useful in treating tinnitus—another condition that affects millions of Americans—in which the individual "hears" a persistent ringing, whistling, or other noise not produced by an outside source. Frequently caused by excessive exposure to noise such as high-decibel music, roaring engines, or gunfire, persistent tinnitus can sometimes lead to severe depression, as it interferes with the ability to sleep, focus on work, and maintain relationships—and these negative feelings only magnify its impact.[18] "The more you worry about it, the worse it gets," explains one high-profile sufferer, actor William Shatner. "I couldn't sleep or think, and I even thought about suicide."[19] Shatner benefited from another form of "tinnitus retraining therapy," in which the noise in his head was masked with low-level broadband sound—a kind of white noise—so that it became less intrusive. Wearing an electronic device that exposed him to the white noise around the clock, and undergoing psychological counseling to help guide his thought processes away from tinnitus-generated noises and combat depression, he reported after four months that he no longer heard the tinnitus ninety-five percent of the time.[20]

Alex Doman experienced ringing in his ears for years, following an acoustic trauma he suffered as a teenager when exposed to loud music at a punk rock concert. After years of experimenting with music listening therapy, he eventually was able to stop the ringing. It continues to recur in one ear from time to time, however, for just a few seconds. "I now understand that this is my body's alarm," he says. The noise serves as a warning that tells him his stress levels are too high and that he needs to do something about it. Most often, the ringing manifests itself when he is working too intensively and not taking enough personal time to recharge.

Scientists are at work on a number of other sonic solutions to tinnitus as well, including pulse generators to stimulate specific areas of the brain,[21] and custom-designed soundtracks—similar to the music listening therapy program that Alex used—to train the brain to filter out the offending sound.[22] In the meantime, however, one sufferer has turned to a more natural source of sound distraction: Famed radio personality and writer Garrison Keillor has discovered that cicadas chirp in the same frequency range as his inner ear and mask the ringing very nicely. "I stood in the park where they were whirring around and I felt relief," he remarks. "Medicine has no remedy for tinnitus. . . . My only alternative, I guess, is to wander the planet in search of cicadas."[23]

The deep neural links between music and the brain that may allow us to use music to block perception of pain may also be related to the decrease in seizure-related electrical activity that some severely epileptic individuals experience when listening to certain classical music selections. Music seems to "call" to the brain on a neuronal level, and the brain responds strongly. Reports regularly surface, too, of favorite melodies or other sounds bringing coma victims back to consciousness—as when fourteen-year-old Justine Cantrell, a member of her high school band, suffered a traumatic brain injury and was roused from unconsciousness only after a classmate played his saxophone in her hospital room.[24]

The physical act of singing, drumming, or playing a musical instrument not only improves overall health by strengthening the immune system, as we have seen, but can also affect the body's condition in specific, positive ways. Many doctors now prescribe singing or wind-instrument lessons for patients with a variety of breathing and pulmonary problems, for instance, because of the workout these activities provide the throat muscles, nasal cavities, lungs, and upper-body muscles. In 2007, for example, a large number of New York City public school children with asthma were able to significantly improve their breathing abilities by studying and practicing the recorder. As a side benefit, they began to feel a greater sense of mastery over their condition. The harmonica, which requires the player to breathe in as well as out, can strengthen the lungs of those with chronic bronchitis, emphysema, and pulmonary disease, and the heart muscles of those who have had open-heart surgery or a heart transplant. Health providers find that daily "harmonica workouts" raise patients' spirits as well, thus speeding their recovery and lowering medical costs.

Sound Profile: Brian Simpson

♫ As a severe asthmatic, Brian Simpson had suffered from his condition every day of his life, and had spent a good portion of his thirty-two years in hospitals, undergoing every available medical treatment, including chemotherapy, without success. In 2002, following an especially harrowing instance of respiratory arrest, his doctors told him that little hope remained for his survival and that, as

Simpson later recalled, "I just needed to be comfortable and enjoy the time I had."

Then a miracle occurred. Lying in bed, listening to a recording by the Pittsburgh Symphony Orchestra's principle oboist, Cynthia Koledo DeAlmeida, Simpson was inspired to pick up the oboe he had played as a music major in college, and begin to play it again. The act didn't make much sense, but as he put it, "I really didn't have much to lose."

At first, he could play the instrument for only a minute at most before losing his breathing capacity. But the more he played, the stronger his lungs felt and the easier it became for him to play—and to breathe.

Doctors later speculated that forcing air through the small opening in the oboe's mouthpiece must have exercised Simpson's abdominal muscles in a unique way. In any case, it seems to have saved his life. Today, he still struggles to walk and must always keep an oxygen tank nearby. But his lung capacity has risen from twenty-five to fifty-five percent, his medication has been reduced, and he hasn't been back in the hospital in more than a year. Best of all, he can now play the oboe two hours a day and perform with a local orchestra—and plans are under way to study the mechanism behind his remarkable recovery in hopes of helping other asthma patients like himself.[25]

Strange as it may seem, an Australian aboriginal instrument called the didgeridoo has helped many people who suffer from sleep apnea, a quite serious condition in which the airways collapse repeatedly during sleep, interrupting breathing and even restricting the supply of oxygen to the brain.[26] This long, pipelike instrument requires the player to develop a technique called "circular breathing"—breathing in through the nose while simultaneously expelling air out of the mouth—which strengthens the throat muscles surrounding the airways, even as the instrument provides healthy vibration throughout the head, throat, and chest.[27] A number of recent studies have shown that, over time, daily playing leads to better sleep and a great sense of daytime alertness as a result.[28]

www.HealingAtTheSpeedOfSound.com/Link39
www.HealingAtTheSpeedOfSound.com/Link40

Here are two demonstrations of the circular breathing technique—the first for use in playing the didgeridoo, and the second, by jazz musician Kenny G, for playing a soprano sax. But, as "America's doctor," Dr. Oz, has pointed out on his celebrated programs, circular breathing can be practiced without an instrument, simply by "playing" an empty roll of wrapping paper or paper towels.[29]

The emotional high experienced by music makers—as evidenced by increased production of immunoglobulin and pain-killing endorphins—is of crucial importance to those with autoimmune disease, allergies (anaphylaxis), eczema, arthritis (including juvenile rheumatoid arthritis), AIDS, or cancer. Dr. Mitchell L. Gaynor, director of medical oncology at New York's Strang-Cornell Cancer Prevention Center, points also to music's ability to decrease stress and increase natural cancer-killer-cell activity as his reason for encouraging his patients to combine singing, drumming, chanting, and verbal expression with the use of other relaxation techniques.[30] These musical activities not only decrease lymphocyte cell counts,[31] but also help cancer patients manage pain[32] and combat depression without pharmaceuticals.[33] "Doctors are finally learning what primitive healers have known for centuries," he writes. By using music, voice, and rhythm to reach "a part of themselves where they can no longer be afraid," patients can bring themselves back toward health.[34]

Listen Up

In his article "Healing: To the Beat of an Inner Drummer," published as part of his Mind over Matter series on the Web site Healthy.net, Dr. Barry Bittman tells of a twenty-two-year-old cancer patient he calls Eric, who had six surgeries in less than a year and was facing yet another round of chemotherapy. At a retreat for cancer survivors headed by Bittman, Eric announced that he'd had enough and was simply going to give up. His listeners, all fellow survivors, could understand better than anyone else the seriousness with which he spoke. How could they argue with him? Eric seemed to be making no progress toward recovery, and all understood that once a patient loses faith in the effectiveness of treatment, its chances of success are sharply diminished.

As an oncologist, however, Bittman had witnessed many such moments of despair, and he remained hopeful for Eric. That evening, he asked the young man to lead the group's drumming circle. As he later recalled, a change began to come over Eric almost as soon as he placed his hands on the drum. "The thought seemed to have passed through his mind that this might be his last chance to fully celebrate the life he'd lived," Bittman writes. "His hands on the drum beat out an unrelenting, driving, urgent rhythm," and the others, surprised by his intensity, responded with enthusiasm. A sense of joy and celebration passed through the group. "Drumming beyond fatigue, beyond their limits and limitations, their sense of camaraderie joined them into a whole."

The next morning, others remarked that Eric looked and acted like he felt better than he had in months, walking about with a bounce in his step and a positive attitude. A short time later, after he had returned home, he described himself to others as "a new person"—and Bittman was not surprised to hear that for the first time, his chemotherapy was working. His prognosis remained serious, but at least for the time being music had rekindled this individual's will to live.[35]

A Healing Resonance—Sound in the Hospital

With all of this research demonstrating the real and remarkable healing powers of the right kinds of music and sound, it is surprising to note how rarely hospital administrators and staff pay serious attention to the sound environment within their facilities. As I have pointed out before, sound can be a two-edged sword in terms of our physical and mental health: Just as the organized rhythms and tones of music can provide enormous, proven support for patients in the hospital, noise can add to an already stressful situation and hinder a patient's efforts to heal. The racket made by paging systems, televisions, monitoring alarms, ice machines, telephones, medical equipment, and the constant conversation of visitors and staff quite commonly—in every single case, according to one 1999 survey[36]—exceed the World Health Organization's maximum recommended background noise level of thirty-five decibels (somewhere between the noise level of a whisper and a humming refrigerator).[37] Amplified by the hard surfaces of hospital interiors designed for durability and ease in disinfecting,[38] the noise level often reaches seventy-two decibels—as loud as a busy highway—and frequently peaks above levels considered safe for healthy employees at work,[39] much less for the seriously ill, who have been shown to be more sensitive to sound than are healthy people.

Hospital patients, weakened by pain and the effects of their medication, and unable to turn down the volume or escape their environment, must sometimes struggle to hear and be heard during the day, and at night are startled awake by sudden or unfamiliar noises. These kinds of conditions exacerbate pain, heighten disorientation, and can easily lead to a state of acute distress, consuming physical resources the patient needs to recover.[40] In intensive care units particularly, noise tends to result in more medications,[41] slower recovery,[42] longer hospital stays, and an increased chance of rehospitalization.[43] Since prolonged or frequent noise often leads to increased heart rate and rises in blood pressure, patients in coronary care units are especially susceptible to noisy environments.[44] Heart attack survivors are more likely to experience additional attacks when exposed to too much noise, and patients with ischemic heart disease, characterized by a reduced blood supply to the heart, can die from overexposure to chaotic sound. Premature or fragile newborns are also particularly vulnerable to this kind of stimulus. Several studies have shown that loud noise levels in the NICU interfere with sleep, elevate infants' blood pressure, increase heart and respiration rates, and lead to an increased need for oxygen support therapy.[45]

Sound leakage, too, is an enormous concern in the healthcare setting. Patients or loved ones who fear that their personal conversations with medical personnel can be overheard may hesitate to talk frankly. Studies have shown that as many as five percent of emergency room patients withhold some of their history or refuse some part of their physical exam because they don't have enough privacy, and their omissions and resistance can lead to errors in treatment plans or administering medication.[46]

Did You Know?

♫ Noise not only affects patients in a hospital or medical facility, but wears on the spirits of the staff as well. High levels of noise have been shown to lead to nursing and medication errors, emotional exhaustion, and burnout among critical-care nurses,[47] who must expend extra energy and time just to communicate effectively and make sure their work standards remain high.[48] A report on noise in the operating room by the Center for Health Design reveals noise levels topping seventy-seven decibels, which forces medical personnel to raise their voices to be heard and leads to decreases in comprehension, mental efficiency, even short-term memory,[49] all of which have serious implications for patient safety.[50] Throughout the hospital, workers report feeling "less pressure and strain" when the volume is kept low[51]—not only because they feel less distracted but also because their patients are happier and more comfortable, and therefore less demanding.

Fortunately, as evidence has mounted of sound's power to harm as well as help patients in hospitals, some administration officials have begun making efforts to increase privacy and reduce noise by replacing overhead paging systems with wireless or cell phone communication; moving noisy machinery away from the patient area when possible, and turning it off between uses; and educating the staff on the importance of maintaining as quiet an environment as possible.[52] More private rooms—one of the most effective ways to combat noise—are also being provided.[53]

As new hospitals are built, architects and designers increase patient privacy by creating examination areas with solid walls instead of curtains, separate conference rooms for medical conversations, and sound-absorbing ceiling tiles and interior finishes in patient areas.[54] They tap into the healing power of nature sounds by installing pleasant-sounding waterfalls and quiet courtyards or gardens where patients, families, and visitors can enjoy special music performances as they have a picnic lunch. In fact, the Marianjoy Rehabilitation Hospital, in Wheaton, Illinois, goes one step further, providing a wheelchair-accessible labyrinth where patients can engage in prayer or meditation , listening to special music selected for this sacred space.

Increasingly, music therapists are present in hospitals. These trained professionals know how to harmonize with the sonic environment, mask ambient noise, and otherwise shape the auditory environment. Companies like DMX, in Austin, Texas, a music sourcing company for public environments, and Aesthetic Audio Systems, of San Diego, have brought specialized programming in a variety of musical styles to hospitals, medical offices, and other health-care environments—all in an effort to, as Florence Nightingale wrote in 1860, "put the patient in the best possible position for nature to act upon him."

www.HealingAtTheSpeedOfSound.com/Link41

Take a tour with me through the Good Samaritan Medical Center, where a sound environment has been created to enhance the experience of patients and staff alike.

Even if you (or a loved one) find yourself in an institution that does not offer these amenities, you can still act in specific ways to improve the sound environment. If noisy machinery and conversations at the nursing station make it difficult to relax and sleep, point this out to staff members in a tactful way, reminding them that people who are ill are especially sensitive to noise and that a relaxed patient not only heals more quickly, but is generally easier to care for. If you have a baby in intensive care, ask the nursing staff whether they are taking steps to reduce noise in that environment. If not, they may be able to play soft lullabies for the infants as a way of calming them and promoting better health.

In other parts of the hospital, if you can't completely change the level of noise, you can at least mask it by listening to music or nature sounds on your personal music device with headphones. Your own specially designed sound relaxation and healing soundtrack can become your greatest ally during a hospital stay. Patients who listen to music report significantly less disturbance from environmental noise.[55] Music helps them tolerate such challenging technology as magnetic resonance imaging machines[56] and mechanical ventilators.[57] Just as listening to music relaxes patients before and during visits to the dentist, so it has proved significantly helpful before surgery and even during minor procedures when local anesthesia is used.[58] When delivered through headphones for thirty minutes before surgery, music has been shown to decrease anxiety as effectively in many cases as antianxiety drugs,[59] making it possible at times to lower the dose of anesthesia.[60] Some studies have even shown that playing music during surgery while the patient is under general anesthesia[61] decreases postoperative pain and medical complications, thereby shortening recovery time.[62] Surgeons and emergency room staff[63] also respond positively to the presence of music while they work. Music of their choice helps surgeons feel more relaxed and focused,[64] and helps create an atmosphere of camaraderie and teamwork.

Many patients are grateful for the soothing music piped into the post-surgery recovery room,[65] as it helps ease their transition to full consciousness.[66] Patients recovering from open heart or bypass surgery especially benefit, since low-volume background music has been shown to reduce stress as they rest in bed.[67] Hospital administrators have begun to note the fact that music's presence often leads to lower doses of drugs, not to mention less stressed and therefore less demanding patients.[68] At the Mayo Clinic in Rochester, Minnesota, music is now used as part of the cardiovascular surgery healing program to promote relaxation, reduce stress and anxiety, decrease pain, help patients sleep, and improve their moods during recovery.[69]

Even in a worst-case scenario, if you find yourself in a hospital without access to music of your choice, keep in mind what I told you earlier about earworms. Music's ability to remain lodged in the brain allows you to benefit from its healing tones and rhythms, even if you are only "listening" inside your own head as you endure an MRI or other uncomfortable medical procedure. I have often told the story of Lorna, a woman who was driving home, listening to act one of a live radio broadcast of Rossini's *The Barber of Seville*, when a truck rear-ended her just before the woman playing Rosina was to sing. As Lorna later recalled, the impact of the accident was sudden and stunning. But even in her state of shock and in great pain, for fifteen minutes, as emergency personnel tried to free her from the wreckage of her car, she continued to listen to the entire aria and the rest of the opera in her mind. The ambulance crew later told her that she had been unconscious until she was placed inside the ambulance. But she clearly recalled hearing Rosina's voice throughout the terrible ordeal. "The music kept me alive," she insisted. "I just kept listening, listening. From the beginning of that aria, I knew I had to finish the opera of my life."[70]

Of course, no one wants to put music to this kind of extreme test. Nevertheless, take a moment to think about what kind of music might "save" you in an accident or severe illness. If you could take only three musical selections to the hospital with you, what would they be?

A Happy Tune

As always when it comes to music, it helps to *create* sound whenever possible, rather than just listen. Music therapists, increasingly present in American hospitals, bring a great deal of pleasure as well as healing to their patients in this way. After participating in music sessions in the hospital, children with serious or even life-threatening conditions often report significant improvement in how they feel.[71] Singing or playing instruments with a therapist in a group setting "gave me something pleasurable to do," one patient said, adding that it distracted her from "the bad things in my life." Another remarked that the music sessions "make me feel relaxed—in fact my headache was gone," and actually helped her to forget for a while that she was ill.[72] Elderly people benefit particularly from this form of therapy, because it stimulates their brains, reduces episodes of confusion and delirium, and decreases their need for pain medication and other drugs.[73]

www.HealingAtTheSpeedOfSound.com/Link42

Music therapist Lillieth Grand helps young hospitalized patients use music as a tool to manage their fear, homesickness, and pain.

Music therapists have helped some patients discover their own strong healing force through the composition of music or writing of songs. Trevor Gibbons, a stroke victim at New York's Beth Israel Medical Center whose therapists encouraged him to put pen to paper, found songwriting to be the ideal way to express feelings of fear, sadness, and frustration, thus working through his negative feelings and finding new hope for the future. "Music is my inspiration, my escape from sadness and loneliness and pain," he says. "When I start to sing it opens up my mind and I think, 'There's nothing I can't do.'"[74] Twelve-year-old Bethany, a victim of a brain injury, shared Trevor's experience after she began creating rhythmic patterns as memory exercises on the software program GarageBand. Quickly moving on to songwriting, she found that the exercise "motivates me to keep going and not quit."[75] Some young patients, such as five-year-old Noel Young, hospitalized repeatedly as he battled a rare blood disease, even create their own CDs. "Like many five-year-olds, Noel loves superheroes," his music therapist explains, "so we wrote and recorded a song that allowed Noel to be the superhero and have superpowers. Opportunities like these allow children to gain back some of the power they have lost in the hospital environment."[76]

www.HealingAtTheSpeedOfSound.com/Link43

Multiplatinum recording artist Moby shows us the many ways in which the nonprofit Institute for Music and Neurologic Function uses music to restore, maintain, and improve people's physical, emotional, and neurologic functioning.

One particularly inspiring story comes from Nashville's Monroe Carell Jr. Children's Hospital at Vanderbilt University Medical Center, where a local songwriter named Jenny Plume was hired to create a music therapy program for young patients. The stated aim of the program was to "help patients express their experience through song," and Plume soon discovered that songwriting provided the best method for the patients in her care. Through their own lyrics and melodies, they could explore their emotions, gain perspective on their situation, and feel more in control. The program proved so effective that it soon drew the attention of a number of country music stars, some of whom agreed to record the children's songs in Nashville's recording studios for a professionally produced CD. The excitement of seeing their private thoughts turned into a finished performance by musicians they admired allowed these ill teenagers to forget their grim circumstances temporarily, and to think of themselves as songwriters instead of simply victims of a disease.[77]

www.HealingAtTheSpeedOfSound.com/Link44

Watch country star Vince Gill record "That's Who I Am," by Chris Weber, a seventeen-year-old with cystic fibrosis.

Music has proved to have such a positive effect that some American hospitals have begun to provide patients with not only recorded music and music therapy but also with occasional live music performances. Singer-songwriter Lanny Sherwin, who performs for children at Cottage Hospital in Santa Barbara, California, admits that singing for children who may be terminally ill is "probably the most difficult and most rewarding gig I do." Still, child specialists at the hospital express gratitude for the joy his music provides in a difficult environment.[78] Meanwhile, hospital administrators at the University of Kentucky Chandler Medical Center have gone even further, commissioning a special auditorium, adjacent to the lobby, for music and other live performances that will be open to the public and live-fed into patients' rooms.

If a music therapist visits a hospital that you or a loved one is in, be sure to take advantage of her services. It is practically impossible to participate in a hospital music therapy session without feeling one's spirits lifted, and music is all it takes to give patients the willpower they need to continue getting well. If no therapist is present, talk with staff and hospital administrators about bringing one to the institution. Many music therapy programs are funded by individual donors or philanthropic programs, and a surprising number of visiting musicians volunteer their services for free.

Fascinating Rhythm

Every single day, music is available to reduce stress, increase our well-being, and bring joy into our lives. When we are ill or in the hospital, it soothes us, heals us, and wraps us in a cocoon of protective sound. Those of us in need of physical or neurological rehabilitation will find, too, that music's rhythms and vibration can bring us back into sync with our bodies, regulating our movements, improving our gait if needed, and even forging new connections and pathways in our brains when the old ones have been damaged. As Dr. Wendy Magee, international fellow in music therapy at London's Institute of Neuropalliative Rehabilitation, explains, music works as a "megavitamin for the brain."[79]

Researchers have found, for example, that the mere act of listening to music for several hours per day can enhance cognitive rehabilitation in stroke victims, as the sounds help activate brain regions related to attention, semantic processing, memory, emotional processing, and motor function.[80] Stroke survivors can begin to restore fine motor skills and coordination by playing the piano, autoharp, or drums.[81] Working with rhythmic patterns on an instrument or computer software helps survivors of stroke or accident-caused brain damage to bolster their memory skills.

Due to the fact that music and language are processed in so many of the same neural regions, singing can help survivors of stroke or brain damage recover crucial speech skills. In an approach called Melodic Intonation Therapy, patients with post-stroke aphasia sing songs with lyrics, with the therapist gradually removing the music over time until the patient is left speaking the lyrics and, eventually, substituting regular conversational phrases in their place. The effort to recall words with meanings similar to those in the songs helps enormously in both word retrieval and in verbal expression.[82] Inside the brain, certain regions on the right side are beginning to pick up the slack for the damaged left side—another demonstration of the brain's amazing plasticity and ability to adapt.

One patient at Beth Israel hospital, a fifty-one-year-old carpenter who had suffered a devastating spinal injury and stroke, experienced a similar process organically through intensive, thrice-weekly sessions of vocal training and piano playing over the course of several years. By the end of these sessions, the carpenter, who had previously sung only in his church choir, could not only speak again, but had fallen in love with music, writing more than four hundred songs, recording three CDs, and performing at a benefit for the hospital. Music had given him two gifts: his power of speech, and a new passion in life. His new relationship with sound "gave me motivation and a chance to look forward to live another day," he claims.[83] Not many other kinds of therapies can do the same.

Amy Price is another individual who owes much in her life to the power of sound. Several years ago, she was involved in a serious automobile accident and suffered brain damage that affected her thinking, memory, speech, hearing, sight, spatial ability, and proprioception (the sense of where the body parts are in relation to each other and whether the body is moving with the proper effort). Neuropsychologists and audiologists informed her that the damage was permanent and that she was unlikely ever to recover her full hearing, sight, or memory abilities. When medical tests showed that her hearing problems lay in the path between the brain and ear, Dr. William Orrison, of the Amigenics Nevada Imaging Centers, suggested she try an intensive course of music listening therapy in hopes that its bone-conduction vibrations, paired with the specially modified music of Mozart and other composers, might reawaken the ear-brain communication. Price took his advice—and experienced marked improvement as the rhythms and natural sequencing characteristics of music helped to carve new neural pathways, literally reorganizing her damaged brain.

Price claimed she would never forget the day, midway through her listening protocol, when for the first time since the accident she was able to hear her cell phone ring as she walked through a noisy shopping mall. Not only could she hear the phone, but she could answer it and carry on a conversation with ease. Soon, she began to notice improvement in her ability to learn new material and retain information. The experience not only allowed Price to recover most of her neural abilities despite the grim prognosis given by the experts, but it also inspired in her a profound fascination with the ways in which the brain functions. In the years since she received treatment, she has become the director of research and development at Thinking Pays, in Boca Raton, Florida, focusing on integrative neuroscience and brain optimization. Much of her current research involves the potential for optimizing brain function through sound.[84]

Just as Amy Price looked to music's complex patterns and rhythms to redesign the neural pathways of her brain, patients with orthopedic and neuromuscular disorders can rely on its guiding beat to support them in their efforts to control their movements, regulate their gait, and recover their sense of their body's movement and where it is in space. The human brain is innately attuned to respond to highly rhythmic music. Sound with a steady beat serves as an auditory timing mechanism, triggering certain neural networks to translate the cadence into organized movement. In this way, people with gait or balance disorders can improve their coordination, and those with Parkinson's disease can better control muscle bursts and involuntary tremors. In some cases, once the rhythm begins, an individual who is frozen can immediately release and begin walking. In his book *Musicophilia*, Dr. Oliver Sacks describes Parkinson's disease patients who are unable to button their own shirts becoming animated by the sounds of dance music and songs from their youth, and he recalls one eighty-nine-year-old wheelchair-bound resident who suddenly rose up to dance when he heard a familiar waltz.[85]

Listen Up

♫ Rande Davis Gedaliah's 2003 diagnosis of Parkinson's was followed by leg spasms, balance problems, difficulty walking, and ultimately a serious fall in the shower. But something remarkable happened when the sixty-year-old public speaking coach turned to an oldies station on her shower radio: She could move her leg with ease, her balance improved, and she couldn't stop dancing. Now, she puts on her iPod and pumps in Bruce Springsteen's "Born in the U.S.A." when she wants to walk quickly; for a slower pace, Queen's "We Are the Champions" does the trick.[86]

Drumming circles, which require coordinating muscle movements and developing an ear for timing, can be quite effective in helping people with neuromuscular disorders control their physical movement. Rick Bausman, a musician and the creator of the Drum Workshop, based in Martha's Vineyard, notes that his disabled participants' motion becomes more fluid—that those with Parkinson's disease "don't shake quite as much, and their tremors seem to calm down."[87] Studies have shown that the same holds true for group music sessions involving pianos, cymbals, xylophones, and other instruments that require participants to move their bodies to the beat.

www.HealingAtTheSpeedOfSound.com/Link45

Watch Jeanne Brinker describe some of her experiences with patients who have found pleasure and improved health and well-being through drumming.

Drumming circles highlight one of music's most important qualities as a tool for rehabilitation: Playing music is so pleasurable that individuals are happy to engage in it for hours, days, and months on end. Patients with disabilities generally so enjoy moving their arms, hands, and fingers to create music on Music Maker computer software, for example, that they exercise longer and reap more benefits as a result.[88] Taking piano lessons, playing music with others, and composing songs on GarageBand have a similar effect, encouraging more engagement, inspiring positive moods, and also providing an emotional outlet to help recovering patients better cope with their condition. Perhaps this is why Bret Michaels, lead singer and songwriter for the rock group Poison, threw himself passionately into performing again after suffering a brain hemorrhage and mild stroke in 2010. "If I have a chance of healing all the way, I need to just be around people and stuff that I feel will help me best. I need to be out on the road," he told one reporter. "I'm hoping the legacy I leave behind is that I'm a fighter, not that I had a brain hemorrhage."[89]

Sound Profile: Nina Temple

♫ Diagnosed with Parkinson's disease at age forty-four, Nina Temple fell into a deep depression, barely venturing out of her house as she struggled to come to terms with her new situation. While brooding on all the things she could no longer do with her life, however, she eventually came up with one activity she loved and still could do: singing. With a friend who also had Parkinson's, she formed Sing for Joy, a choir consisting of singers with Parkinson's disease and multiple sclerosis, and survivors of stroke, cancer, and other deadly conditions, along with their caregivers. Rehearsing weekly and performing for the public, from Cole Porter classics to "ethnic punk," Temple and her new friends found that singing provided them with many physical and neurological benefits: combating voice loss (a common symptom of Parkinson's disease), strengthening throat muscles typically affected by neurological conditions, and regaining their own sense of inner rhythm. Best of all for Temple, however, were the social and psychological benefits the activity brought to all the members, including herself. "It's quite easy to get overwhelmed by the disease," she says. "Having something that you do every week that makes you forget all your troubles and keeps you from feeling isolated is a great pleasure."[90]

Some people with Parkinson's find great pleasure in getting together to dance to rhythmic music. The internationally known, Brooklyn-based Mark Morris Dance Group gives back to its community by providing dance lessons for neighbors with Parkinson's disease.[91] Participants love the challenge of working with highly skilled instructors in a professional setting. They benefit, too, from meeting others who share their experience. Moving to live piano music, they must focus closely on detailed movement and coordinate mind and body—a perfect workout for individuals with this condition. "It's really like bliss, in a way," says one participant.

www.HealingAtTheSpeedOfSound.com/Link46

Watch this PBS report on the Mark Morris Dance Group's dance classes for people with Parkinson's disease.

In recent decades, a growing number of scientists, musicians, and educators have experimented with ways to employ vibroacoustic therapy—music combined with barely perceptible low-frequency sound vibration transferred directly to the human body—in easing pain and improving performance in patients with a variety of conditions. In Norway, beanbag chairs were designed with embedded speakers, delivering music and full-body vibration to relax and stimulate the muscles of severely disabled children. Individuals with Parkinson's disease, cystic fibrosis, cerebral palsy, and autism were found to benefit as well. Postoperative heart patients who received this form of vibroacoustic therapy, via speakers attached to their hospital beds, required less time on ventilators, cutting the length of their hospital stays almost in half.

Since then, health providers have created other ways to deliver this healing double dose of music and vibration. Sarajane Williams, a Pennsylvania-based harpist and former nurse, designed a "vibroacoustic harp"—an amplified harp with speakers attached to a chair or massage table. Playing her harp and channeling the amplified sound through the embedded speakers to the patient, she was able to reduce nausea in some patients undergoing chemotherapy, mitigate others' chronic pain, and calm patients with post-traumatic stress. Other medical personnel began using the therapy to relax patients undergoing in vitro fertilization procedures, finding not only that the practice reduced stress but that more successful pregnancies resulted.[92]

Dr. James B. Hopkins, a Los Angeles chiropractor, dispensed with the speakers altogether, turning the bed itself into a musical instrument capable of surrounding the patient in a cocoon of vibration. In a process he calls Pythagorean Harmonix Healing (inspired by Pythagoras's conception of the "harmony of the spheres"), he places his patients in a hollow wood resonating "bed" of his own design—in essence, a gigantic harp. Stretching out underneath, he strikes the elongated strings, occasionally hitting specially designed percussion instruments that he calls "planet gongs."[93]

The idea of finding relief from symptoms inside a musical instrument may strike many as unusual or even laughable. As Williams acknowledges, such experiments represent a paradigm shift for those accustomed to traditional treatments. "But it's clear that the body reacts to certain wave forms in specific ways," she insists. "I believe that the harp itself, and its healing qualities, will be better understood in twenty years."[94]

Pack Up Your Sorrows

Music and singing are a spiritual activity—a way to evoke the truth in one's heart and soul.[95] Musicians agree: The noted jazz guitarist Stanley Jordan has called music a four-dimensional healing force, working on physical, mental, emotional, and spiritual levels all at the same time. Psychotherapists, too, have long understood its power to uncover past experiences of trauma, pain, grief, and joy so that individuals can examine them openly and bring health to their inner worlds. Even in their present lives, many find music to be a powerful tool in managing anxiety, depression, and addiction to alcohol or illegal substances, because music not only delivers pleasurable endorphins in the brain but also connects people socially and emotionally with others. Young people suffering from depression or violent or suicidal behavior find catharsis through music—often the very forms of grunge, emo, and heavy metal of which their elders disapprove.

In recent years, listening training and other forms of music therapy have been used to help returning American soldiers manage a number of neural and psychological challenges as well. Occupational therapist Debra DeHart and other therapists are currently pilot-testing a listening-training program for wounded soldiers in the U.S. Army, using specially modified music combined with brain fitness software technology developed by Advanced Brain Technologies to treat those with mild traumatic brain injuries, post-traumatic stress disorder, and depression—conditions often coupled with limited memory and attention and concentration problems. The compositions by Mozart and other composers help "retune" the brains of these soldiers just as they do those of children with ADHD and other neurological conditions, helping these men and women regain their ability to meet appointments, take needed medication, follow commands, manage their moods, and perform other tasks required before they can return home or redeploy.

This is the case, too, for civilians with psychological disabilities. Studies have shown that biweekly sessions of individual music therapy can improve functioning in those diagnosed with depression.[96] In psychiatric wards, patients' anxiety often decreases when listening to recorded music or nature sounds, while the opportunity to play musical instruments can provide a sense of transformation and temporary escape from even psychotic symptoms.

Listen Up

♫ In recent years, a groundswell of scientific opinion has surfaced questioning the effectiveness of pharmaceutical antidepressants (everything from the original tricyclics to new SSRIs). For decades, physicians and their patients have been influenced in their medical decisions by scientific studies purporting to demonstrate the effectiveness of these drugs.

Yet recent groundbreaking research by scientists, including the University of Connecticut's Irving Kirsch and Guy Sapirstein, has revealed that taking a placebo, or a fake pill, is seventy-five to eighty-two percent as effective as taking antidepressants for all but those with very severe depression.[97] In other words, as science columnist Sharon Begley wrote in *Newsweek* in 2010, antidepressants work for the most part only because patients *believe* they work. Because of that belief, these patients are willing to endure the drugs' sometimes severe side effects.[98]

As a result of this research, physicians and scientists are looking more closely and seriously at non-pharmacological options for treating depression—including music-based therapies. Listening training has been among the most effective in this area.[99] At the Paracelsus Medical University Salzburg, in Austria, for example, Vera Brandes, director of the university's MusicMedicine Research Program, has designed a listening-training program called I-MAT. The music used in the program is composed in accordance with the latest research on the ways music can resynchronize the physical and neural functioning that causes depression. Researchers observed that after only ten listening sessions, patients' exhaustion, feelings of burnout, and other symptoms of depression were significantly reduced. After a full course, most participants claimed to feel profoundly different—less listless or restless, more clearheaded and emotionally balanced, and more motivated and positive in mood.[100] It will be fascinating to see what new developments come from this area of research, now that it is receiving more scientific attention and support.

Many psychologists and physicians have pointed to the human voice as perhaps the most telling indicator of an individual's emotional and psychological state. Sigmund Freud, Carl Jung, Willhelm Reich, and countless others have discussed the ways in which the voice serves as a kind of psychological membrane between the inner and outer worlds, capturing and retaining the emotional content of joyful and traumatic experiences and reflecting them back in the form of rhythm, pace, volume, fullness of range, richness of quality, strength, clarity, and other characteristics, along with the accompanying facial expressions and body language. As psychologist Morris Brody wrote in *The Psychoanalytic Quarterly* in the early 1940s, "The voice is a sensitive vector of emotional states, and is used by the ego as a vector for neurotic symptoms and defense mechanisms. To hear the voice solely for what it has to say and to overlook the voice itself, deprives the analyst of an important avenue that has led to emotional conflict. The voice constantly acts out those resistances."[101] And just as the voice expresses the emotional life of every human being, so it can be used to heal the emotions, address psychological problems, and reforge connections with others.

Voice therapy has been around formally for more than half a century. In chapter three, I described Dr. Alfred Tomatis's groundbreaking work in using the mother's voice to treat patients' vocal, psychological, and cognitive disabilities. Today, psychologists use a variety of vocal techniques to help individuals resolve issues from their past and solve problems they are currently experiencing. Music therapists show patients how they can express through song all kinds of fears, hopes, and other emotions they wouldn't normally. Victims of post-traumatic stress disorder find relief by repeating a personal mantra at times of stress or anxiety.[102] Silvia Nakkach, director of the accredited certificate program in Sound, Voice, and Music Healing at the California Institute of Integral Studies, describes the benefits of these practices as comparable to those of listening to classical music or singing Indian ragas or other sacred songs. "We enter a state akin to meditation, where singing becomes a doorway to the most inner silence," she writes. "Singing medicine melodies connects us with our true energetic and emotional nature."[103]

As people learn to improve their own voices, they experience an incredible affirmation of being, their confidence increases, and their health stabilizes. Particularly for disempowered people—including those with physical, cognitive, emotional, or psychological disabilities—there is something very exciting about being heard and getting validation. These positive feelings can be extended throughout an individual's personal network when he or she joins voices with family members and friends. Family therapists, for example, have found group singing and music making a productive way to improve communication in family or couples therapy. Family grudges, they find, are often forgotten in the process of making music together, and the music prevents members from mentally dropping out of the therapy session. When improvisation is encouraged, along with solo musical turns, each participant enjoys the opportunity to perform for and gain recognition from the family.

In similar ways, group singing or music-making sessions can prove enormously helpful for soldiers and others with post-traumatic stress disorder. Choruses, drumming groups, and even hand bell choirs—an increasingly popular activity for some veterans—can offer emotional release to individuals experiencing psychological distress, and perhaps most important, they create a sense of community. "I can easily be distracted from my everyday stressors," one grateful drummer comments, "and become consumed with the emotion and the music."

Similar effects can be experienced through sound healing, in which groups of individuals sing, chant, or hum together in a darkened room. Participating in such sessions "just gives you a sense of peace and makes you feel that you can help yourself through a lot of emotional and physical issues. It makes you feel you have that power," explains one participant.[104] While no specific goal is named—as it is in music therapy—sound healing does help individuals unlock negative energy and achieve inner balance.

Rhythm, tone, melody, vibration, words—every aspect of music and song works not only to make us who we are, but to keep us physically healthy, emotionally balanced, and mentally alert as we move through our lives. Truly, sound is the miracle cure for what ails us, freely available, free of negative side effects, and as pleasurable as it is beneficial. Now that we have seen the many, many ways in which music helps each individual experience life to the fullest, we will explore how it also connects us to one another, strengthening family ties, spreading joy through our communities, and binding people together around the world.

CHAPTER SIX

Let Music Ring

Creating a Sound Community at Home, in the Neighborhood, and in the World

Life is a symphony, and the action of every person in this life is the playing of their particular part in the music.

—Hazrat Inayat Khan

After the day's work, most of us look forward eagerly to returning to our own private retreats, where we can relax, exchange news of the day with friends and loved ones, and restore our energy for tomorrow. Increasingly, though, that journey home—and even the evening hours spent within our own walls—is fraught with a level of noise so constant and pervasive that we fail to find the peace and refreshment we seek. From the car alarms beeping in the parking lot as we leave work, to the loud music in the sports bar where we meet friends in the early evening, to the roaring trucks we pass on our homeward trek and the lawnmowers or blasting stereos that greet us when we arrive home, noise assaults us so consistently that we sometimes fail even to realize the degree to which our ears are under attack.

Of course, there has always been noise in the world, even if it used to consist of a single rooster's annoying crow signaling the approach of dawn. But with the expansion of the industrial age, decibel levels have soared. New York City resident Julia Barnett Rice marked this change at the turn of the twentieth century with her creation of the Society for the Suppression of Unnecessary Noise, a reaction to the shrill whistles of tugboats in the waters surrounding Manhattan Island.[1] Ironically, in the century since then, Rice's hometown has remained one of the noisiest cities in the country—and not just on the notoriously clamorous subway platforms, where passing trains cause real pain to commuters' ears and permanently damage their hearing, but on the sidewalks and plazas aboveground as well. A study released by Columbia University researchers as recently as October 2010 revealed that the level of background noise exceeds healthy levels in ninety-eight percent of Manhattan's public spaces. Out of sixty sites tested by the researchers, most measured background noise levels of more than seventy decibels, with some of the highest noise spikes coming from passing trucks.[2]

But noise is no longer a problem limited to our largest and most technologically advanced cities. Elsewhere, it has also become a source of resentment, and is high on the list of reasons cited in the United States for selling a home and relocating.[3] In his book *In Pursuit of Silence,* George Prochnik describes a competition among boom-car drivers in the parking lot of Explosive Sound and Video, in central Florida, where the cars' huge sound systems emit blasts loud enough to shatter windshields.[4] Even on America's farms, the noise of harvesters, sprayers, and other machinery has left half of older farmers with hearing loss.[5] And on the once-tranquil island of Vinalhaven, Maine, residents who initially cheered the installation of giant wind turbines for the production of green energy now claim that the ultralow-frequency sound and vibration of the 123-foot blades may be harming the health of those who live nearby. "I remember the sound of silence so palpable, so merciless in its depths, that you could almost feel your heart stop in sympathy," Art Lindgren, an island resident, told a *New York Times* reporter. His wife, Cheryl, added, "I grieve for the past."[6]

People respond to such sound impositions in different ways. Some, like George Michelsen Foy, author of *Zero Decibels*, view chronic urban background noise, which Foy calls the city's "monster breath," as an inevitable if loathsome part of modern life.[7] Garret Keizer, author of *The Unwanted Sound of Everything We Want*, characterizes noisemaking as a form of arrogance and contempt. "A person who says 'My noise is my right' basically means 'Your ear is my hole,'" he writes. Yet he, too, acknowledges the view of noise as an unavoidable, "baked-in" aspect of modern technology.[8] Prochnik, who worries that he may actually be a borderline "noise crank," admits to having "snitched on contractors who started work early" and "battled neighbors who hold large parties."[9] Others have responded to noise more aggressively, in ways that sometimes end in violence. Eighty-two-year-old Frank Parduski, dubbed "the world's first anti-noise martyr" by *New Scientist* magazine, was run over and killed by a young motorcyclist whom he tried to stop from driving back and forth repeatedly in front of his house one afternoon.[10]

Of course, one person's noise is another's serenade. Most of us remember the furor that arose during the World Cup competitions in 2010 over the use of vuvuzelas, those long, plastic hornlike instruments with which South African soccer fans made an ear-shattering racket throughout the games. To most witnesses, the noise was intolerable. As *New York Times* columnist Roger Cohen acknowledges, entire Facebook pages were dedicated to banning the instrument, and earplugs sold briskly to Europeans in the stands. Nevertheless, writes Cohen, who spent part of his childhood in South Africa, "I have news for the discomfited: This is actually Africa. The horn sounds to summon. From the kudu horn made from the spiral-horned antler to the plastic horn is not such a great distance." Most significantly, the sight of black and white South African citizens blowing the horns in unison symbolized "an affirmation of a nation's miraculous (if incomplete) healing" after fifty years of apartheid. "I'm sorry, French players will have to suffer their headaches: These are not minor political miracles," Cohen concludes.[11]

www.HealingAtTheSpeedOfSound.com/Link47

Long after the 2010 World Cup games become a distant memory, people may still recall their response to the sound of the vuvuzela.

In this book, I wish to focus not on the particular type or genre of the sound, but on its decibel level and duration. Any sound, from the most evocative performance of Schumann to the greatest Metallica hit to the voice of a parent or spouse, becomes noise when its decibel level and/or duration rise to unacceptable levels. Those who object to its proliferation can call on scientific evidence to back up their complaints. As

Dr. William H. Stewart, former Surgeon General of the United States, asserts, "Calling noise a nuisance is like calling smog an inconvenience. Noise must be considered a hazard to the health of people everywhere."[12]

Fortunately, as we have seen throughout this book, sound's effects depend entirely on how and when it is used. In this chapter, we will discuss ways to peacefully work around the sound-related needs of neighbors and family members while using music to strengthen bonds, create community, and reach out to others around the world.

Gone Are the Days

When you think of home, what comes to mind? An evening in front of a crackling fire, curled up with a good book? Cooking dinner while chatting with your partner or listening to the radio? The half hour spent tossing a Frisbee in the backyard with your dog? Or do you see yourself shouting at your kids over the noise of the television to get them to do their homework, or trying to focus on a book or e-mail despite the noise of construction outside your window?

Chances are, merely conjuring up these scenarios is enough to affect your mood. Research has shown that the sounds we hear directly influence our emotional outlook,[13] but we don't need science to tell us that traffic noise makes us tense while a child's laughter lifts our hearts—or that music in a minor key tends to slow us down while upbeat music cheers us up.[14] The good news is that we can take control of sound to create our own emotional climate, as effectively as film score composers create a flow of moods for their audiences. Music has the power to boost your energy just as effectively as your favorite caffeinated drink, and to act as an evening tonic to help you unwind—all without the side effects of coffee or alcohol.

Now, in the evening, consider the ways in which you can expand on the sound concepts you've learned from this book to orchestrate a nourishing soundtrack that will carry you toward the conclusion of your day. One way to begin is by creating a "sound journal," in which you record the times of day you and your family experience the most stress, frustration, or discomfort at home, and those times you find most enjoyable. Then consider the sound context of each of these situations. As you arrive home and open your front door, for example, does your cat's welcoming meow or the clatter of dinner preparations lift your spirits as it signals your return to those you love? Or do you typically walk into a household filled with loud music and the sound of people arguing—making you feel instantly tired and putting you into a bad mood? At dinner, does family conversation relax you or make you feel tense? How do you feel when the phone rings during a conversation with your partner and she answers it? What is your emotional response to the sound announcing the arrival of a text message for you? Is it different if the message is for your teenager? Identifying the sounds that make you feel good and those that spoil your mood is the first step toward designing a new aural environment as you would create a decorating scheme. With sound (and sometimes silence) you can establish a generally serene, pleasant atmosphere, provide a bright patch of aesthetically pleasing stimulation here and there, and mask ugly or intrusive sounds that cannot be eliminated.

First, as in any decorating project, it helps to start with as neutral a palette as possible. In chapter one, I urged you to turn off the television, turn down the stereo, and otherwise decrease the noise level as much as you can. You can continue this practice in the evenings, closing windows and perhaps installing heavy curtains if the outside noise is loud; asking teens to close their bedroom doors to muffle the sound when they are talking on the phone, and asking them to use headphones when they wish to listen to music individually; adding carpets to the floor, and even felt liners to the bottoms of furniture legs if the scraping of chairs irritates you.

Next, think of the types of aural textures—like the color schemes of your home—that you would like to lay over this neutral palette to positively influence the mood and tenor of your family's daily life. Start with the sounds that will greet you and others as you come through the front door in the evening—sounds that should signal and enhance the transition from the workplace to home. If you are single, a playlist of your favorite upbeat reggae or Latin songs might work best to usher you back to your own world. Those who share their home with other adults might choose a less personalized, less obtrusive selection of light jazz, world, or classical music that pleases everyone. If you are a single parent with young children, you may choose ethnic folk music, whose melodies please old and young alike. Generally, unless you live alone, it's best to stick to instrumental music that doesn't distract or hinder conversation. Be sure to vary the music style frequently to avoid a feeling of stagnation, and to keep the volume low enough so that its effects are almost subliminal.

Sound Break: Sound Samples

♫ Often, we listen to the same radio stations and albums day in and day out, from force of habit. Now, though, while you're thinking of ways to redesign the sound texture of your home, take a moment to explore the radio dial, sample some of your family members' favorite albums, and try a few unfamiliar musical genres for a change. How does the classical station make you feel? What about your partner's jazz music—does the music shut you down or lift you up? Who are you as you listen to hip-hop, to old-time blues, to Top 40 tunes? Does a particular type of sound make you feel the way you are, or how you want to be? By becoming more aware of the community of sound around you, you can add richness to the sound palette inside your own home.

Now, continue selecting other sonic "colors" to set the mood and enhance other activities that take place throughout your evening. Lively music with a strong beat—anything from Vivaldi to James Brown to Rihanna or AC/DC—can turn second-shift duties such as making dinner or doing housework into dance-time fun.[15] Adding Mozart and Bach or folk music to young children's playtime—or the funny tunes of such children's-music creators as Dan Zanes or They Might Be Giants—will keep young imaginations active and tempers calm. (When this music is used regularly, your children will also begin to associate it with how they feel at playtime, so playing it at other times will automatically lift their moods.) At dinner, light jazz, pop vocals, or other soft but lively background sounds with a quick tempo will help create a sociable atmosphere.

When it's time for homework, teenagers are likely to have their own sound ideas. If you can't get them to stimulate their minds with Salieri's "Danse" from *Tatare* or Mozart's Andante from Piano Concerto no. 21, let them experiment with their own favorites and observe for themselves what works best. Remember, the strong beat that teenagers often prefer may help keep them awake and focused, as long as it's not too loud, but songs with lyrics tend to distract. It's worthwhile for you and your teens to explore the expanding world of instrumental "tributes" to popular rock, rap, and punk heroes, like the adaptation of the Eminem song "Lose Yourself," below.

 **www.HealingAtTheSpeedOfSound.com/Link48**

Teenagers tend to resist any tinkering with their favorite music—often with good reason—but once your teen hears the high-quality instrumental punk, rap, and hip-hop tributes produced by Vitamin Records and similar companies, she may agree that this kind of music can help her get her homework done.

The final step in designing a sound environment for your home is to toss in a few bright, invigorating sonic "throw pillows" to address specific situations or needs. Keep on hand recordings of Gregorian chants, or the slow movement of Beethoven's Piano Concerto no. 5, "The Emperor," for times when you feel especially stressed and want to lie down, close your eyes, and relax. For a romantic evening, create a sense of bonding and intimacy with the music of Antonio Carlos Jobim, Ella Fitzgerald, Bon Jovi, Willie Nelson—or any music with special meaning or loving associations for the two of you. Mothers or others with too little free time might enjoy an exotic vacation in their minds by playing some entrancing Spanish, Moroccan, or other world music while soaking in the tub. If you're feeling depressed or have experienced an emotional blow, then the blues, an operatic lament, or other sad music may work best to help you work through your feelings. As music psychology researcher Patrick Hunter, of the University of Toronto, has found, sad music often provides cathartic release, allowing people to work toward equilibrium at their own pace.[16]

 **www.HealingAtTheSpeedOfSound.com/Link49**

Each of us has our own idea of what makes for a "romantic" song, but these suggestions from eHarmony may give you some ideas for creating your own playlist.

Don't forget that silence also works well as a decorative accent. Establish certain "time-outs"—brief periods of silence, or privacy with headphones, that may be interrupted only in emergencies. Time-outs are especially useful when stress tends to be high, such as the first ten minutes after arriving home; for the first half hour after the kids' bedtime, to help them fall asleep; or during the half hour before your own bedtime, when your partner agrees to use headphones while watching television so you can wind down. If the neighbors in your apartment building have noisy habits, ask tactfully whether they might agree to a "sound curfew," reducing the decibel level after, say, ten p.m.

Family Rhythms

Beautiful sound can provide more than a soundtrack for your family life. At times of crisis or difficult change, making music together can help strengthen bonds and open communication among family members. Family therapists and marriage counselors frequently recommend music making as a way to "tune the ears" of individuals, improving their ability to really listen to what others are saying to them. Playing music together also reminds a family that it's possible to literally create a sense of harmony together, while letting family members take a solo turn gives each a chance to be heard and encourages him or her to stay engaged.

Even in happy families, without a therapist present, the act of singing or making music together brings separate beings into sync—a kind of entrainment that inspires feelings of harmony and love. Music making is no longer limited to playing the piano and singing together or sharing old tunes around a campfire. Initiating casual, spontaneous drumming sessions on plastic wastebaskets or whatever is at hand, playing *The Beatles: Rock Band* or *DJ Hero* together, or singing along with *American Idol* on TV can also be fun. It's not the form of music, but the act of doing things together, that creates some of our favorite memories of family life.

www.HealingAtTheSpeedOfSound.com/Link50
www.HealingAtTheSpeedOfSound.com/Link51

Experience Music Project in Seattle and Rock 'n' Roll Camp for Girls in cities nationwide aim to help school-age children express themselves and find camaraderie through music. Enrolling your children in such programs, and participating yourself as a volunteer, are excellent ways to deepen your musical connection with your own children and with others in the community at large.

One more vital aspect of the sound environment at home, touched on lightly in earlier chapters, is the tone, quality, and volume of our own vocal expressions. As a parent, spouse, son or daughter, or partner, you convey as much meaning through your tone of voice and inflection as with your words. (To understand the power of the "music" in our voices, think about how much we are able to communicate to those who don't understand the meaning of our words—preverbal children, pets, and people who don't speak our language.) In chapter three, we explored the crucial role the mother's voice plays in the development of a child's verbal, emotional, and social skills. Keep this in mind as you communicate with your children of whatever age, as well as with other family members. Try to hear yourself: Does your voice express impatience or love, criticism or acceptance, dissatisfaction or joy in being together as a community at home? Note the visual and vocal feedback you get from your family members to ensure that your tone is congruent with your feeling and intent. As you did at work, consider recording one or more conversations, and then thinking as you play them back about how you might communicate more effectively.

In One Voice

Once you have improved the atmosphere of your home and the communication among family members, the natural next step is to expand that sense of connectivity outward to the community. As at home, the best way to begin is to consider first how to tone down the dissonance in our neighborhoods, and then look for ways to create a positive sound environment for all to share.

Some solutions fall within the realm of local government. In New York, the noisiest of cities, Mayor Bloomberg attacked the problem of urban noise pollution with Operation Silent Night, launched in 2002. In this effort to crack down on unhealthy sound, the city responded to nearly one hundred thousand noise complaints in a one-year period. Documenting violations with sound meters, officials then enforced noise regulations by seizing audio equipment, towing vehicles, and issuing a flurry of summonses and fines. The program was given partial credit for a decline in the city's crime rate that year to the lowest level since 1968, and Bloomberg has since gone on to attack the issue of traffic congestion in the city center and to try to reduce noise in other ways.[17] The city of Santa Ana, California, launched a similarly directed effort to deal with the regular convergence of boom cars in one particular neighborhood every Sunday evening, which was leading to the abandonment of the area by families and businesses. Once the police department focused on enforcing the regulations in this area, the boom cars dispersed and the quality of life for everyone dramatically improved.[18]

If your local government has not yet targeted noise issues that you feel are important, consider creating or joining a neighborhood action committee to draw attention to the problem. Do your research—collect studies that demonstrate the negative effects of noise on health, crime level, social climate, and business activity. Submit opinion pieces on the topic to your local newspapers and community radio stations. Approach your friends and neighbors for consensus and support. This type of group approach is often preferable to confronting individual noisemakers on your own. Complaints about sound, felt by so many of us as a particularly personal form of expression, can give rise to angry and even violent responses, as we saw with Mr. Parduski and the young motorcycle rider. They often require special tact and a willingness to negotiate; immediate issues are often best resolved through official channels such as a complaint line or the police.

www.HealingAtTheSpeedOfSound.com/Link52
www.HealingAtTheSpeedOfSound.com/Link53

For up-to-date research on environmental noise, tips on how to counter noise in your community, and opportunities to advocate for a quieter world, check out the Web sites of the Noise Pollution Clearinghouse, based in Vermont, and the Right to Quiet Society, based in Canada.

Sound on the streets is not always a nuisance. Studies have shown, and many civic leaders and law enforcement officials have demonstrated, that just as repairing broken windows and planting trees improves the social climate of a given neighborhood quite quickly, so certain types of music can be used to discourage crime. In one poor Brooklyn neighborhood, for example, members of the Crown Heights Community Mediation Center recently assembled on a street corner to ring a large brass bell once for every victim who had been shot in the neighborhood, while solemnly chanting, "No more," as a way to call public attention to their anti–gun violence program.[19]

In another memorable experiment, police installed speakers on the roof of an abandoned bar in a neighborhood plagued by drug dealers, and broadcast recordings of Beethoven string quartets until the dealers fled the area. Easy listening, Barry Manilow, country tunes, and other non-"criminalized" music—that is, music that has not been associated with this type of antisocial activity—has been used in similar projects. Not surprisingly, such efforts remain controversial, as they merely relocate crime without solving it, and because they impose music that strikes many locals as alien, unpleasant, and culturally offensive. Nevertheless, it is interesting to note their effectiveness and to brainstorm about how to use similar approaches in more acceptable ways.

 **www.HealingAtTheSpeedOfSound.com/Link54**

Listen to this account of the Venezuelan-born conductor Gustavo Dudamel, whose commitment to classical music as an engine of social change led him to work with El Sistema, Venezuela's system of youth music education, and—after he became music director of the Los Angeles Philharmonic—with the Youth Orchestra Los Angeles (YOLA). Through these organizations and others, Dudamel and his colleagues have been able to change the lives of countless numbers of children living in poverty, who might otherwise have fallen into a life of crime.

On other occasions, prison officials have improved the social climate of their institutions by piping classical music into the public areas or giving inmates the opportunity to make music. One study of a thirteen-year program conducted in more than fifty British prisons, in which inmates were offered the chance to study and perform music, revealed that ninety percent of the inmates who participated were more likely to enroll in literacy and other education programs afterward—thus improving their chance of successful rehabilitation.[20]

 **www.HealingAtTheSpeedOfSound.com/Link55**

In this podcast from the Library of Congress's Music and the Brain series, Jacqueline Helfgott, chair of the Criminal Justice Department at Seattle University, discusses the sometimes controversial ways in which music has been used to deter crime in Seattle and elsewhere in the United States.

Music can be used to create positive change in ways other than crime fighting. Think of the wonderful sense of shared ritual or ceremony you experience when Christmas caroling door-to-door or participating in a community choir. Thanks to the recent popularity of such television shows as *Glee*, *American Idol*, and *The Sing-Off*, community singing has become fashionable again. All over America and internationally, people are coming together to sing as they never did before—in vocal ensembles, gospel choirs, barbershop quartets, college glee clubs, socially active ensembles such as the Vermont-based Good Earth Singers, and single-gender groups such as the all-female Sweet Adelines and Sweet Honey in the Rock.

Surveys conducted by Chorus America show that eighteen percent of American adults and children now sing in church, school, or professional or community choirs. For those who participate in such music-making activities, raised levels of endorphins and oxytocin in the bloodstream make for a heady feeling that singing coach Helen Astrid calls "almost indescribable. You feel like you've got a spring in your step. You feel like you're being totally true to yourself. You're using your whole body; everything is involved."[21] As singers, we become intensely aware of ourselves, each other, and the environment in which we're singing, as we focus on our own voice, on getting the notes and words right, and on the voices around us. The entrainment phenomenon—the kind of phase locking of hearts and minds that takes place wherever music occurs—brings a sense of unity to virtually any group, forging emotional, mental, and spiritual connections. Even karaoke nights lift our spirits and make us feel part of a joyful group.

www.HealingAtTheSpeedOfSound.com/Link56

Watch how song can create in even that most mundane of environments, an airport baggage claim area, an atmosphere of community and joy.

Lifting our voices together not only makes each of us feel better, but creates what musician Brian Eno calls "civilizational benefits." When you sing with a group of people, particularly without musical accompaniment, he writes, "you learn how to subsume yourself to the group consciousness—because a cappella singing is all about the immersion of the self into the community. That's one of the great feelings: to stop being me for a little while, and to become us. That way lies empathy; the great virtue." It's no wonder, as Colette Hiller, director of Sing the Nation, asserts, that "singing bonds people. There's a goose-bumpy feeling of connection."[22]

Best of all, this sense of cohesion occurs regardless of the individual identity of each participant. "The point about singing," remarks Professor Grenville Hancox, director of music at England's Canterbury Christ Church University, "is that it is something we all did when we were born, regardless of color, creed, or anything else. All the billions of us on the planet sang and for the first nine months of our lives relied on the manipulation of our voice's pitch to meet our basic and fundamental needs. . . . Even if a person does it only once a month, [singing] makes an extraordinary difference. It's a staggering thing."[23] This is true even for those of us with less-than-average vocal talent, as long as we're willing and eager to learn while we sing—and community music groups have proven to be excellent places for authentic learning.[24]

Sound Profile: Susan Brink

♫ Susan Brink, a reporter for the *Los Angeles Times*, had been told all through childhood that she couldn't sing. Like many others in her situation, she learned to lip-synch early on. Still, as an adult the desire persisted for her to join with others in song, particularly as research surfaced regarding singing's physical and psychological benefits. Searching for an "inclusive, nonjudgmental group-singing experience," she came across "How to Sing in the Shower," a workshop for amateur singers held at a rustic Oregon retreat. With mixed feelings, Brink signed up, joining six other equally ambivalent, untrained adult singers in a hand-hewn yurt to practice breathing, volume, and vocalization under the guidance of singing coach Cathleen Wilder.

Wilder, adept at creating an open, accepting atmosphere, not only taught her students technique, but constantly reminded them that singing was their birthright and that the work they were doing together was "about the joy." She showed the participants how standing next to a better singer could help them sing in tune, and demonstrated that breathing for singing is "just inhaling and then making sound with the exhale—nothing more complicated than that." As the students continued to practice an accessible, enjoyable repertoire of songs such as "Buffalo Gals" and "Amazing Grace," their voices grew stronger and more confident. "To my ears, we got better with every song," Brink writes. "Most important, I learned that I've got a voice, like everyone does, that blends with others. . . . Claiming our birthright, we sang. And it felt good."[25]

Playing in a community orchestra offers rewards similar to those of singing with others, elevating mood and instilling a wonderful sense of shared values. As one clarinetist commented during a study of the effects of music making on mood, "Everyone is working together towards the same goal, and we are usually trying to evoke some kind of emotion through our music. In a really focused rehearsal, I can easily be distracted from my everyday stressors and become consumed with the emotion and the music."[26] The experience can create an almost spiritual state of transcendence; certainly it is always uplifting and joyful, and the feeling lasts for hours after the last note has ended.[27] The musicologist Christopher Small suggests that music makers' collaborative experience—and the relationship between the orchestra and its music—affirms the larger relationships between individuals and society and between humanity and the natural world. "That, I believe, is the reason why when we have been present at a good and satisfying musical performance we feel more fully ourselves, more fully realized, and more in tune with ourselves and with our fellows," he writes. "We feel we have been afforded a glimpse of how the world really is."[28]

The tradition of community music making dates back to America's earliest days, when "jamming circles" would form with more experienced musicians in the center shouting out the name and key of each song, while players with less experience surrounded them and played along. In this way, the experienced musicians were able to enjoy a good session while the others followed along and learned.[29] "Slow jams," in which everyone in the circle played a particular song at a slower speed, were also held to allow young participants to learn in an open, nonjudgmental atmosphere.

In these kinds of inclusive activities, no dividing line existed between teacher and student, or even between performers and audience. And until recently, as the author Barbara Ehrenreich points out in her fascinating book *Dancing in the Streets: A History of Collective Joy*, this collective, nonhierarchical, celebratory form of music making, song, and dance was the rule rather than the exception. From Paleolithic times at least, she tells us, people have made music and danced together, often ecstatically, usually in large groups, and preferably with music or drumming and even masks. When the Roman Catholic Church put an end to ecstatic dancing as part of its service in the thirteenth century, the practice was reborn as Carnival. By the Victorian era, as Western explorers began going all around the world and finding natives dancing in that pre-Inquisition manner, they found it sexual, intoxicated, out of control, and possibly devil inspired. Even today, in many parts of Africa there is still a single word for "speak," "sing," and "dance."[30]

Today, largely thanks to the democratizing influence of new technology, nonhierarchical community music making is staging a comeback. The ecstatic dancing of ancient times has been replaced by today's mosh pit, rave experience, and annual Carnival celebrations. Via Craigslist, Facebook, and other Internet services, increasing numbers of people are able to find fellow singers or musicians for their choruses, choirs, or bands, or to draw people together for neighborhood jamming circles and other music events, singing and playing together with instruments ranging from electric guitars to ukuleles, harmonicas, and spoons. Others are using social-media music groups to share music experiences online. The genealogy blogger FootnoteMaven, for example, creates an annual forum for sharing favorite Christmas carols, called Blog Caroling, in which participants contribute the lyrics to a favorite carol and tell a story of why it means so much to them.[31] Others routinely benefit from user-generated or crowd-sourced playlists. These kinds of communities have no geographic limits. They demonstrate that the potential for reinventing the ecstatic, joyous, healing music making of our ancestors is as boundless as our imaginations.

 **www.HealingAtTheSpeedOfSound.com/Link57**

Listen to this Christmas music created from congregation members' iPhones and iPads at Northpoint Community Church, in Alpharetta, Georgia.

The Tapping Point

In earlier chapters, I pointed to the increasing popularity of drumming circles, another form of nonhierarchical music making, which also serves to unify a group into an ecstatic, bonded whole. The drumming circle creates common ground. It invites cultural sharing, listening, collaboration, and collective action. Since almost anyone can beat a drum, practically anyone can participate in drumming circles. For this reason, they serve as an ideal tool not only for psychological balance and health, as I discussed earlier, but also for community building, team building, family or community rite-of-passage celebrations, diversity training activities, and for easing the kinds of tensions that can arise in our multicultural society.

Increasingly, drumming circles can be found in any midsize or larger community in the United States. If one does not exist in your area and you have some musical experience, consider creating one to help further your community goals. Information on finding drumming-circle facilitators for hire or training to become a facilitator yourself is available in appendix two at the end of this book.

Community choruses and orchestras, folk-based music-making events, and drumming circles all work naturally to strengthen group identity and bring a community in tune with its own shared values and aims. It should hardly surprise us, then, to learn that according to surveys choristers tend to be leaders in civic engagement, community activism, arts education, and preserving community heritage,[32] and that the robustness of the choirs in a particular region correlates highly with its people's level of civic engagement.[33] Perhaps this is why so many nonprofit organizations have made an effort to develop a musical community that brings disadvantaged youth, neglected elders, and as many others as possible into the fold.

The links between group musical activity and community service are everywhere. The National Institutes of Health Philharmonia, in Washington, D.C., for example—comprising volunteer musicians from the medical community, including some of the highest-caliber scientists and doctors in the country—gives half a dozen or more free performances per year, with earnings donated to such charities as the Patient Emergency Fund.[34]

The Boston Minstrel Company, an all-volunteer choir formed in 1991,[35] performs almost weekly in Boston-area homeless shelters, hospitals, and correctional institutions, with the aim of providing entertainment, an emotional lift, and perhaps even catharsis for listeners, along with the sense of community so often painfully lacking in their lives.[36] These songfests are interactive performances, with audience members given hand percussion instruments and strongly encouraged to play and sing along. At the end of each performance, the Minstrels and the audience join together in a closing circle, holding hands and singing together with soloists or speakers taking turns at the microphone.

Dr. Peggy Codding, music therapy professor at Berklee College of Music, who sings with the Minstrels and is a member of their board of trustees, points to the positive change she sees in audience participants' energy and social interaction as these evenings progress. "Minstrel nights matter. Participants comment afterward about the meaning the event has had for them," she writes. "The uplifted spirit is visible to the eye."[37] She concludes, "It's hard to say 'I love you,' but you can do it in a song. . . . When you bring it all together, music is a very powerful tool."[38] It is no wonder that some of the homeless audience members have wound up joining the choir and contributing to the musical outreach efforts themselves.[39]

Music can bridge divides. In Melbourne, Australia, a performing-arts project called Yallah Shabiba! ("Come on young ones!") helps Arab and non-Arab teenagers explore issues of racism, self-esteem, and the nature of friendship through collaborative, high-energy music, dancing, drama, rap, beat box, Arabic drumming, spoken word, belly dance, video, and comedic monologue.

Music can empower. In Charlottesville, Virginia, Rachel Bagby, author of *Divine Daughters*, a book addressing the subject of women coming into their full voices, has launched a movement she calls Choral Earth, dedicated to organizing the millions of choir members worldwide in support of global sustainability and combating climate change.[40] Choral communities have traditionally organized movements for social change, she points out, and can now harness and expand their vocal power using the twenty-first-century tools of technology and outreach.

It is easy to understand how music groups and leaders are moved to transform their deep feelings of community into concrete action to help others in the world. If you are part of such a group yourself, consider the ways you might direct the power of your goodwill and your sheer numbers toward a worthy goal. The good feelings we experience creating sound together only expand when we share them with others. By working together, we can make our voices heard throughout our neighborhoods, in our cities, and around the world.

Listen Up

 **www.HealingAtTheSpeedOfSound.com/Link58**

One cause sorely in need of volunteer advocates strikes close to the heart of every music lover: music education in American schools. Despite the plethora of scientific evidence demonstrating the benefits of music education, music and arts classes are usually the first to be eliminated as school budgets shrink—even as the need for music and music-enriched curricula grows in our media-drenched, economically constrained society.

If you are concerned by this issue, check out the NAMM Foundation's SupportMusic Coalition Web site for the latest news, the most recent relevant research, and information on how to make a difference in your neighborhood schools.

As well-known education expert Howard Gardner wrote in 1997, "Music is as vital nourishment for the mind as school lunches are for the body," both as an educational tool and as an academic pursuit in its own right. And as Mike Huckabee, former Arkansas governor and former chairman of the Education Commission of the States, stated, "If we don't provide an arts education, at least an arts opportunity for every child, we are leaving a lot of children behind. . . . [L]eaving the arts out is beyond neglect and is virtual abuse of a child."

Good Vibrations

One interesting aspect of community participation is that the more involved we get, the better we feel. As we spend more time with our neighbors, we tend to expand our good work outward into the larger population. Music is an excellent vehicle through which to connect in positive ways with other cultural groups and nations, as it transcends language and draws all participants into a joyful union. The ensemble consciousness practiced by musicians, blending their voices with others often very different from themselves, makes them natural diplomats, able to blend the ideas and traditions of different cultures, form sonic alliances with indigenous musicians, and exchange knowledge in other ways.

Recognizing this fact, the United Nations recently joined with the International Council for Caring Communities to host a compendium titled "Music as a Natural Resource." The program focused on music's potential value in helping to create sustainable communities, working with trauma survivors and treating those with other mental and physical health issues, particularly in nations decimated by war or natural disaster. In the United States, our government has long recognized music's power to reach out and heal the people of other nations. Since 1843, it has funded performances by American musicians in foreign countries. One of its most memorable recent efforts was the New York Philharmonic's visit to North Korea, in February 2008.

But powerful international and national organizations are not alone in striving to put the music's power to work for the global good. In 1999, a

Los Angeles composer and music teacher named Liz Shropshire was so shocked by photographs in the media of the refugee camps in Kosovo—whose traumatized women and children had endured a brutal, decade-long ethnic cleansing campaign—that she was moved to take action in the best way she knew how. Emptying her personal savings account and soliciting donations from musical instrument companies and private donors, she amassed a total of 140 harmonicas, 130 pennywhistles, 50 pairs of drumsticks, 4 electric keyboards, 60 beginning piano books, 500 pencils, a portable stereo, and a portable tape recorder and took them all to Kosovo to create the Kosovo Children's Music Initiative, a program of music instruction for refugee children. The daily classes in singing, drumming, pennywhistles, harmonica, and sing-alongs, and the performances presented for families and friends brought a sense of normalcy and community to a shattered population, and helped begin the healing process.[41]

The following year, Shropshire formally organized the nonprofit Shropshire Music Foundation, through which she has been providing musical instruments and music education to children in war-struck areas ever since.[42] Music therapists Davida Price and Vanessa Contopulos, creators of a project called ChildSong Uganda, which brings music to children displaced by the decades-long Ugandan civil war, are among those who have received instruments from the Shropshire Foundation. Price tells us, "For the child soldiers rehabilitated from the bush, it is a huge privilege to study and sit and rest. The children had a great appreciation for simple things." Music gives these children a renewed sense of hope, she believes. It inspires pride in culture, self-esteem, leadership, and social interaction. "They need it just as much as food and shelter. It reminds us of why we want to live, gives meaning to life, and without this, the other things are just not as important." Price voices her hope that they might continue with programs elsewhere in Africa and other places where the need is great, including the United States.

Another pair of musicians, Cameron Powers and Kristina Sophia, began their musical diplomatic careers, oddly enough, singing Iraqi love songs on the streets in Baghdad in 2003. As they later wrote, their love for and understanding of Iraqi music and culture had prompted them to "stand in solidarity with Iraqis" by honoring their ancient music in public, even as the U.S. military invasion began. Their listeners were amazed and delighted by the young Americans' ability to play the oud, a traditional Middle Eastern instrument, and to perform popular Iraqi songs for Iraqis and even the Jordanian soldiers guarding the border. The joy and mutual appreciation blossoming during these sessions contrasted sharply with the bombings taking place not far away.

Their experience of a lifetime in Iraq inspired Powers and Sophia to create the nonprofit Musical Missions of Peace back home in Colorado, with the aim of promoting peace worldwide through the power of music. In the years since, as the violence in Iraq has continued, Musical Missions of Peace has helped to create music schools for Iraqi refugee children, where skilled local musicians pass on the basics and nuances of their ancient *maqam* music to the next generation. The organization has also helped to establish mobile music schools in Syria and Jordan and drum circles in Kurdistan, and has raised funds for a children's cancer hospital in Cairo.[43]

Powers and Sophia have demonstrated that sharing music and learning the music and languages of other cultures can serve as one path toward peace. They don't attempt to make a political statement, but rather work to build bridges between two cultures. "We go over to represent the America that appreciates the Arabic-speaking world—their music, their language, their culture, and their ancient wisdom," says Sophia. Music is the ultimate icebreaker, which comes "on a heart level" that everyone understands; words aren't even necessary. "The benefits? Let's list a few: A foundation of deep trust is laid, as people who sing and dance together form deep natural bonds. Musical soundscapes are preverbal; friendships develop on the most primal levels, and cultural stereotypes shatter on both sides and the healing of fear-ridden legacies of conflict can begin. When we are deeply engaged in a musical chant, we are given a break from the endless cycles of negative and positive judgment making. In short," she concludes, "music is a key that just opens their hearts."[44]

Christine Stevens, the internationally acclaimed music therapist, speaker, founder of UpBeat Drum Circles, and author of the book *The Art and Heart of Drum Circles*, has translated her own understanding of music-centered interventions for conflict resolution to peacemaking efforts in Iraq. "Drumming is a proven, potent tool for peace," she tells us. "Just as it works to bring together individuals within a family, classroom, or community group, so it can positively affect relations between tribal units and even nations."

In past years, Stevens has provided workshops and seminars worldwide, including in Hong Kong, Brazil, South Africa, Japan, and Western Europe, and has drummed with a gamut of groups, from schoolchildren at 9/11's Ground Zero to survivors of Hurricane Katrina in New Orleans.[45]

Convinced by scientific research showing that the type of group drumming Stevens facilitates has real, measurable benefits, an international relief organization recently invited her to facilitate a music-based conflict-resolution effort in Iraq. This made sense to her, she later wrote, "drumming is the language of global diplomacy." For five days, she reported, groups that would otherwise never have had any reason to meet each other convened and trained together in drum schools. Following the program, the feedback from the participants was extraordinarily positive, helping them feel more connected as a community. Because of this success, ongoing weekly drum circles have since been established in youth centers across Iraq.[46]

Stories like these are inspiring, to say the least. Now that you have read them, take a moment to think about how you might be able to support these efforts to reknit the world's community of people through the power of music and sound, or to make independent contributions of your own. Working for the global good improves the lives of others, but it enhances your own life as well.

www.HealingAtTheSpeedOfSound.com/Link59

"Music is our tradition. Even war cannot take it from us," says a refugee child in northern Uganda, a country ravaged by more than two decades of civil war. Watch these excerpts from *War Dance,* the Academy Award–winning documentary featuring three Ugandan children living in a displaced persons camp who find a path toward hope and spiritual healing after they are invited to compete in an annual music and dance competition.

CHAPTER SEVEN

"Imagine You Are Humming to God"

A Sound Voice

After silence, that which comes nearest to expressing the inexpressible is music.

—Aldous Huxley

As a teenager, I had the privilege of studying in France under the great music pedagogue and conductor Nadia Boulanger. One day in my harmony class, I showed her a copy of some handwritten chant I had found, a page of unfamiliar, small square notes on a strangely scripted page. It was nothing like the Bach fugues or Debussy *Préludes* I was studying. She told me to sing it in syllables.

"It only has four lines," I protested, "and I don't know how to read this kind of music without a clef and a staff."

She sang "re, mi, fa, fa, mi, fa." I repeated it. She told me to try again with the Latin word *Kyrie*. "Close your eyes and imagine that you are humming to God," she said.

I did as I was told. Singing with my eyes closed, I could feel the sound reverberate within my body like the sounds of a pipe organ inside a great cathedral. I had a sudden inner awareness. I was close to something I had not experienced before. Was this the reason they called it "harmony" class?

Mlle. Boulanger appeared satisfied. "Now make up a chant," she instructed me. "Use only those three notes. Learn to feel it. Listen deeply as you sing. Then, it will become easy to read." Next I learned five, eight, and ten notes in a variety of ancient modes. Boulanger told me they each had a different spiritual feeling. I did not understand, but I have never forgotten what she said.

Throughout recorded history, mankind has intuited a spiritual aspect to sound and vibration, and has sought to harness its power to connect with the universes within and without. In ancient Greece, Pythagoras used the word *kosmos* to refer to the alignment between the heavens and the earth ("as above, so below"), and spoke of the "harmony of the spheres," the symphony created by the mathematical correspondence between music and the movements of the planets and stars. Galileo, a masterful lute player, was frequently guided in his explorations of the physical world by the precise mathematical properties of music. The eighteenth-century German poet and philosopher Novalis suggested that each disease had a characteristic "sound," or temperament, that could best be treated by a physician well trained in music.

Today, thanks to such modern techniques as positron-emission tomography (PET scans) and functional magnetic resonance imaging (fMRIs), we can see the brain harmonize with sound and music on a neuronal scale—scientifically demonstrating the concordance of inner and outer worlds that mankind has subjectively experienced for centuries. We now know empirically that sound and rhythm in proper proportion can realign and regulate the mind and body. We can watch musical sounds expand the mind as they stimulate areas associated with visual imagery or other senses—possibly explaining the phenomenon of synesthesia, in which some people "see" certain sound frequencies as colors or experience them as tastes, textures, weights, or scents.[1] Researchers have observed, too, the ways in which specific tonal sequences entrain the brain, creating altered states of consciousness that can inspire and heal.

www.HealingAtTheSpeedOfSound.com/Link60

Dr. Richard E. Cytowic, M.D., discusses the phenomenon of synesthesia in this podcast from the Library of Congress's Music and the Brain series.

The Sound of the Spirit

We are immensely fortunate to live at a time when we can benefit from this scientific analysis of a world of spiritual practices both past and present. We no longer need to rely solely on the assurance of a teacher or guru that the daily practice of meditating to music, vocalizing in conscious ways, or moving our bodies to certain rhythms will sharpen our focus, heal our spirit, and raise our consciousness to a higher level. These effects have been objectively demonstrated. We know now—as we have seen from the studies and personal experiences presented throughout this book—that sitting quietly while listening to music will positively affect the body and mind by lowering blood pressure and encouraging the production of immunoglobulin A; that singing or vocalizing makes us feel euphoric because the act of making music floods our bodies with dopamine and other positive hormones; and that certain kinds of drumming or other rhythmic activity can create altered states of consciousness by affecting our brain wave activity.[2]

Another wonderful aspect of music is that it happens in the here and now: Listening carefully requires you to exist entirely in the moment. Throughout the world, meditation groups, prayer circles, healing practitioners, and therapists are using bells and crystal bowls to bring us to a more contemplative state. That quality of attention sets the stage for greater mental and emotional clarity and even, if desired, altered states of consciousness.

Sound Profile: Ostad Elahi

♫ When it comes to the passionate expression of divine love through music, few if any practitioners have ever surpassed the Persian musician and mystic Ostad Elahi (1895–1974). Having mastered the art of the tambour (an ancient Kurdish lute) at a young age as a step on his own spiritual journey, Elahi went on to reassemble its scattered repertoire and, with his intricate musical ornamentations and complex playing technique, to almost single-handedly revive a seven-hundred-year-old mystical tradition. A prolific musician who would play for hours on end during meditative retreats, Elahi never performed in public. Yet Jean During, an acclaimed ethnomusicologist and the director of research at France's National Center for Scientific Research (CNRS), called him a veritable virtuoso, and musicians as prominent as Yehudi Menuhin, the master violinist, traveled to Iran to hear him play. "Never had I heard anything like it," Menuhin later recalled. "It was very sensitive, very intense music, but also very precise and pure. I almost couldn't believe what I was hearing."[3]

Only a few hours of amateur recordings of Elahi's music remain, but since their release in the mid-1990s a surge of interest has developed in the music's therapeutic effects as well as its ability to express various spiritual states. The music's rich high-frequency spectrum, complexity of tempo and rhythms, and abundant overtones and harmonics create in the listener a sublime, relaxing, yet awakened state of mind. For this reason, Elahi's music is now being used in listening-therapy treatment programs aimed at optimizing peak performance while also allowing listeners to experience the music spiritually. Two of these therapeutic listening programs, "Music for the Mind" and "Music for the Mind II," not only modify the sound according to the latest psychoacoustic techniques, but add authentic nature sounds from Elahi's native village for a full spiritually and scientifically grounded experience.

Altered States

Sound has always been there, ready to open new vistas in our awareness and to serve as a compass to guide us in our spiritual lives. As long ago as the seventeenth century, the German mathematician, astronomer, astrologer, and musician Johannes Kepler explored in his book *Harmonices Mundi* ("The Harmony of the World") the relationship between the harmonic proportions in music and the physical harmonies in planetary motion—and suggested that perhaps at the moment of creation all planets sang together in "perfect concord." Three hundred years later, German composer Paul Hindemith expressed this idea of universal congruence with *Die Harmonie der Welt*, a mystical opera based on Kepler's text and life. In the opera, the chorus sings as the dying astronomer succumbs to feverish hallucinations:

Our gaze into the infinite cosmos
Encircling us with rich and gentle harmonies
Inclines us through vision, ardor, and faithful prayer
To uplift our imperfect selves
Higher than through logic and erudition;
Until the spirit of ultimate majesty
Grants to our soul
The grace to be merged
Into the exalted harmony of the World.[4]

Today, with the help of science, we continue to explore the links between sound and human spirituality. Every day, new miracles occur in the experimental realms with singing crystal bowls, tuning forks, improvisation, chanting, and movement, as researchers attempt to identify the mechanisms that allow us to access altered states of consciousness and to heal ourselves through tone, vibration, and rhythm. In a sense, through science we are working our way back to what we knew as listeners in the ancient world: that different modes of music spark different human emotions; that some rhythms warm us up while others cool us down; that carefully constructed rituals involving prayer, chant, and rhythmic music, song, and dance can enable us to shed our everyday personalities and become one with God or some other form of ultimate truth—knowledge preserved only in the mystic branches of the Persian, Hindu, Jewish, Muslim, Buddhist, and Christian traditions today.[5]

Music's documented chemical effects on the brain provide part of the answer to the mystery of its power to take us outside ourselves, allowing us to experience a sense of euphoria and even to transcend ordinary reality. According to researchers at McGill University, in Montreal, the goose bumps or the chills up our spines that we experience when listening to beautiful sounds are signs that our brains are responding to this neurological stimulation with a surge of the reward chemical dopamine—much as they would respond to a pleasurable meal or, in extreme cases, a psychoactive drug such as cocaine. "Anytime we do something our brains want us to do again, dopamine is released," the scientists explain. Music taps into this circuitry, which seems to have evolved to drive human motivation. The pleasure response prompts us to listen to more music like this, which in turns spurs the brain's development so that it can better comprehend, anticipate, and appreciate similar music in the future—thus prompting a greater surge of dopamine in an endless, even addictive cycle. Valorie Salimpoor, leader of the research team, suggests that this dopamine release, which engages ancient reward circuitry and sparks intense emotional responses, may explain why music can be so effectively used in rituals to create ecstatic or "hedonistic" states.[6]

 **www.HealingAtTheSpeedOfSound.com/Link61**

The McGill University researchers studying the brain's pleasure response to music named Samuel Barber's "Adagio for Strings"—in its original form, as performed here, or even in a dance, trance, or techno remix—the most popular selection among their subjects.[7] Listen to this recording of the piece on our Web site. Can you tell why the brain loves this music so? Does the experience of listening sweep you away to other realities, other worlds?

Science has not yet uncovered all the fundamental links between music and the spirit. Much remains to be learned. And much will remain that must be taken on speculation or faith. When we consider the ways in which music can help us connect to realms outside our ordinary lives, let's not hesitate to venture beyond our daily experience. This is the greatest duty of all the arts, to take us to the "other world" of perception and sensation, so that we will continue to seek and find solace in this world.

Expressing the Self

Listening daily to beautiful sounds naturally inspires us to express ourselves musically—to use the voice to experience harmony with our surroundings. In chapter five, we discussed the ways in which the voice serves as a kind of conduit between our inner state and the outer world, helping us to release repressed emotions, trauma, or grief. We noted some of the ways in which voice analysis and voice therapy techniques involving singing or chanting can be used to treat individuals for emotional, psychological, and communication problems, and how creating sound as part of a group can help establish a healing sense of mutual acceptance and community. Now, alone at home, you can use the power of sound to regain your own sense of emotional balance, by literally expressing yourself in the liberating forms of song, chant, and tone.

For eons, singing has served as a way to release blocked energy, express emotion, and achieve catharsis; as a means through which to harmonize with the environment and with others in society; and as a form of worship and adoration. Song connects us to the roots of our common humanity, allowing us to experience the present in the context of the past, and to experience in the present our hopes, dreams, and expectations for the future. As the Islamic scholar Abu Hamid al-Ghazali observed in *The Revival of Religious Sciences*, singing is a spiritual act that evokes the truth in one's heart and soul.[8] Even if you are self-conscious about your voice and resist singing with others in a public forum, you may find welcome release from the stresses of the day by singing along with some of the music to which you listen at night.

Expressing yourself vocally may be easier than you think. The biggest part of a singer's training is learning how to direct the voice as desired, and having a mental image of what's going on inside the body to produce sounds helps us work better and learn more quickly how to improve. With a relaxed throat, sing or hum a low sound. Now make the sound go up. As the pitch rises, notice how your throat tightens. That's the power of breath passing through your voice box as it obeys your mental direction. Note that the harder you contract your abdominal muscles, the louder the sound becomes.

As the sound waves generated by these vibrating vocal cords pass through the open areas in your mouth, throat, and chest, they cause the walls of these spaces to vibrate, too, at various related frequencies. As you sing, you can feel this vibration throughout your upper body, even in your bones. As your song enters the room, the space around you vibrates as well, absorbing or deflecting the sound depending on the materials in the walls, floor, and ceiling. "Anything that can vibrate or resonate can change the way singing is heard," the Canadian singer and music writer Edward Willett tells us, "and everything vibrates to some degree."[9]

All singing takes place according to this process of breath filling the spaces in your body with vibration and sound. Of course, some singers sound more beautiful than others, depending on the quality of the vibrato, the "cleanness" of the overtones, and the rich mixture of those bright and dark resonances that bring fullness and depth to the sound of the voice. By maintaining a relaxed and lifted posture and breathing deeply and freely, you will find yourself naturally capable of reproducing the beautiful sounds you hear in a gratifying and fulfilling way, no matter what you've thought about your singing before.[10]

From time immemorial, shamans and other spiritual and religious leaders have used vocal and percussive sounds to channel spiritual energy from one state of consciousness to another. This type of music springs from all traditions—including Indian ragas, Gregorian chants, healing songs from Africa and South America, music from the Tibetan, Hebrew, Sufi, and Buddhist traditions, and even Western lullabies—and shares certain characteristics, such as simple tonal configurations, that reflect a sacred unity with nature. Musician and faculty member of the California Institute of Integral Studies Silvia Nakkach calls these types of archetypal music "medicine melodies," capable of healing body, mind, and spirit by clearing our internal channels and allowing for the free passage of energy between the worlds without and within.[11]

Medicine melodies "induce concentration and sharpen our capacity for self-awareness, allowing us to see not only what is there, but also what is felt, and what others feel," Nakkach writes. Singing is transformative "because it liberates self-expression, promotes physical and emotional balance, and engenders a sense of devotion and happiness. . . . When the voice wanders through ancient sounds, trancelike melodic repetitive patterns, and textural prayers, it creates an optimum coordination between brain, breath and heart, which helps to reduce stress, clear emotions, and sharpen intellectual focus and creativity. . . . Awakening the whole body of the voice becomes a spiritual practice that involves both the body and the mind—the ultimate aim being the experience of divine remembrance and transcendence."[12]

Researchers have confirmed that devotional and other forms of meditative or ecstatic singing produce measurable effects in the physical body, strengthening the immune system, improving blood pressure, breathing, and blood circulation, and thus enhancing our sense of well-being on both the physical and spiritual planes. Whether we choose Christian hymns, Buddhist chants, or Elizabethan ballads, medicine melodies immerse us in the present moment and provide us with release through spontaneous, simple, and passionate song.[13]

 **www.HealingAtTheSpeedOfSound.com/Link62**

Join Silvia Nakkach as she demonstrates her concept of medicine melodies and discusses their powers.

The Spiritual Power of Tone

For many, a daily session of listening to music, and perhaps producing song as well, can suffice as a welcome source of joy and comfort at the beginning or close of each busy day. Some, however, may wish to focus more intently on expanding the range and quality of their vocal expression as a way of growing more in touch with their own spirituality, and of communicating more effectively with others.

We may not always think about what we sound like to ourselves or others, but it's hard to imagine communicating via speech without the accompanying tone of voice. Tone reveals so very much—sometimes, whether we want it to or not. We can tell a person's mood by their tone of voice, and they can tell ours. The most skillful among us can control tone to either express or conceal our feelings. Once we become aware of our voice and develop some skill at modifying it, we can all, to some degree, choose what our voice reveals as easily as we choose what to say with our words. Sometimes we put on a happy tone just to make others around us feel good. People with acute hearing and listening skills understand that the tone of voice in its most natural state reveals true joy, true passion, and true love as well as depression, stress, and complete despondency.

The voice and tone of voice can express pain within the body. Voice and tone show how much breath is being used to give out to the world. Are we strangled by our thoughts, our innermost tensions? The tone of the voice gives us a sense, a barometer, of how the atmospheres of our mind and body are communicating with each other. Like no other instrument, the voice is able to weave breath, sound, and expression for emotional release.

Daily toning—the conscious vocalizing of elongated vowel sounds for extended periods of time—is an ideal way to get in touch with your own voice, both literally and metaphorically. Laurel Elizabeth Keyes, author of *Toning: The Creative Power of the Voice*, defines the centuries-old practice as "the right use of the natural breath and allowing the full flow of life within."[14] Like all forms of vocalization, toning helps oxygen to circulate through the body, relaxes muscles, and stimulates the flow of energy. As Mark Rider points out in *The Rhythmic Language of Health and Disease*, the effects of toning are more pronounced, eliciting significantly lower heart rate and higher immune response than merely singing, and the experience is more intense. Observing people as they toned on a syllable and pitch of their choosing for a period of ten minutes, Rider found that the tone's harmonics seemed to "provide subjects with a continuous high frequency stimulation," constituting "a natural form of biofeedback" and perhaps enhancing brain wave activity.[15]

Perhaps the best aspect of toning is that it requires no particular skill, no special instrument or equipment, and no musical training. You needn't know an A flat from an F sharp. You just need your voice and a little nudge in the right direction. Take this five-day turn through your own toning capabilities and see how you feel after spending just a few minutes a day exploring your voice and sounding your own kinds of medicine melodies. You may be surprised to discover how this one activity can positively affect your outlook and sense of well-being for the entire day.

Day 1—*Do some humming.* Sit comfortably in a chair, close your eyes, and just hum for five minutes with a very relaxed jaw and your teeth slightly apart. Hum at any pitch that feels comfortable, not necessarily a particular melody. Feel the buzzing, vibrating energy throughout your body. Take a few deep breaths when you're done, and smile.

Day 2—*Make the "ahhhh" sound.* A stress-relieving sound if there ever was one, it's what you naturally do when you yawn. Begin with a quiet *ah* anytime you're feeling tense, and move your jaw around to relax it. Breathe in, breathe out on a long, slow *ahhhh*, take another breath, repeat. This isn't a song or even a melody—just the soft sound of relaxation emerging from your mouth. If you're among others you don't wish to disturb, you can even do this in your head, breathing in, then thinking *ahhhh* while breathing slowly out. Instant relaxation, especially if you can close your eyes too.

Day 3—*Go, "Eeee."* This one will wake you up! Very helpful while driving or if you're in that midafternoon slump, sounding an *eeee* is more useful than a jolt of caffeine. Take three to five minutes to explore this invigorating, playful sound. Smile, but don't strain, as you make your *eeee*-energizing sound.

Day 4—*Say, "Ohhh."* The *oh* and *om* are the rich, deeply connected sounds prized by many folks who make a practice of chanting or toning, and you will come to appreciate this round, full *oh* too. For an instant tune-up, spend five minutes sounding *oh*, breathing in deeply, letting the *oh* slide up and down in a spontaneous, unscripted melody, or simply holding whatever pitch emerges from your lungs. Your chest, jaw, and head all vibrate when you make the *oh* sound, and practicing this particular sound can change muscle tension, brain waves, and skin temperature. It can even alter your breath and heart rates.

Day 5—*Experiment!* Beginning at the very lowest pitch you can reach (without straining), let your voice glide upward slowly on relaxing vowel sounds that arise without effort and resonate throughout your body. Use your hands to slowly trace where in your upper body (skull, throat, chest) you feel the vocal massage of your voice as you change from *ahhhh* to *ohhh* to *eeee* and back again so you can see which vowel elicits the best stress-releasing energy as you sound. Most of all, enjoy your voice and the feelings of well-being generated by using your very own sonic tonic in this way.

 **www.HealingAtTheSpeedOfSound.com/Link63**

Listen to me demonstrate proper toning technique. Then try it yourself and experience its effect.

Years ago, motivated by the desire to express myself more fully and effectively as a public speaker, I spent much time exploring the differences I felt between singing, chanting musically, and limiting my utterance to a single tone. Toning was not particularly a musical experience. It was fully energetic, vibrational, and massaging to the inner landscape of my reality. For months, I wrestled with my left brain's criticism of making such absurd, nonmusical, uncontrolled, nonaesthetic sounds. I realized my voice was not creating music so much as it was creating a deep and profound awareness of the energy inside my body through sounding. My enthusiasm for the practice expanded so much as a result that I spent a number of years researching, writing, and lecturing about toning's beneficial effects. If your experience with toning has sparked your own curiosity and interest, you can learn more about the technique and its history in my books *The Roar of Silence* and *Creating Inner Harmony*, my recorded lecture Healing Yourself with Your Own Voice, and the new edition of Laurel Keyes's *Toning.*

The Phrase That Calms

Chanting—rhythmically repeating a phrase, sentence, or rhythmic sequence in a meditative manner—is another way to maintain psychological and spiritual balance, as well as to simply wind down at the end of the day. As we saw in earlier chapters, quietly repeating a healing phrase, or mantra, when faced with personal conflicts or stressful situations can help keep our blood pressure down and allow us to feel more in control of our lives. Chanting a phrase with personal positive significance or a calming effect has been shown to benefit those with post-traumatic stress disorder[16] and to improve the psychological state of people in high-stress or tedious jobs. As a daily practice, it can go further, enhancing our spiritual well-being and connecting us with our true energetic and emotional nature in much the same way as listening to music, singing sacred songs, and toning.

The words we choose to chant—whether they are a phrase as simple as "All is well" or a fragment of prayer from your religious background—are less important than their personal significance for us and their power to bring us out of any temporary emotional turmoil, and to create a space within which to reconnect with ourselves. Choose a phrase that is imbued with a positive meaning for you, not something imposed by someone else. In the evening, half an hour before bedtime, retreat to a quiet place in your home, dim the lights, and sit comfortably in a chair, on your bed, or on the floor. Repeat your chosen phrase or word slowly and steadily, allowing its energy to seep down inside you on an ever-deeper level, creating a sense of serenity, strength, and calm. By making a daily habit of this practice, you can ensure that your soothing phrase will surface in your mind automatically when you need it during stressful periods of the night or day. Your own voice will gently nudge away the cares of the moment, so that you can move forward unburdened by negative emotion and choose the action best suited to your needs.

Listen Up

♫ Of all the forms of song meditation created in the history of humankind, Gregorian chant remains among the most beautiful and transcendent. For centuries, monastic communities have gathered together seven times a day to mark the Sacred Hours—times of song, meditation, and prayer—which in turn formed a part of the ecclesiastical calendar, with its fixed and movable feasts heralding the seasons and tonalities of the liturgical year. If you find that you rarely have the opportunity or desire to chant alone at home, listening to recordings of Gregorian chant might make for a satisfactory alternative. The beauty of the chants will bring a sense of timelessness and tradition to your ears and heart. If you feel moved to chant along now and again, you will find that the elongated tones and vowel sounds, made with the correct posture, charge your brain with oxygenated blood—stimulating as powerfully as coffee, but with healthier results.

A Transcendent Beat

Drumming, used for eons to open the door to altered states of consciousness in order to manage pain and heal the sick and suffering, has become another popular form of meditation in the modern world as scientists confirm the power of repetitive rhythm to coordinate brain function and regulate biological functioning. The shamanic drum pattern of approximately 4 to 4.5 beats per second increases listeners' levels of alpha brain waves, associated with relaxation and general well-being, and/or theta waves, associated with a drowsy, near-unconscious state. Exposure to these rhythms, particularly when they're used in conjunction with imagery therapies, can reduce tension, anxiety, fatigue, pain perception, and depression, and can relieve insomnia by helping you to relax. Many participants also report experiences of trance states or other altered state of consciousness, even when the experience does not occur within cultural ritual, ceremony, or intent.

In chapter six, I discussed the benefits of participating in a drumming group in one's community. Even if you have not been able to join such a group in your area, you can benefit from the power of rhythm by listening to recordings of drumming sessions. Studies have shown that doing so, and drumming along as you feel so moved, can be nearly as effective as participating in a live session. Try it for yourself this evening: Light some candles, dim the electric lights, put a recording of shamanic drumming on the sound system, and play along. You'll be amazed by how relaxed these rhythmic time-outs can make you feel.

www.HealingAtTheSpeedOfSound.com/Link64

Use a drum, an upside-down plastic bucket, a book, or any other handy surface and start drumming along with this simple rhythm. As you grow comfortable with the beat, add your own more complex rhythms. Try chanting along, inventing a positive, self-affirming phrase to lift your spirits. Once you've tried this, you're likely to want to make it a daily practice!

Music serves to evoke the prayer, the praise, and the pulse of the known and the unknown. The voice is the tool for invocation, whether it be emotionally provocative or almost silent and contemplative. The rhythmic imprint of your soul and spirit may not be defined by a clinical study, but it is important for your own testament of inner peace.

CHAPTER EIGHT

The Melody Lingers

Music and Aging

There is nothing more notable in Socrates than that he found time, when he was an old man, to learn music and dancing, and thought it time well spent.

—Michel de Montaigne

Sound and music shape our development from pre-birth through adulthood, influencing our mood, our health, our spiritual and emotional balance, and our ease in communicating with those we love. They can also profoundly influence the quality of our mental, physical, and psychological functioning in later life, even as they add inestimable beauty and joy to the passing years. In this chapter, we will examine ways to use the power of rhythm, vibration, melody, and tone to sharpen our minds, keep ourselves active, and mitigate the effects of illness and other challenges of aging. Whether you have parents or grandparents who could benefit from the healing and stimulating properties of sound, or you yourself have passed the midpoint of life, the techniques presented here can create a bridge from a full, productive middle age to the type of rich, engaged, lively maturity we all hope to enjoy in our senior years.

 **www.HealingAtTheSpeedOfSound.com/Link65**

After sixty-two years of marriage, Fran and Marlo Cowan find making music more enjoyable and stimulating than ever. Watch as they perform an impromptu piano duet in the atrium of the Mayo Clinic!

Music for Life

Some of the best news to emerge from the recent advances in brain-imaging technology is the discovery that, contrary to previous belief, the brain does not stop growing in our later years. Rather, as long as we keep learning new skills, refining old ones, and engaging in creative activities, the neural connections in our brains continue to strengthen and new connections can even be made.[1]

Dr. Gene Cohen, author of *The Mature Mind: The Positive Power of the Aging Brain* and the former director of the George Washington University's Center on Aging, Health & Humanities, produced much of the recent groundbreaking research on creativity and brain power in the second half of his life. He tells us that throughout adult life—including well after age fifty—the mind experiences measurable and important surges of creativity and brain function. During these periods, older brains can draw on areas underused in earlier years and actually "resculpt" themselves as certain genes are activated by experience gained over the years.[2] In fact, he adds, for those who maintain a basic level of physical fitness and do not suffer from such diseases as dementia or Parkinson's disease, the brain's information processing center reaches its greatest density between the ages of sixty and eighty.

Research has shown that mature brains are different from younger ones, but they have their own unique strengths. For instance, many middle-aged and older individuals demonstrate superior "developmental intelligence"—that is, the ability to synthesize disparate views, to hold opposing viewpoints in their minds at the same time without judgment, and to comprehend the bigger picture without getting hung up on details or on personal issues.[3] These are just the skills needed to accomplish what Cohen calls the "four developmental phases of the second half of life": to reevaluate and reconsider our lives; to experience liberation and a new desire to experiment as we realize, "If not now, when"; to sum up what we've learned over time and share this knowledge with others; and finally to restate and reaffirm to ourselves the truths and major themes of our lives.[4]

The key to accomplishing these goals—and to continuing to expand our brain capacity and creativity in the older years, Cohen emphasizes—lies in the old bromide "Use it or lose it," a principle as applicable to mental abilities as to physical ones.[5] As we continue to engage in challenging leisure activities, to exercise both our brains and bodies, to work toward mastery of skills in any area of our choosing, and to build and maintain strong social networks, our brains really will improve with age and our lives will become richer and more fulfilling as a result.[6]

What better way to accomplish all of these aims than through music? By listening closely to our favorite sounds or, better, singing, playing instruments, or dancing with others, we engage more areas of the brain simultaneously than through almost any other activity. Music making allows us to interact with others and make new friends. It gives us an engaging and enjoyable activity to look forward to. It stimulates our emotions and our intellect, adding meaning and fulfillment to our lives. It connects us to our own past and present, to our culture, and to life.[7]

In recent decades, a host of wonderful music-related programs have been developed for those in midlife and older. Across the country, Road Scholar (previously known as Elderhostel) organizes "music and seniors" educational programs around annual classical music festivals, which include attendance at symphony rehearsals, lectures by the artists, and the opportunity to meet other music lovers of one's own age. In Brooklyn, New York, the Mark Morris Dance Group provides physically and artistically demanding dance instruction for seniors,[8] stretching participants' minds and bodies, encouraging new friendships, and facilitating a genuine sense of accomplishment and artistic expression.[9]

 **www.HealingAtTheSpeedOfSound.com/Link66**

Take inspiration from this Web site for the Mark Morris Dance Group's wonderful community outreach program, which provides professional-style dance instruction for seniors, individuals with Parkinson's disease, and young students.

New Horizons International Music Association[10]—the brainchild of Roy Ernst, professor emeritus of the Eastman School of Music, in Rochester, New York—has created more than 170 community music ensembles, orchestras, and bands for older adults with little or no prior musical training, thus providing them with the same type of musical experiences that high school and college students enjoy.[11] Participants find that playing music with others—reading musical notation, working with rhythm and pitch, exercising fine muscle movements to play an instrument, and exploring emotion and memories through sound—provides wonderful intellectual challenges and keeps them feeling young. Deep friendships are formed as the groups practice, perform, and attend concerts and other events together—there have even been several marriages among members. One participant points to the exceptional dedication that her group's older members bring to the activity. "This comes at a [point] in life when you have the time to devote to it," she explains. "Not many people drop out. It's something that holds you. Next to my family, certainly, the musical activity is the most important thing in my life."[12] Ernst also points out that players middle-aged and beyond often have something extra to bring to a performance. "High school kids could never do what we do, because they haven't lived enough; they haven't seen enough joy or sorrow," he insists. "We have a special ability to play music expressively and with feeling."[13]

Aside from these larger organizations, many churches, community centers, and other local groups host swing-dancing or square-dancing nights, support choirs or choruses, or encourage instrumental ensembles for participants middle-aged and older. Meeting with others to pursue a shared creative goal is an excellent way to widen your social network (and sometimes to fall in love), and is crucial in maintaining a healthy lifestyle for the future.

www.HealingAtTheSpeedOfSound.com/Link67

In this TED talk, musician and researcher Charles Limb discusses his efforts to scientifically study the process of musical creativity and its implications regarding brain functioning.

Good Vibrations

Many of music's benefits for young people, examined in earlier chapters, can prove even more advantageous for those of us who are middle-aged and older. Men and women in their thirties may appreciate being able to lower their blood pressure and fortify their immune systems by listening to soft music or recorded nature sounds, for example, but for those who are older these improvements can be crucial and even lifesaving. Likewise, while college students no doubt appreciate music's power to get them moving during exercise, older people may truly depend on music to motivate them to work out regularly—whether through tai chi, aerobics, bicycling, dancing (ballroom, line dancing, swing), or even actively conducting music—to maintain coordination, prevent falls, and perhaps even delay certain types of decreased brain function.

www.HealingAtTheSpeedOfSound.com/Link68

Watch how energized this group of seniors becomes as they "conduct" a John Philip Sousa march under the direction of retired symphony conductor David Dworkin—and imagine how effectively they're improving blood circulation in the body and brain.

Older people with arthritis are likely to find that daily sessions spent listening to classical or other relaxing music on headphones—a universal de-stressor—can significantly reduce their perception of arthritis or other pain[14] without the cost and negative side effects associated with medication.[15] Patients undergoing knee or hip replacement procedure can decrease the likelihood of postoperative confusion or disorientation by listening to music following surgery, and can speed their recovery by continuing their listening sessions for an hour or so four times per day.[16] And older individuals with poor blood circulation, stiff muscles, chronic pain, insomnia, or the nausea that often accompanies chemotherapy can benefit as much from vibroacoustic therapy's "internal massage" as children with autism, cystic fibrosis, and other conditions.

In all of these instances, the ability to use sound to moderate their own symptoms helps these individuals to feel more in control of their lives, and thus also improves their mood, increases their energy level, and gets them out socializing more. "This is energy medicine we're working with," explains the vibroacoustic harp therapist Sarajane Williams. "Patients feel energized by it—there's a lot of emotional processing." Frequently, people who begin their sessions feeling anxious or despondent finish with a renewed sense of purposefulness and joy.

As with those who are younger, older people often discover that playing music or singing, as opposed to simply listening, leads to even greater benefits. Playing virtually any instrument, from harmonica to keyboard to electric guitar, strengthens muscles and can improve dexterity and mobility.[17] Practicing and performing music also leads to decreased anxiety and depression, fewer falls, fewer doctor visits, a stronger immune system, and better health overall.[18] These effects are not just psychological—they occur chemically as well. A major study called the Music Making and Wellness Project, organized by Frederick Tims, chair of music therapy at Michigan State University, revealed that after two semesters of group keyboard lessons, retirees showed significantly increased levels of human growth hormone (HGH), the decrease of which in the elderly has been linked to osteoporosis, lower muscle mass, an increase in aches and pains, decreased sexual function, and other symptoms associated with aging. No wonder, then, that middle-aged or older people report that playing music or singing together allows them to "relive" their youths—or that the grown children of participants in one such singing program, led by Dr. Gene Cohen as part of a study for the National Endowment for the Arts, mob him following each concert, insisting, "Please. This must never stop."[19]

Listen Up

♫ It's impossible to enjoy music to its fullest if you can't hear well. As we age, our hearing ability tends to decrease—about one-third of people over sixty and half of those over eighty experience age-related hearing loss—so it's important to have our hearing checked as regularly as our vision. If you are one of those who shy away from hearing examinations, dreading a prescription for an unattractive hearing aid, the good news is that in recent years scientists have developed highly sophisticated new ways to cope with this disability, and still more devices will be available soon.

Whereas the standard analog hearing aids of the past amplified all frequencies equally and had to completely plug the ear in order to prevent feedback, new, "open-fit" digital devices use a narrow, inconspicuous tube to carry amplified frequencies into the ear, and can be tuned to respond only to the frequencies needed, while the ear remains open to other frequencies. Some of these devices have multiple microphones that can filter out background noise and tune in human speech. These new devices work like tiny computers, whose microchips allow them to convey more subtlety of sound and music, and whose software can be adapted to the user's individual needs.[20]

John House, president of the House Ear Institute, in Los Angeles, predicts that within five years doctors will be able to implant hearing devices that don't require an external aid at all. Researchers are also exploring methods to regenerate lost or damaged hair cells in the inner ear, and looking at ways to identify and manipulate the genes responsible for age-related hearing loss to prevent, rather than simply treat, the condition. Within the next twenty years, House predicts, as many as one-third of older people with significant hearing loss will be able to recover their hearing in this way. And in fifty years, doctors may be able to prevent or cure hearing loss in nearly everyone.[21]

 **www.HealingAtTheSpeedOfSound.com/Link69**

Here, on the Web site of the National Institute on Deafness and Other Communication Disorders, you will find the latest findings on hearing loss and new developments in diagnosis and treatment.

Remember That Tune

If you saw Nick Cassavetes's film *The Notebook*, you may remember the moving scene in which Gena Rowlands, in the role of Allie, a woman with Alzheimer's disease, is encouraged by a nurse to try playing the piano. Allie has forgotten that she used to love to play the instrument—or that she even knew how to play—but once she places her hands on the piano keys, the music flows from her fingers with astounding ease, bringing with it encapsulated memories of her younger days.

Music's power to capture experience, and to re-create it in the listener's mind long after it has faded from conscious memory, is certainly one of sound's most fascinating properties. In the scientific literature, stories like Allie's abound. In *The New Yorker*, Oliver Sacks describes the strange case of Clive Wearing, an eminent English musician and musicologist who in his mid-forties was struck by a brain infection that left him with the worst case of amnesia in recorded medical history. As an amnesiac, Wearing forgot virtually everything from moment to moment—his wife's name, his friends' identities, the workings of such modern devices as cell phones and the Internet. Each moment, he felt as though he was waking from a coma. Yet when he sat down at the piano, all the while insisting that he didn't know how to play, his memory of the instrument and of the music returned the moment his fingers touched the keys. In the same way, Wearing could still sing, conduct his choir, and engage in other musical activities with full passion and engagement. Music served as his only anchor in an otherwise fathomless, blank world.[22]

www.HealingAtTheSpeedOfSound.com/Link70

Oliver Sacks, author of *Musicophilia*, discusses music's power to reawaken memories in people with Alzheimer's disease.

One doesn't have to be forgetful, or even have a minor case of amnesia, to understand the almost magical power of music to transport us to another time in our lives. We've all had this experience many times. Do you recall the first time you heard James Taylor's "You've Got a Friend," Talking Heads' "Once in a Lifetime," or any other song with which you connected emotionally? A survey of more than three thousand people around the world, conducted by researchers at the University of Leeds, showed that most respondents were able to pinpoint where and when they first heard a particular Beatles song, and could often provide a vivid, upbeat anecdote related to that first exposure. "The first time I ever heard 'Lucy in the Sky with Diamonds' was when I was six years old at a friend's house," reported one young woman. "We spent all day dancing, laughing, and singing to the song, memorizing the words and having the time of our lives." Another recalled, "I heard 'She Loves You' for the first time when I was eleven years old. . . . The sounds came from the neighbor's bedroom window. . . . I still remember that particular night, lying on the bed and hearing the words loud and clear."[23] More recently, *New York Times* columnist Bob Herbert responded to the news of Aretha Franklin's pancreatic cancer with a recollection of hearing her song "I Never Loved a Man" played over and over at his sister Sandy's eighteenth birthday party, in 1967. "[A]ll these beautiful teenagers, their lives about to get going in earnest, were doing intricate dance routines to the music," he recalled with evident emotion. "Aretha was an ecstatic presence in the house as surely as if she'd been there in person. She was like a sister to every one of the kids."[24]

The strong emotional content of all of these acts of recollection—Allie's in *The Notebook*, Wearing's at the piano, the survey respondents' and Bob Herbert's remembrances of popular tunes—provides a crucial clue in understanding the link between music and memory. Researchers including Petr Janata, a cognitive neuroscientist at the University of California, Davis, explain that the prefrontal cortex—the region of the brain most likely responsible for the task of recalling a melody[25]—is also key to the response and control of emotions and the place where the individual's autobiographical information, or sense of self, is stored. Probably for this reason, as a melody carves a memory pathway into this neural region, it encapsulates along with the sound the emotional impressions and sense of self the listener experiences as he hears it at that particular time. Most recently, we saw a vivid and memorable illustration of this concept in the director Jim Kohlberg's wonderful film *The Music Never Stopped*, in which a young man suffering from severe amnesia caused by a brain tumor can only access his memory, and connect emotionally with his father, through the music of the Grateful Dead and other bands he loved in his youth in the 1960s.

This rich neural resonance between music, emotion, and personal identity has been demonstrated scientifically, via magnetic resonance imaging. Researchers at the University of California, Davis, have noted, for example, that while the prefrontal cortex responds to rhythm and key signature in any song, it's particularly active when a song has autobiographical relevance[26]—that is, when it touches on our own memories or sense of ourselves. Some scientists have suggested that music's power to stimulate activity in this way may explain why, as surveys have shown, professional musicians are less likely than nonmusicians to experience Alzheimer's in later life, after decades of this type of stimulation.

It is also most likely the reason why we tend to respond most viscerally to music we first heard and loved during adolescence, as evidenced by the survey respondents mentioned earlier. As Dr. Janata points out, the early teenage years are when our autobiographical sense begins to solidify, so songs first heard during that period connect firmly with that fresh sense of self forming in the prefrontal cortex. Hearing one of these songs now, our hearts start pumping, our feet start moving, our adolescent energy reasserts itself like magic, and we almost feel fourteen or fifteen again. But aspects of our identity formed in emotionally potent periods in later life can also be vividly resurrected through music, as in the case of one woman with dementia so severe that she could not identify a song she used to sing to her children, but she still responded to its melody with the words, "I have to go; the children will be home from school soon."[27]

 **www.HealingAtTheSpeedOfSound.com/Link71**

Dr. Petr Janata discusses music, memories, and the brain in the Library of Congress series Music and the Brain.

Clearly, these connections between music, memory, and self-identity carry strong implications for treatment of the more than five million Americans who suffer from Alzheimer's disease, as well as those with other forms of dementia or memory-related disorders. Because the prefrontal cortex is among the last brain regions to atrophy, music can often connect with these individuals, even in advanced stages of illness. It is exciting to witness the ways in which familiar tunes from crucial periods of such a person's life—childhood nursery rhymes, dance music from adolescence, wedding music or religious hymns—can pluck her out of the fog of senescence and awaken her personality, if only for a moment. This type of musical stimulation may also delay symptoms in some cases. Studies have shown that many individuals with Alzheimer's who listen to two or three hours of music each day demonstrate improved memory, comprehension, and cognitive abilities. Equally important, points out Suzanne Hanser, founder of the music therapy department at Berklee College of Music, in Boston, and a practicing therapist at the Dana-Farber Cancer Institute, is the way in which listening to such songs can renew the bond between patients and their loved ones, helping them relive meaningful moments from their past while also creating new ones. Such experiences can be a godsend for couples whose relationships have been strained or damaged by the onset of this challenging condition.

If you care for or know an elderly person—with or without some form of dementia—think about the ways in which music can serve as a supplemental support at times when his or her cognitive or communication skills falter. Many older people suffer from sleep irregularities, for example. Maintaining a regular, predictable routine, with strict delineation between periods of wakefulness and sleep, can lift the spirits and increase alertness for anyone with sleep problems, and has been shown to delay the progression of dementia. As we have seen in earlier chapters, music is a wonderful tool for building structure into a day—beginning with lively, light melodies on the stereo in the morning as you open the curtains to let the sunshine in; switching to a familiar melody (something soft and stimulating—perhaps a little Bach or Schumann, or Chick Corea) to signal the times for meals; putting on some strongly rhythmic, upbeat music to set the mood for an exercise session; and, finally, marking bedtime with dimmed lights and the soft and beautiful sounds of the "Moonlight Sonata."

Listen Up

♫ When caring for an elderly person, it's important to keep in mind the changes in sound perception that take place in the later years. The sound of the television, radio, fluorescent lights, conversation, and even live music can be distracting and confusing to older people—or else they may not be able to hear them at all. Prescribed drugs can heighten sensitivity to certain sounds, making their presence more annoying. An older person's psychological state can affect sound perception as well, requiring a greater-than-average degree of silence in many cases, particularly near the end of life.

Even those who are unable to keep track of the flow of activities will respond to the emotional content of each musical selection. Researchers have found that the right kind of music played during meals soothes patients with dementia in nursing homes and hospitals, decreasing their confusion and minimizing conflicts so they can focus on eating a healthy amount of food.[28] Lively, upbeat music may draw a reluctant individual into conversation, or persuade him to go out with you for a walk. You can even use melody in the form of soft, cheerful whistling or humming to reassure a loved one with dementia as you first enter the room. Even if his brain initially responds to your appearance with confusion or fear, the emotional content of your happy tune may make him *feel*, even if he doesn't *know*, that you are his friend.

There is no limit to the ways in which you can communicate with an elderly loved one musically, through the emotions rather than the intellect. Singing a familiar nursery tune as you help with a change of clothes, or humming a lullaby as you hold hands, stroke hair, or embrace your loved one, tells her that she is loved even if she is no longer able to comprehend your words. Loneliness is a danger for the elderly, particularly because many are too embarrassed to admit to it, or because they have no one to tell. It is especially common among people with Alzheimer's—seventy percent of whom live at home in relative isolation—and has been shown to lead frequently to depression, anxiety, aggression, and even thoughts of suicide.[29] By connecting through music, you can literally save an older person's life. If you have been feeling despondent or exhausted by your caregiving duties, you may be amazed by how uplifting these music sessions can be for you, too.

www.HealingAtTheSpeedOfSound.com/Link72

Watch me demonstrate the "Paper Plate Payout," the most popular and beneficial music exercise I have ever used in residential settings with the elderly, using simple paper plates as percussion instruments to stimulate the brain and share a joyful experience.

Group singing, dance, or music-playing or -listening programs, whether provided by a church organization, a community group, a cultural series designed for retirees, or a music therapist in an assisted-care facility, are a great idea for all seniors. They are especially crucial for those with any form of dementia, since research has shown that these conditions progress more slowly when people remain active and in regular contact with others. A weekly music session allows elderly people to connect—even those who have lost the ability to converse successfully—and thus greatly improves the tenor of their lives.

Even relatively young participants in music programs at assisted-living facilities report feeling happy and invigorated after socializing at such sessions. Brigette Sutton, a music therapist in Pittsburgh, observes that as music sparks memories, it moves participants to share their reminiscences with one another. "It takes time to develop a relationship," she points out. Music gets people to talk, enhancing their social lives even as it stimulates cognitive functioning. As a result, their depression lifts, they become more aware of themselves and their surroundings, they find themselves better able to manage their pain and discomfort without prescription drugs, and thus they enjoy a greater sense of control over their lives.[30] No wonder that a recent study at Stanford University found that elderly patients who were diagnosed with depression gained self-esteem and saw an improvement in their mood following sessions with a music therapist,[31] and that the subjects of a 2002 study in the UK—all residents of a long-term care facility—reported increased "life satisfaction" in addition to improved balance, flexibility, and cognitive abilities while participating in regular sessions of musical exercise therapy.

www.HealingAtTheSpeedOfSound.com/Link73

Kindermusik Village, a music program designed for babies and preschoolers, has extended its reach to include seniors as well. Watch the ways in which music helps the members of three generations connect, communicate, and share the joy of living for an hour each week.

It should come as no surprise at this point to learn that drumming circles and other rhythm-based music therapy programs can benefit nearly all seniors, including those with neurological challenges. Drumming provides an invigorating cardiovascular workout, a wonderful, joyful environment for social interaction, and neurological stimulation that can help improve cognition and other brain functions. Best of all, these cost-effective rhythmic activities require no special skill or previous musical experience, and they're rewarding for everyone, from those with their first gray hairs to people in later stages of Alzheimer's.

In 1991, the pioneering researcher Barbara Crowe, director of the music therapy department at Arizona State University and one of the leaders of the rhythm-based therapy movement, joined with former Grateful Dead drummer Mickey Hart, who's also a musicologist and social activist, to urge the Senate Special Committee on Aging to actively promote drum circles for the elderly, citing drumming's beneficial effects for those with

Alzheimer's and Parkinson's diseases as well as for those who have survived stroke or brain injury. As Hart has pointed out, "We know that music, rhythm, sound, and controlled vibrations affect brain wave function." Inevitably, once the mechanisms and methods for music-rhythm therapy have been further codified, "the neurological applications of music and rhythm for Alzheimer's, dementia, and all the motor impairment diseases will be affected."[32]

Memory Drummers, of St. Louis, coordinated by the local Alzheimer's Association, serves as one interesting example of a therapeutic drumming group. The group's members—educators, surgeons, and other "high-functioning professionals" who once traveled the world, participated in seminars, and otherwise took part in public life in important ways—now find themselves in early stages of Alzheimer's. Their drumming circle, whose specially trained facilitator has adapted the program to ease the learning process and to compensate for memory problems, provides them with what Abhilash Desai, director of St. Louis University's Center for Healthy Brain Aging, calls a "holistic intervention" consisting of cognitive stimulation, a physical workout, cultural enrichment, and social interaction. The highly educated participants appreciate the chance to experience the music of other cultures, and greatly enjoy the chance to let loose and beat the drums. More important, though, is the inclusive, nonjudgmental, nonhierarchical nature of this type of group, which allows them to let down their guard, share their experience with others diagnosed with Alzheimer's, exchange emotional sustenance and moral support, and thus begin to adjust to the reality of their condition. The friendships that have resulted are perhaps the greatest benefit provided by the group. As one member's wife observes, "He doesn't get depressed, and I think it's because of [drumming]. He seems more comfortable with those people than even with me."[33]

Listen Up

♫ Recent research conducted by Dr. Barry Bittman and colleagues revealed that group drumming and keyboard accompaniment not only improves the lives of the elderly but also decreases burnout and improves mood among the health-care workers who care for them. Their study of 112 long-term-care workers who participated in such a recreational music-making program showed statistically significant improvement in scores on the Maslach Burnout Inventory and the Profile of Mood States assessments. A refreshed, invigorated staff is less likely to make mistakes, feel demoralized, or leave the job, the authors of the study pointed out—leading to considerable savings in cost and efficiency for medical institutions while creating a better environment for everyone.[34]

When the Time for Words Is Past

"I was asleep when he died," writes the iconic singer and poet Patti Smith of her former lover, the artist Robert Mapplethorpe, in *Just Kids*, Smith's deeply moving memoir of their friendship. "I had called the hospital to say one more good night, but he had gone under, beneath layers of morphine."[35] Hanging up the phone, knowing she would never hear her friend's voice again, Smith drew the blanket over her baby daughter in her crib, kissed her young son as he slept, and then fell asleep, grieving, beside her husband.

The next morning, she awoke early and, going downstairs, found the television left on from the night before, tuned to an arts channel. An opera, Puccini's *Tosca*, was playing. "I was drawn to the screen as Tosca declared, with power and sorrow, her passion for the painter Cavaradossi," Smith writes. Soon afterward, as she raised the blinds, smoothed the fabric covering of a chair, and leafed through a book of paintings, the telephone rang. It was Robert's younger brother, giving her the news she fully expected that day: Robert had died.

Smith stood motionless, then slowly, as in a dream, returned to her chair. "At that moment, Tosca began the great aria, 'Vissi d'arte,' *I have lived for love, I have lived for Art*," she writes. "I closed my eyes and folded my hands. Providence determined how I would say goodbye."[36]

Nothing can meet life's most profound moments as effectively as music. These magical sounds, in sync with the universe and all its workings, are perfectly designed to usher us into life, nourish us through every stage of our time on earth, and comfort us and our loved ones as we make the transition out of this world. In recent years, interest has spread regarding the use of pastoral music therapy—that is, the use of music to provide solace to those with severe or terminal illnesses and their loved ones. Especially when confined to a hospital, nursing home, or other institution, people nearing the end of their lives often experience deep feelings of hopelessness, observes Charles Gourgey, director of the nonprofit music therapy organization Sounds of Hope Inc. Pastoral music therapists draw upon the music of different cultures and traditions to address such individuals' emotional and spiritual needs, helping them mobilize their inner resources and strengthen their connections with family members or friends even when verbal communication is no longer possible.

This approach is made easier by the increasing use of hospices as a place of repose for the dying—a place where patients can come to terms with the end of life and spend their last days lovingly tended to by family, friends, and compassionate, specially trained staff. The term *hospice*, dating back to medieval times, when it referred to a stopping place for weary travelers, was adopted in the 1960s by physicians and psychologists promoting the concept of death with dignity. Since then, gradual changes in government regulations and insurance coverage have made it possible for more individuals to find comfort and serenity in this way at the end of life—and to greatly improve their quality of life through music.[37] As one pastoral singer explains, "The human voice is a sound that comes between where we're headed and what we know." With its spiritual and emotional content carried through the air, "Music is a metaphor for what it feels like to not have a body. Music is vibration." As such, it makes the perfect vehicle for transition.

The spiritual benefits of music at times of crisis are no doubt clear to anyone who has had access to it. Scientists have begun to back up this intuitive sense with objective observation. Lisa M. Gallagher, a music therapist at the Cleveland Clinic's Harry R. Horvitz Center for Palliative Medicine, demonstrated in a recent study of two hundred patients receiving care for cancer, AIDS, aneurysms, and other conditions that listening to live piano music of the patient's choice for twenty-five minutes per day "helps improve mood while decreasing pain, anxiety, depression, and even shortness of breath." In survey after survey, a large majority of patients report improvement in their mood and increased relaxation after participating in end-of-life music therapy programs—and researchers observe corresponding evidence of improvement in their facial expressions and conversation as well.

For these reasons, most hospices and even some hospitals and nursing homes welcome music therapists, musicians, and singers to comfort the ill and dying whenever possible. Sometimes the music is provided by a solitary singer or instrumentalist. The harp is a particularly popular instrument, no doubt due to its classic significance as an ancient healing instrument. In any case, its soothing palette of tone colors and the glissando effects of the strumming of its strings seem to cast a spell on listeners, bringing them to a place of reflection and repose, while its wide pitch range sends healing vibrations through the body. "We can see things changing before our eyes—people grow less anxious, blood pressure goes down," says California therapist Barbara Rose Billings.[38] In her book *Harp Therapy Manual: Cradle of Sound*, Christina Tourin—a second-generation harpist, mentor to thousands of harpists worldwide through the International Harp Therapy Program, and developer of bedside programs for hospice, hospitals, and homes—explains that these effects can be magnified by combining each patient's resonant tone, musical preference, mood, and rhythm to help them in emotional, mental, physical, and spiritual healing.[39]

The healing extends to family members and to the medical staff as well. Neurologist Richard Mendius says the sound of Billings's harp "changes the whole tone" at the nursing station, and that he, too, feels more at ease after hearing her play.[40] Therapists themselves, including Jennifer Hollis, at the Lahey Clinic in Burlington, find the experience profoundly rewarding. "I see people who have to say good-bye to each other, who are coming to terms with what it means to leave this world, or this life that they've known," she says. "For me, it's a real education in what it means to be human."[41]

www.HealingAtTheSpeedOfSound.com/Link74

When Christina Tourin was called to the bedside of Geri, a terminal cancer patient at San Diego Hospice who was paralyzed from the waist down, she found a former dancer weeping, "How I wish I could dance again!" Tourin came up with a plan to help Geri realize her dream by dancing with her hands and arms to the music of the harp, recording her performance on videotape as a gift for her loving family. Tourin was surprised at the enthusiasm with which Geri took up the idea, preparing for her performance by supervising the creation of the set, discussing special effects, giving it the name "DANCE in the Clouds," and applying makeup before the cameras rolled. Here, you can see the result—an artistic expression that not only provided her family with a precious memento, but greatly improved Geri's sense of physical well-being in the process, boosted her morale, and thus may have contributed to her surviving for more than a year longer than expected.

Increasingly, musicians have gathered together in chamber groups or choral ensembles to help the dying prepare for the transition out of life. The demand for the all-female, nonprofit Threshold Choir, based in California, has grown so great that more than seventy associated choirs have sprung up in nearly every American state as well as overseas. Like similar ensembles, including the all-volunteer Trillium[42] and Wellspring[43] choirs in Vermont, the Threshold Choir provides gentle, introspective selections designed to suit the patient's taste and to lead him or her gently and steadily out of the concerns of daily life and toward contemplation of its end. Some of the Threshold Choir's several hundred selections date back to the ninth century; many others were composed by choir members. "There's an amazing community when we're singing among all of us who are mortal, sharing what we have to give to each other," one singer remarks. "The human voice in harmony—one voice supporting another—that's what it's supposed to be."[44]

It is hardly surprising to learn that many of the musicians who work with the dying were originally inspired by their own experience with the death of a friend or family member. Kate Munger, creator of the original Threshold Choir, was visiting a close friend in the hospital who was dying from AIDS when she spontaneously began to sing to him a song titled "There's a Moon." The act of singing had a profoundly calming effect on both her friend and on her, Munger later recalled. "Two hours later, he fell into a serene sleep. I realized that I had given him a gift"—and thus the idea for the Threshold Choir was born. While working as an undergraduate orderly at a Montana geriatric home, musician and educator Therese Schroeder-Sheker had been struck by the cold and insensitive treatment of those facing their final hours. Instinctively, she began using her singing voice and a harp to comfort these patients. In time her involvement expanded to a thirty-year career as a practitioner and teacher of music thanatology (music care and ministry for the end of life) and, in 1992, the creation of its premier organization, the Chalice of Repose Project.[45]

Of course, one needn't rely on professional musicians or singers to provide music in a hospital or hospice. What could be more moving than for friends or family to join together in softly singing or playing music that was significant in their loved one's life? Putting together a list of songs to play at the patient's bedside, or assembling a compilation of others' recordings, can prove as therapeutic for caregivers as for the patient. Not only does this bring to mind your most meaningful moments together, but it also masks some of the very noisy mechanical life-support systems. Often, hearing is the last sense to remain before death, and silence may also be appropriate at this powerful time for both family and patient.

Music therapists often help hospice patients and their families in such endeavors. A therapist can demonstrate how playing a song in time with a patient's breathing pattern and then gradually slowing the tempo will help the patient regulate his or her breathing. The therapist can also demonstrate how to nonverbally support a patient who is unconscious by singing or playing gentle lullabies or other melodies at the bedside. "When [family members] see even in a nonresponsive state that the client is responding to the music in some way, whether it's with a facial expression or their breathing is in time with the music, it gives the family a feeling that something is being done," one therapist explains. Some music therapists even help patients or family members write or record songs to express their feelings about this time of transition. Canadian music therapist Louise Cadrin recounts the story of one elderly patient who fulfilled a dream of having his singing recorded. "He'd been given a small tape recorder and he had sung into that so it could be left as a gift for the family," she reports. "The next morning he awoke with some clarity, so we recorded four songs." Within forty-eight hours, the man had died; the songs were played at his funeral service.

Of course, the choice of music is as significant in this context as it is when ushering newborns into the world. Priscilla Baker, coordinator of the Wellspring choir, observes that patients in the earlier stages of their end-of-life journey, particularly those who are still able to communicate and perhaps even sing, often benefit most from the songs that take them back to their youth—to happier, healthier times in their lives.

As the patient grows weaker and less communicative, the quiet, contemplative sounds of lullabies and laments—those gentle, introspective musical pieces sung in operas by dying characters, such as "Dido's Lament" from Henry Purcell's *Dido and Aeneas*—usually prove most comforting to the terminally ill and give solace to those left behind. Dr. Clare O'Callaghan, an Australia-based psychologist and researcher at the University of Melbourne, suggests creating "lullaments"—combining patients' and families' favorite lullabies with laments, which allows them to express their grief and begin to move toward new awareness and adaptation.[46]

Near the end of the patient's life, Baker suggests, it's time to change the tone. "At that point, we don't sing songs [the patient] would recognize," she explains, "because in a way, that person is in passage. That person is really leaving this world. . . . We don't want to pull him back by singing a song he's going to recognize, that some part of his brain is going to attach itself to a memory."[47] Ancient music; the simplest of chants, with no words; the slow, quiet strums of a few chords on a guitar; or even long moments of silence can all be of value as we pass and transform. As Baker points out, "We [in the choir] are not in this time and place. We've entered a space of divinity and sacredness and we've touched the divine by singing, coupled by being invited into that space by someone's dying. The last thing we do in life is we leave—we pass and transform."

www.HealingAtTheSpeedOfSound.com/Link75

Hospice musician Marcia Guntzel Feldman describes various types and purposes of music used in hospices and provides a link for obtaining recorded music.

Contemplating the ways in which music and sound can stimulate, support, and comfort us through the latter half and last stages of life, we cannot help but feel inspired to put music to work in making the most of our remaining time on earth. As we have seen, a growing body of evidence tells us that it would be practically impossible to come up with a healthier, more fulfilling resolution.

In addition, many of us find that giving to others magnifies our own joy in life. If you have a musical bent, consider joining or initiating a music, singing, or drumming group in your own neighborhood, or for adults, teens, or children less fortunate than you. And always, always make music a part of your daily life. Start the day with focused listening to music you love—whether it's Bach, Led Zeppelin, the Beatles, or Glenn Miller—and then build your own sonic tapestry to carry you through the day. The process *and* the experience will open your heart to more new ideas, feelings, and opportunities than you ever imagined. In large events throughout the world, such as "Sing London," hymns, chants, and love songs are bringing people of all ages and beliefs together in harmony. "Thousands of people within multicultural communities are sharing new ways to experience a unique 'singing field' where everyone is welcomed, heard and inspired," says Chloë Goodchild, director of the Naked Voice Foundation. Like the billions of people who heard the grand music of Westminster Abbey play at the wedding of Kate Middleton and Prince William, may we also find time in our lives to raise our own voices and instruments of inspiration.

As Charles Darwin writes in his autobiography, "If I had my life to live over again, I would have made a rule to . . . listen to some music at least once every week; for perhaps the parts of my brain now atrophied would thus have been kept active through use." Try it yourself and see.

CHAPTER NINE

A Soundtrack for Life

Creating Your Own Sound Diet

Throughout the course of this book, you have considered a wide variety of ways in which sound can enrich your life. You've learned how and why an improved sound environment can help you start your day in a better mood and with increased energy. You've explored the ways in which sound and sometimes silence can increase your own and others' productivity and comfort on the job. You've considered music's profound effects on brain development and health from pre-birth through adulthood, its positive effects on family and community relations, its emotional and spiritual benefits, and its helpful impact on the aging.

Now, at the end of your day, think about how you can use what you've learned about sound to relax yourself and your family and prepare for a good night's sleep. Did you find that waking to the recorded sounds of birds chirping cheered you up this morning? Perhaps this evening a recording of ocean waves and seagulls can turn an hour's reading into a mini-vacation—at least in your imagination. Did you enjoy assembling a sequence of songs, music, and artists for your family, work, and daily commute? You can use one piece of music at soft or loud volumes to see how different it sounds during a workout, on a drive, or at dinner. Look for some of your old favorites to use as "oasis music"—a perfect nightcap with which to avoid the dreaded end-of-day meltdown. If you have silent or sullen teenagers at home, use what you've learned about the bonding effects of drumming circles: Pass around some buckets or plastic bins one evening and try communicating through rhythms rather than words. And if you were intrigued by the effects you experienced when toning, singing, or chanting, a nightly session before bedtime could become a wonderful way for you to reconnect with yourself, reintegrate, and shed the cares of the day.

Increasingly, in recent decades, a good night's sleep has become an almost insurmountable challenge for many adults as well as children. If you or someone you know has difficulty sleeping, use what you've learned in these chapters to make the sound environment more relaxing. Mask traffic or other noise with some American Indian flute music, Bob Marley, or Debussy. Wear earplugs to block the sounds of a snoring partner, and if the symptoms are severe, urge him or her to seek help from an ear, nose, and throat doctor or a sleep specialist.

Researchers have found a strong correlation between children's sleep problems and the number of hours spent with video or computer games in the evening hours,[1] so call a moratorium on these overstimulating devices well before bedtime and replace them with soothing audiobooks, music, or nature sounds. If you yourself feel jumpy from too much computer or television time, or you are prevented from sleeping by your own racing thoughts, dim the lights in your bedroom, lie still, breathe deeply and rhythmically, and let your personal mantra or soothing phrase float weightlessly in your mind. Don't forget the power of rhythm to relax and regulate the body. Babies fall asleep more easily when gently rocked. For the rest of us, neuroscientist Seth Horowitz and composer Lance Massey have developed a type of advanced sound-technology device, now under study at Oregon State University, that triggers the same type of motion-induced sleepiness in both children and adults.

Certainly, in the evening, it's useful to recall the words of the composer R. Murray Schafer in his book *The Tuning of the World*: "If we have a hope of improving the acoustic design of the world, it will be realizable only after the recovery of silence as a positive state in our lives. Still the noise of the mind: that is the first task—then everything else will follow in time."[2]

www.HealingAtTheSpeedOfSound.com/Link76

Even pets have been shown to respond positively to lullabies or to soft, soothing sounds. Watch how easily these puppies fall asleep when sung to in low, soft tones.

Your Sound Diet

Now, as you relax in the evening, is a good time not only to sum up what you've learned about what music brings to you, but to think more deeply about what you bring to every piece of music you hear. Listening is a subjective act. The sounds we hear, and the ways they affect us, have as much to do with our own inner qualities and state of being as with the sounds themselves and the context in which they are produced. Our background and life experience, our thousands of memories and emotional associations, our musical knowledge and understanding, and our willingness to set aside preconceptions and listen actively with open ears—all profoundly influence the degree to which we benefit from what we hear.

This, of course, is why parents so often hate the music their teenagers love, and why one partner in a marriage loves country while the other listens only to jazz. It's why some of us live to attend the opera and others can't bear it. It's why customers in restaurants are forever asking the waitstaff to turn the music up . . . or to turn it down. It's also why, throughout this book, I have urged you to create *your own* sound diet based on the general principles I have taught you, rather than insist on off-the-shelf music selections for each situation in your day. By calling up from memory the music that touches you most deeply as a unique individual, you can create soundscapes with the power to truly transform every part of your day and your life.

One of the best ways to come up with these nourishing "sound nuggets" is to look back over our lives and think about what sounds accompanied some of the most emotionally potent times of our lives. Below, I've provided some queries designed to spark your memory. As songs come to mind, write them down. You'll be surprised how many tunes begin to surface once you get started.

- What were your ten favorite songs in high school?
- What is your favorite musical instrument?
- What are the best three concerts you ever attended?
- Of all the films you've seen, which four had the best music?
- Is there a song that always makes you sad?
- What kind of music always relaxes you?
- Which five pop artists do you love most?
- What songs remind you of the last person you dated?
- Which songs most often get stuck in your head?
- What music do you remember from a sports event?
- Who is your favorite guitar hero?
- What kind of music always makes you feel good?
- What one piece of music would you want at your funeral?
- Which of your friends plays a musical instrument? What would you most like to hear him or her play?
- Which artist and which style of music from your past would you most like to hear now?
- What are the five most-played albums in your car?
- What are your three favorite classical pieces?

Now do you have some ideas of what you most want to hear while driving to work, dining with your loved one, or falling asleep at night? We are lucky to live in an era when some terrific musical tools are available to help us expand outward from these bits of autobiographical inspiration to create entire playlists for any situation. For example, if Miles Davis's classic album *Kind of Blue* makes you happy because you first heard it the night you met your husband, go to Amazon.com and wander through the site's "Customers Who Bought This Item Also Bought" list. You'll find Bill Evans's *Portrait in Jazz,* Charles Mingus's *Mingus Ah Um,* and music from a dozen similar players. Click on the more appealing selections, sample the songs, and then follow *those* pages' links to more songs. It's easy to build an entire library of musical resources this way.

For instance, if you like Carole King's vocals, try building what's called a "radio station" around her on Pandora.com and seeing what other singers pop up (Joni Mitchell, Laura Nyro, and Paul Simon, when I tried it).

As one song after another plays, tell the program that you like selections by the artists who conform to the concept of the soundscape you're creating, and give a ruthless thumbs-down to everything else. Quickly you'll find yourself with both familiar and new sounds in your ears.

On Rhapsody and iTunes, the process is much the same. These services have spent millions creating algorithms that can help you work your way through nearly all the music in the world—every instrument, artist, genre, period, and kind to discover exactly the sound, tempo, and timbre you need to give you stimulation, regulation, or inspiration. Take advantage of them to create the mood and degree of aural stimulation you desire any time of the day or night.

It's great to have lots of selections on hand, particularly when many of those musical choices bring back wonderful memories or stimulate you emotionally or intellectually. Our subjective experience of music goes even deeper than our preferences for certain genres or artists. I first began to understand this decades ago, while working as a classical music critic for an English weekly newspaper in Tokyo. One evening, on entering the Bunka Kaikan for an all-Mozart concert with the Tokyo Philharmonic Orchestra, I was surprised to see how many chairs and music stands had been placed on the stage. It was clear to me that the size of certain sections of the orchestra was nearly triple the size of those called for in the original composition, in order to give the performance a fuller, richer, more romantic sound. I disapproved of these modern additions to Mozart's original orchestration.

Sitting next to me, with her grandson, was an elderly Japanese woman dressed in a formal kimono. The young man was studying violin, and had brought his grandmother to the hall to hear his teacher play in the orchestra. The woman sat forward during the Mozart piano concerto that followed in what seemed almost a Buddhist meditation posture. When it was over, she had tears in her eyes and simply said, "The most beautiful moment in my life."

My filtered listening, based on the history of the music, the criticism I had read relating to this piece, and my own personal preferences, actually robbed me of the full moments of beauty that she experienced. I realized that my classical, conservative upbringing in music, my ear training, and my harmony classes had limited my understanding of music in the great scheme of the world. In a sense, I was actually wearing "sunglasses" on my ears. Neither one of us was wrong in the way we interpreted what we heard; we were simply listening from different hemispheres, both neurologically and geographically.

This experience sparked my interest in the subjective aspect of listening—the ways in which our manner of hearing and *registering* sound measurably influences its physical and emotional effects. Our brains do not respond mechanically to music, in uniform and predictable ways across the population. Instead, a melody or musical phrase infiltrates each individual's unique neuronal network, tripping a memory from decades past, sparking a unique physical response, and thereby, within seconds, either broadening our sense of space around us or making us feel irritated or overwhelmed.

Next time you attend a concert, observe for yourself how the same musical performance sparks responses as varied as the number of ears that hear the sounds. Some listeners lean forward in an intense state of alertness and excitement; others sink into their seats, enjoying an expensive nap. The audience member to one side of you may seem to have difficulty sitting still as she listens, while the person on your other side sits perfectly silently, with an expression of profound peace. Music also affects people differently outside the concert hall. While I cannot bear to have any music in the room while I am writing this chapter, hundreds of my students have insisted over the years that it's impossible for them to study without music in the background. (I can only beg them to remember to protect their ears by listening using headphones, not earbuds, or to a stereo at low volume.)

For the past four years, I have given Saturday morning classes for the SuperListening™ Club associated with our local philharmonic orchestra. Before each concert, we explore the ways music affects our emotions and why we like and dislike certain kinds of music—exploring recently, for example, how listening to Frank Zappa, Rachmaninoff, and a tango made us feel.

We have also spent much time discussing the subjective state in which different listeners experience sound, and we've identified twenty attitudes or tendencies with which people typically listen to music. A "tone bather," for example, comes to music with no agenda; he simply leans back and lets the music happen. He often uses music as sonic wallpaper, letting it play in the background as he moves through his day. The "rhythmic listener" responds strongly to the beat of the music, tapping her foot and getting into the groove. As a result, her mood tends to be more quickly and easily affected than the tone bather by music's presence: Upbeat music easily lifts her spirits, but she finds it harder to ignore background music in order to focus on her work. A "musicological listener," on the other hand, comes to the music with knowledge of the composer's life and oeuvre, knows when it was composed and what is unique about its compositional style, and analyzes it as she listens in terms of harmony, melody, and other aspects. Sometimes, as I've pointed out, all of this information can get in the way of fully experiencing the music—but at other times the shades of understanding "color" the music in myriad ways and greatly enhance its effects on our emotions, body, and mind.

Identifying the kind of listener you are is the second step in creating a sound diet that works best for you. Realizing that you are a rhythmic listener, for example, can help you remember to choose music with a toned-down beat for work or relaxation time, so that your body's natural response doesn't interfere. Understanding your tendencies as a tone bather may inform your decision to include periods of silence in your day. Once you understand your habitual listening approach to music, you can experiment as well with other ways to listen, expanding your experience and versatility until you become what I call a SuperListener, able to take advantage of all that sound and music have to offer.

Listen Up

♫ Here are twenty types of listeners, with brief descriptions of the subjective ways in which each is likely to experience the same piece of music. Which type are you? Does your type change depending on the day, your mood, or the circumstances? Would you like to try being one or more of the other types of listeners for an hour or a day?

The Tone Bather	Lets the music wash over and through her. There is no agenda! Often uses music as sonic wallpaper.
The Instrumental Listener	Picks out the clarinet, the piano, or another instrument when a group is playing. Focuses on one tonal color or voice.
The Performer or Audience Watcher	Watches the conductor, the instrumentalists, the singers or solo guitarist, and checks the responses of other audience members. All of the visual cues become part of the music experience for this listener.
The Visual Listener (Eyes Closed)	Closes her eyes and visualizes the music as it plays, thus allowing another level of listening to take place.
The Story Listener	As with *Peter and the Wolf* or a movie soundtrack, he imagines a narrative while listening to the music. His sense of the music's "story" amplifies his emotions and sense of spaciousness and suspense as he listens.
The Rhythmic Listener	The rhythm picks him up. He taps his foot and syncs physically with the beat. Listening, he almost exercises to the music. Music easily speeds him up or slows him down.
The Dancing Listener	She can't be still. She *must* move to the music. Music makes her want to express, interpret, dance!
The Listening Conductor	Moves his arms and body to reflect the music and mold or shape it. Anticipates what will happen next in a symphonic piece.

The Melodic Listener	Follows the flow of the expressive musical line. Often, when the music is over, the tune lingers. She may suddenly start to hum or sing the melody hours later.
The Harmonic Listener	This listener is attuned to the richness, emotion, mood, and texture of the music underneath the melody and framed by its rhythm and speed.
The Form and Structure Listener	A left-brained listener especially attuned to the music's structural framework, whether it's the sonata allegro form or a Brazilian bossa nova.
The Emotional Listener	Feeling, feeling, feeling . . . whether it's love, grief, rage, or ecstasy. Emotional catharsis is key to this listener's enjoyment.
The Sleeping Listener	Relaxes deeply into the music—often to the point of sleep.
The Musicological–Historical Listener	Reads every word of the program notes at a concert, has informed herself on the composers' lives and works, is knowledgeable about the performers' lives and styles. Enjoys music appreciation classes and/or blogs about music.
The Meditative Listener	Acquires a still mood, a sense of deep presence, when listening to music. When the music is slower, more spacious, or even religious, this listener enters a very focused state of awareness not dominated by rhythm, emotion or movement.
The Resistant Listener	A listener who's enduring music she doesn't like, whether it's classical, rock, country, or any other genre. This listener's body and mind clench tightly as she mentally shields her ears from sounds that clash with her sensibilities.

The Cultural and Social Listener	Listens for the indigenous, spiritual, religious, or cultural context of the music. While listening, imagines the social context in which the music was created, and this enhances his enjoyment.
The Inventive Listener	Listening to music on the subway, she imagines her fellow passengers as the singers. Mowing the lawn while wearing noise-reduction headphones, she pictures the lawn as a tropical forest with charming dancers. Listening to Bach, she sees mathematical equations. She listens to jazz as a way of "escaping" a frustrating traffic jam, and cooks to different music genres as a way to inspire experimentation with spices and other ingredients.
The Modified Music Listener	Listens to electronically filtered or modified music, as in a music listening training program. This type of listening exercises the brain for therapeutic, cognitive, or communication purposes.
The SuperListener™	This is the goal of my teaching and training: to help listeners accurately assess their auditory environment and use the tools I provide to improve every moment of life "through the wink of an ear."

It should be clear in reviewing these many types of listening that none of them are unhealthy, nor is there any single correct way to listen. Our hearing ability, age, physical and emotional health, social background, education, mood, and so many other factors determine how we filter the sound of the world around us—making us one type of listener one day and another type the next, and sometimes during a single musical performance merging two different types of listening (emotional and meditative) or moving from one type to another (from the melodic listener to the story listener).

Experiment with this idea yourself by retreating to a quiet spot this evening to listen on headphones to any music of your choice. As you listen, write down the style in which you seem to be listening every five minutes or so. After a while, switch to a different musical genre and see whether your listening style changes with the music. Next, follow the instructions in the next three exercises to intentionally change your listening approach and experience another way of hearing.

SuperListening: the Instrumental Listener

 **www.HealingAtTheSpeedOfSound.com/Link77**

Close your eyes and listen to the famous second movement of Antonin Dvořák's *New World Symphony.* Focus on the beautiful, melodic sound of the English horn playing the American spiritual "Goin' Home." Through the entire recording, try to listen only to that single instrument, filtering out the other sounds. As you listen, your own thoughts, ideas, and emotions will compete for your attention. Don't fight their attempts to distract you, but do your best to remain engaged with the sound you have chosen and to maintain your concentration. As you listen, how does the sound of the instrument make you feel? Does the familiar melody call up personal memories? Do you "see" the music in your mind? Feel your body relax as this beautiful music carries you to another world.[3]

 **www.HealingAtTheSpeedOfSound.com/Link78**

After you have finished listening, switch to this vocal arrangement of the same melody, performed by the boys' choir Libera. Does this version affect you in different ways?

SuperListening: the Meditative Listener

 **www.HealingAtTheSpeedOfSound.com/Link79**
(Free Download No. 6)

Retreat to a quiet room in your home, or listen with the best sound system you have. This time, instead of simply listening, allow me to guide you through a meditation as we focus on a recording of my own composition, "Crystallite," from *Crystal Meditations/Essence.*

SuperListening: the Listening Conductor

 **www.HealingAtTheSpeedOfSound.com/Link80**

Do you remember the video we watched of the three-year-old conducting Beethoven's Fifth Symphony with such joy and abandon? Now it's your turn.

Stand up and move to the music. Express what you hear with your entire body. This is not so much about getting an aerobic workout, as was the conducting exercise presented in chapter one, as it is about *feeling* the music, *anticipating* its movement, and *expressing* it in gesture, movement, posture, and even facial expression. If you feel the need, take your cues at first from Arturo Toscanini's movements as he conducts in this video; google music conductors on your computer and study how different conductors move in different ways; or even return to the video of the three-year-old for a more active, enthusiastic experience! Soon, you will feel confident enough to move away from these examples to create your own unique conducting style. Just as each person's way of listening to music is unique, depending on that person's history and mood, so each conductor must lead the orchestra in her own personal way—and at the same time discover more about who she is as an individual.

Following each experiment, assess how you feel. Did actively listening to music in all of these different ways improve your emotional and/or physical state? Do you feel more balanced? Are your thoughts better organized? Has the constant inner chatter—so often a litany of self-criticism or worry—turned off, even if only briefly? This is the magic of music—learning to digest it in different ways, to filter it, to focus within it, and then to modify the physical and emotional reactions we have to sound. By listening more consciously, actively, imaginatively, and healthfully in this way—that is, by becoming a SuperListener with a variety of listening approaches at your command—you can literally change your perception, improve your ability to focus your attention, and begin the journey toward a new self-awareness. I use these skills in every class and in every concert I attend. As my teacher Nadia Boulanger said, "The only thing boring in life is yourself." There is always something amazing in good music. There is always something nutritious. Don't over-listen; just take the world and turn it into your own amazing, balanced diet.

A World of Sound

So what do you have now? You have resources to help you create soundtracks for every part of your day and your life, as well as an understanding of how music affects your body and mind. What can you do with these? First thing when you get out of bed, put on the music you've chosen to start your day. If you're usually a tone bather, make the deliberate choice to become a conductor on this day. I guarantee that you'll find yourself eager to move, not only to the music, but joyfully out the door.

When you've loaded the groceries in the car and are heading toward home, put on the playlist you made of your favorite songs from your youth, but this time instead of registering the music as an emotional listener, pay attention to the songs from a cultural and social point of view. You'll still feel enjoyment, but your mind will also be stimulated by new intellectual associations and ideas.

If you're usually a resistant listener on the job, thanks to your coworker's poor taste in music, try being more analytical. Seek out the deeper patterns in the music, anticipate where the rhythm is going to go next, laugh when you realize that the musician is quoting a bit of another song's melody in his improvisation or that the composer has just played a clever

Epilogue

Sound and Healing in Times to Come

In the pages of this book, we have learned a great deal about music's power to heal, to enlighten, to educate, invigorate, stimulate, and inspire. Of course, there is so much more to know about music and about the wealth of research that is being conducted daily, even as I complete this chapter. In writing this book, I screened more than ten thousand studies, articles, books, and other sources of fascinating and relevant information. These writings represent the stepping-stones leading us from age-old knowledge to the scientific understanding that can create transformation, growth, and health—yet so much more work is being done. There are dozens of organizations that I have not mentioned, from hospices to health-care institutions, fully dedicated to making the arts a pathway through which science is delivered and administered. Unfortunately, I also could not include the names of all of the wonderful musicians, researchers, teachers, shamans, speech therapists, healers, and entertainers who truly do the hands-on work in this field. I honor all of them and their myriad contributions to the integration of the spiritual, musical, and tonal bases of health and wellness.

Beauty, expression, and harmony are timeless. As we move forward in the twenty-first century, let us hear the mathematical structure of music underlying the chaos and cacophony of our cities. Let us counter the war songs with transcendent chant and song. Let us open our ears to tunes sung in the darkness of the night, and celebrate the radiant sounds of the ancient hymns, chants, and ballads. Whoever we are, in whatever city or nation in the world, each of us has a unique song to sing, a voice with which to express the joy we experience in our lives. With music, we can join with others and, together, bring harmony and health to this world.

www.HealingAtTheSpeedOfSound.com/Link81
(Free Download No. 7)

Allow us to leave you with a parting gift. This Irish blessing, by Buvana Gerlach and Christina Tourin, courtesy of Emerald Harp Productions, will inspire you day and night and fill your heart with the great Spirit of Music.

Appendix One

Learning, Listening, and Experiencing Healing at the Speed of Sound™

May the new vistas of using music that you have learned from this book provide a fresh beginning. By using your computer or electronic reader, you can continue this mission by signing in to our Web site:

www.HealingAtTheSpeedOfSound.com

At this site you will find:

- Free music downloads so you can immediately put sound to work in your life
- An extended library of resources, articles, and clinical studies that will deepen your knowledge of how music and sound can improve your life
- All the Web links for the dozens of icons used to make this book a living, singing, and informative resource. Meet the authors, watch demonstrations, and find links to experts in the world of neurology, music, and sound therapy.

The ear icons ( ) will take e-readers to sound recordings and informative audio podcasts.

The eye icons (👁) will link to videos, lectures, exercise demonstrations, and documentary excerpts.

The lightbulb "idea" icons (💡) will connect you to organizational Web sites, newsletters, and other resources that will help you implement the suggestions we provide.

- Join a community of people interested in making the world a better place through music and sound.
- Read in-depth articles and studies in the field of environmental noise, music therapy, and sound healing.
- Begin your Healing at the Speed of Sound program, which will guide you step-by-step to understand how you can use music—and silence—to become more efficient, productive, relaxed, and healthy.
- Stay up-to-date in the world of sound and listening through online classes and webinars.

Appendix Two

Sound Resources

Organizations

American Music Therapy Association
8455 Colesville Road, Suite 1000
Silver Spring, MD 20910
(301) 589-3300
Fax (301) 589-5175
http://www.musictherapy.org

Foundation for Music-Based Learning
P.O. Box 4274
Greensboro, NC 27404
(336) 272-5303
lheyge@aol.com

The Foundation for Music-Based Learning (founded in 1993) is a non-profit educational and charitable corporation that encourages and supports individuals and organizations in research, development, and outreach pertaining to music- and movement-based learning.

The Healing Music Organization
P.O. Box 3731

Santa Cruz, CA 95063
(831) 588-7498
http://www.healingmusic.org

The Institute for Music & Brain Science
175 Cambridge Street, Suite 340
Boston, MA 02114
http://www.brainmusic.org

Interdisciplinary Society for Quantitative Research in Music and Medicine
Weber State University
3848 Harrison Boulevard
Ogden, UT 84408
(801) 626-7340
qrmm@weber.edu
http://www.weber.edu/ISQRMM

The Interdisciplinary Society for Quantitative Research in Music and Medicine is a society of scholars and researchers pursuing studies on the effects of music on the health of the human mind, body, and soul.

International Association for Music & Medicine
314 Woodward Way NW
Atlanta, GA 30305
http://www.iammonline.com

The International Association for Music & Medicine was founded to promote an integrative perspective to applied music in health care. It disseminates high-level research through the IAMM journal, *Music & Medicine*, published by SAGE.

International Society for Music in Medicine
Paulmannshöher Str. 17
D-58515 Lüdenscheid, Germany
http://musicmedicine.net

A leading international organization involved in research, conferences, and publishing, coordinated by Dr. Ralph Sprintge, executive director.

MENC: The National Association for Music Education
1806 Robert Fulton Drive
Reston, VA 20191
(800) 336-3768
http://www.menc.org

The National Association for Music Education is the largest organization that addresses all aspects of music education, with more than sixty-five thousand members.

Musical Missions of Peace
http://www.musicalmissionsofpeace.org

This nonprofit based in Colorado practices and champions the use of music to create peace throughout the world.

National Association for the Education of Young Children
1313 L Street NW, Suite 500
Washington, D.C. 20005
(202) 232-8777 or (800) 424-2460
http://www.naeyc.org

National Guild for Community Arts Education
520 Eighth Avenue, Suite 302
New York, NY 10018
(212) 268-3337
http://www.nationalguild.org

Society for the Arts in Healthcare
2437 Fifteenth Street NW
Washington, D.C. 20009
(202) 299-9770
http://www.thesah.org

Society for the Arts in Healthcare is an outstanding organization for artists and professionals in health care. Subscribe to the free monthly newsletter.

Sound and Music Alliance
http://www.soundandmusicalliance.org

Sound and Music Alliance, a 501(c)(6) nonprofit membership organization, is an interdisciplinary alliance of therapists, clinicians, educators, musicians, researchers, sound and music practitioners, indigenous teachers, program developers, and product manufacturers.

Sound Healers Association
P.O. Box 2240
Boulder, CO 80306
(303) 443-8181
http://www.soundhealersassociation.org

Sound Healers Association offers New Age resources and activities in sound healing.

PUBLICATIONS

Hearing Health E-News
http://www.drf.org/Hearing+Health+E-Newsletter
This monthly e-newsletter of the Deafness Research Foundation has many interesting articles on music and healing.

Hearing Health Magazine
http://www.drf.org/magazine

Hearing the World
http://www.hear-the-world.com/en/the-magazine.html
The magazine for the culture of hearing.

Tinnitus Today
http://www.ata.org/about-ata/news-pubs/tinnitus-today
The magazine of the American Tinnitus Association.

Other Resources

Advanced Brain Technologies
5748 South Adams Avenue Parkway
Ogden, Utah 84405
(801) 622-5676
info@advancedbrain.com
http://www.advancedbrain.com

Information on professional courses and classes taught by Alex Doman, as well as music, learning enhancement, and music listening therapy programs, including the Listening Program.

The Children's Group, Linus Entertainment
14-3245 Harvester Road
Burlington, ON L7N 3T7
Canada
(905) 831-1995 ext. 22
lhunter@childrensgroup.com
http://www.childrensgroup.com

Recording, research, and other valuable links on the benefits of classical music.

Hospital Audiences Inc.
548 Broadway, Third Floor
New York, NY 10012
(212) 575-7676
http://www.hainyc.org

Offers hope and inspiration through music and the arts for the culturally underserved.

Institute for Music and Neurologic Function
Beth Abraham Hospital
612 Allerton Avenue
Bronx, NY 10467

(718) 519-5840
http://www.bethabe.org/news/readmore/events

Offers a wide range of therapies, research, and education under the guidance of Concetta M. Tomaino, ACMT-BC, music therapy director, and Oliver Sacks, M.D., founding member.

Kindermusik International
203 South Church Street
Greensboro, NC 27401
(336) 273-3363
(800) 628-5687
info@kindermusik.com
http://www.kindermusik.com

Information on music and families, parent-teacher training, and Music Together class locations nationwide.

The Listening Centre
599 Markham Street
Toronto, ON M6G 2L7
Canada
http://www.listeningcentre.com

The oldest North American center and principal Canadian resource for the Tomatis Method.

The Mozart Effect® Resource Center
P.O. Box 800
Boulder, CO 80306-0800
(800) 721-2177
http://www.mozarteffect.com

Lectures, workshops, research, and additional materials on music, health, and education from Don Campbell.

Music for People
(877) 44-MUSIC (877-446-8742)
http://www.musicforpeople.org

Promotes music making and improvisational performance, led by director David Darling.

Music Together LLC
66 Witherspoon Street
Princeton, NJ 08542
(800) 728-2692
http://www.musictogether.com

Musikgarten
507 Arlington Street
Greensboro, NC 27406
(800) 216-6864
http://www.musikgarten.org

Nordoff-Robbins Center for Music Therapy
82 Washington Square East, Fourth Floor
New York, NY 10003
(212) 998-5151
http://www.steinhardt.ngu.edu/centers/norduffrobbins

Offers outpatient treatment programs for children, adolescents, and young adults with various disabilities.

Paracelsus Medical University
Research Program MusicMedicine
Vera Brandes, director
Strubergasse 21
5020 Salzburg
Austria
+43 664 255 01 02
http://www.music-medicine.com

Remo Drum Circles and Drumming Resources
Remo Inc.
28101 Industry Drive
Valencia, CA 91355

(661) 294-5600
http://www.remo.com

Suzuki Association of the Americas Inc.
P.O. Box 17310
Boulder, CO 80308
(888) 378-9854
info@suzukiassociation.org
http://www.suzukiassociation.org

American headquarters for the Suzuki Method and training.

UpBeat Drum Circles
25220 Steinbeck Ave., Number H
Stevenson Ranch, CA 91381
(310) 770-3398
http://www.ubdrumcircles.com

Village Music Circles
719 Swift Street, Suite 65
Santa Cruz, CA 95060
(831) 458-1946
http://www.drumcircle.com

Notes

Chapter One: Awake and Energize

1. Cell Press (Neuron), "News, 2007 Press Releases: Music Hath Charms to Probe the Brain's Auditory Circuitry," Stanford Cognitive and Systems Neuroscience Laboratory, http://stanford.edu/group/scsnl/cgi-bin/drupal_scsnl/content/news.
2. V. Penhume, R. Zatorre, and W. Feindel, "The Role of the Auditory Cortex in Retention of Rhythmic Patterns as Studied in Patients with Temporal Lobe Removals Including Heschl's Gyrus," *Neuropsychologia* 37, no. 3 (1999): 315–31.
3. G. Schlaug, K. Schulze, and J. Mandell, "Congenital Amusia: An Auditory-Motor Feedback Disorder?" *Restorative Neurology and Neuroscience* 25, no. 3–4 (2007): 323–34.
4. "Definitions of Human Brain Components," Disabled World, http://www.disabled-world.com/artman/publish/brain-definitions.shtml.
5. "Music and the Brain: Institute Scientists Show How We Process Complex Sounds," *Brain Matters, the Publication of the Neurosciences Institute* 2, no. 1 (2001).
6. Sarah Rodman, "Can Science Explain Why ABBA Is So Catchy?" *Boston Globe*, July 13, 2008.
7. Sherill Tippins, *February House: The Story of W. H. Auden, Carson*

McCullers, *Jane and Paul Bowles, Benjamin Britten, and Gypsy Rose Lee, Under One Roof in Wartime America* (Boston: Houghton Mifflin, 2005), 31.

8. M. Suda, K. Morimoto, A. Obata, H. Koizumi, and A. Maki, "Cortical Responses to Mozart's Sonata Enhance Spatial-Reasoning Ability," *Neurological Research* 30, no. 9 (2008): 885–88.
9. Emily Singer, "Molecular Basis for Mozart Effect Revealed," *New Scientist*, April 23, 2004, http://www.newscientist.com/article/dn4918-molecular-basis-for-mozart-effect-revealed.html.
10. Gretchen Reynolds, "Phys Ed: Does Music Make You Exercise Harder?" *New York Times*, August 25, 2010.
11. Ibid.
12. Ibid.
13. Steven Kurutz, "They're Playing My Song. Time to Work Out." *New York Times*, January 10, 2008.
14. Kelsey McQueary, "What Music Pumps You Up for a Workout?" *Arkansas Traveler*, April 1, 2009.
15. M. Z. Goodman, "A Workout Space for Hard-Core Pedaling," *New York Times*, December 16, 2010.
16. Reynolds, "Phys Ed."
17. Ibid.
18. Brunel University, "Jog to the Beat: Music Increases Exercise Endurance by 15%," ScienceDaily, http://www.sciencedaily.com/releases/2008/10/081001093753.htm.
19. Larry Granillo, "Trevor Hoffman & Hell's Bells," Wezen Ball, http://www.wezen-ball.com/2010-articles/may/trevor-hoffman-a-hells-bells.html.
20. *San Diego Union-Tribune*, quoted in Granillo, "Trevor Hoffman & Hell's Bells."
21. Ibid.
22. Kurutz, "They're Playing My Song."
23. Len Kravitz, "The Effects of Music on Exercise?" University of New Mexico, http://www.unm.edu/~lkravitz/Article%20folder/musicexercise.html.
24. K. D. Kryter, quoted in the American Speech-Language-Hearing Association's "Noise Is Difficult to Define—Part 1," Hearing Loss Web, http://www.hearinglossweb.com/Medical/Causes/nihl/diff.htm.
25. "Noise and Hearing Loss," American Speech-Language-Hearing Association, http://www.asha.org/public/hearing/disorders/noise.htm.

26. George Prochnik, *In Pursuit of Silence: Listening for Meaning in a World of Noise* (New York: Doubleday, 2010), 18.
27. "New Hearing Protection Campaign Targets Tweens and Their Parents," National Institute on Deafness and Other Communication Disorders, http://www.nidcd.nih.gov/health/inside/spr09/pg1.html.
28. Adapted from "Decibel Levels of Many Common Sounds," Soundbytes, http://www.soundbytes.com/page/SB/CTGY/decibel-levels.
29. Randy Shore, "Pet Sounds: Soothing Techno Hits for Dogs Selling Like Milk-Bones," *Vancouver Sun*, January 7, 2009, http://www.vancouversun .com/Sounds+Soothing+techno+hits+dogs+selling+like+Milkbones/ 1152355/story.html.
30. "International Noise Awareness Day," Center for Hearing and Communication, http://www.chchearing.org/noise-center-home/international-noise -awareness-day.
31. Simon Jenkins, "It Can Conjure Up a Mood for Sex, and Might Just Curb the Need for Drugs," *Guardian* (UK), October 5, 2007.

Chapter Two: Out in the World

1. Thomas Carlyle to Geraldine E. Jewsbury, June 15, 1840, quoted in The Carlyle Letters Online: A Victorian Cultural Reference, vol. 12, 163–66, http://carlyleletters.dukejournals.org/cgi/content/full/12/1/ lt-18400615-TC-GEJ-01?maxtoshow=&hits=10&RESULTFORMAT= &fulltext=%22in+a+thousand+senses%22&searchid=1&FIRSTINDEX=0& resourcetype=HWCIT.
2. *London Observer*, "Carlyle's Soundproof Room," *New York Times*, February 24, 1886.
3. John M. Picker, "The Soundproof Study: Victorian Professionals, Work Space, and Urban Noise," LIT@MIT, http://lit.mit.edu/publications/jPicker -3Soundproof.pdf.
4. *The Times* (London), May 2, 1856.
5. Picker, "The Soundproof Study."
6. Ibid.
7. *London Observer*, "Carlye's Soundproof Room."
8. Jane Welsh to Thomas Carlyle, July 27, 1852, quoted in The Carlyle Letters Online: A Victorian Cultural Refence, vol. 27, 189–90, http://carlyleletters

.dukejournals.org/cgi/content/full/27/1/lt-18520727-JWC-JAC-01?maxtoshow=&hits=10&RESULTFORMAT=&fulltext=%22it+is+amazing+how+little+I+care%22&searchid=1&FIRSTINDEX=0&resourcetype=HWCIT.

9. American Speech-Language-Hearing Association, "Noise and Hearing Loss."
10. "Cell Phone Use Causes High Frequency Hearing Loss," Medical News Today, http://www.medicalnewstoday.com/articles/83116.php.
11. A. Veverka, "Loud Earbuds Sound like Trouble Ahead," *Charlotte Observer*, May 18, 2009.
12. American Speech-Language-Hearing Association, "Noise and Hearing Loss."
13. Ibid.
14. Pete Townshend, quoted in "Pete Townshend Quotes," BrainyQuote, http://www.brainyquote.com/quotes/authors/p/pete_townshend.html.
15. J. Ringen, "Music Making Fans Deaf?" *Rolling Stone*, November 18, 2005.
16. "Bad News for Loud Music," StarTribune.com (Minneapolis–St. Paul), September 7, 2007, http://www.startribune.com/world/11619851.html.
17. Gary White, "Hazards of Striking Up the Band: Daily Exposure to Thunderous Sounds Can Damage Music Directors' Hearing," *The Ledger* (Lakeland, Fla.), October 16, 2007, http://www.theledger.com/article/20071016/NEWS/710160347.
18. Edeltraut Emmerich, Lars Rudel, and Frank Richter, "Is the Audiologic Status of Professional Musicians a Reflection of the Noise Exposure in Classical Orchestral Music?" *European Archives of Oto-Rhino-Laryngology* 265, no. 7 (2008): 753–58, http://cat.inist.fr/?aModele=afficheN&cpsidt=20426580.
19. Gordon Marc le Roux, "'Whistle While You Work': A Historical Account of Some Associations Among Music, Work, and Health," *American Journal of Public Health* 95, no. 7 (2005), http://www.ajph.org/cgi/reprint/95/7/1106.pdf.
20. "Mice and Music Experiment Mozart: Hard Rock Makes Killer Mice, Teen Finds," Educational CyberPlayGround Inc., http://www.edu-cyberpg.com/Music/Mice_and_Music_Experiment_Mo.html.
21. S. Whitall, "Sharing Cool Music and Creative Ideas Is What Keeps Ford Designers Fueled," *Detroit News*, June 6, 2009, http://www.detnews.com/article/20090606/ENT04/906060354/Sharing-cool-music-and-creative-ideas-is-what-keeps-Ford-designers-fueled?imw=Y.

22. Barbara Rose, "Employees Plug into Music and a Different Workplace Dynamic," *Los Angeles Times*, March 12, 2006.
23. Anneli Beronius Haake, "Music Listening Practices in Workplace Settings in the UK: An Exploratory Survey of Office-Based Settings," *Proceedings of the 9th International Conference on Music Perception & Cognition* (2006), http://www.shef.ac.uk/content/1/c6/05/52/50/ICMPC9%20ABH%20.doc.
24. Rose, "Employees Plug into Music and a Different Workplace Dynamic."
25. Ibid.
26. Haake, "Music Listening Practices in Workplace Settings in the UK."
27. Ibid.
28. Teresa Lesiuk, "The Effect of Music Listening on Work Performance," *Psychology of Music* 33, no. 2 (2005): 173–91.
29. Rose, "Employees Plug into Music and a Different Workplace Dynamic."
30. Haake, "Music Listening Practices in Workplace Settings in the UK."
31. Laura Marcus, "Desk Jockeys," *Guardian* (UK), July 7, 2008, http://www.guardian.co.uk/money/2008/jul/07/workandcareers.
32. Haake, "Music Listening Practices in Workplace Settings in the UK."
33. Ibid.
34. M. K. Culp, "Music in the Workplace Isn't Always in Tune," *The Dallas Morning News*, March 17, 2008.
35. A. North, D. Hargreaves, and J. McKendrick, "The Influence of In-Store Music on Wine Selection," *Journal of Applied Psychology* 84, no. 2 (1999): 271–76.
36. "Certain Music Makes Us Buy Specific Brands," *Parade*, Janurary 4, 2009.
37. Judy Foreman, "Environmental Cues Affect How Much You Eat," *Boston Globe*, August 18, 2008, http://www.boston.com/news/health/articles/2008/08/18/environmental_cues_affect_how_much_you_eat/.
38. Vincent P. Magnini and Emily E. Parker, "The Psychological Effects of Music: Implications for Hotel Firms," *Journal of Vacation Marketing* 15, no. 1 (2009), http://jvm.sagepub.com/cgi/content/abstract/15/1/53.
39. Alan Mozes, "Loud Music in Bars Hastens Drinking," HealthDay, http://www.hon.ch/News/HSN/617602.html.
40. N. Hurst, "Delta: Right Tunes Make Boarding Faster," *Detroit News*, August 18, 2008, http://www.detnews.com.
41. Mimi Rawlinson, quoted in Delta Blog: "Full Throttle Fun . . . the Music of Delta Pride," Delta Air Lines, http://blog.delta.com/category/tunes-onboard/.

42. Jenkins, "It Can Conjure Up a Mood for Sex."
43. Elaine Sciolino, "Allegro, Andante, Adagio and Corporate Harmony; A Conductor Draws Management Metaphors from Musical Teamwork," *New York Times*, July 26, 2001.
44. Ibid.
45. Russ Riendeau, "Use the Power of Music to Create Positive Change," Russ Riendeau.com, http://www.russriendeau.com/topics.htm; D. Anfuso, "Try Music to Jump-Start Creativity in the Workplace," *Daily Breeze* (Los Angeles), http://www.dailybreeze.com.
46. Alia Blackwood, "A Song in Her Heart," *Spry Living*, April 23, 2002, http://www.spryliving.com/article/42302.html.
47. Ibid.
48. Nalani Ambady, D. LaPlante, T. Nguyen, R. Rosenthal, N. Chaumeton, and W. Levinson, "Surgeon's Tone of Voice: A Clue to Malpractice History," *Surgery* 132 (July 2002): 5–9.

Chapter Three: Music of Life

1. The Royal Institution, "The Royal Institution Presents New Research at First Public Conference on 'The Musical Brain'; London Gathering Marks Turning Point in Music-Brain Science," *PR Newswire*, July 12, 2002.
2. Fred J. Schwartz, "Perinatal Stress Reduction, Music and Medical Cost Savings," Transitions Music, http://transitionsmusic.com/Spintge%20article.htm.
3. Adam Eshleman, "Probing Question: Can Babies Learn In Utero?" Penn State Live, http://live.psu.edu/story/37888/nw1.
4. Ibid.
5. Brandon Keim, "Baby Got Beat: Music May Be Inborn," *Wired*, January 26, 2009, http://www.wired.com/wiredscience/2009/01/babybeats/.
6. Al Letson, "Father Figures," The Moth, http://castroller.com/search/?cx=006301784352006871957%3A4dq3tss8al4&cof=FORID%3A10&ie=UTF-8&t=e&q=%22al+letson%22&sa=Search#1311.
7. Norman M. Weinberger, "Lessons of the Music Womb," Musica, http://www.musica.uci.edu/mrn/V6I1W99.html#womb.
8. J. A. Sloboda, quoted in *The Music Instinct: Science & Song* (Roxbury, CT: Mannes Productions Inc., 2009), film.

9. Weinberger, "Lessons of the Music Womb."
10. L. R. Leader, P. Baillie, B. Martin, and E. Vermeulen, "The Assessment and Significance of Habituation to a Repeated Stimulus by the Human Fetus," *Early Human Development* 7, no. 3 (1982): 211–19.
11. D. Spelt, "The Conditioning of the Human Fetus In Utero," *Journal of Experimental Psychology* 38, no. 3 (1948): 338–46.
12. ICT Results, "Babies Learn Music While Sleeping," ScienceDaily, http://www.sciencedaily.com/releases/2009/02/090226082517.htm.
13. Nancy K. Dess, "Music on the Mind," *Psychology Today*, September/October 2000.
14. "Soothing Music Reduces Stress, Anxiety and Depression during Pregnancy Says Study," Medical News Today, http://www.medicalnewstoday.com/articles/124336.php.
15. Giselle E. Whitwell, "Benefits," Center for Prenatal and Perinatal Music, http://www.prenatalmusic.com/pages/benefits.php.
16. Ibid.
17. Tate Gunnerson, "Newborn Babies Feel the Rhythm," ProHealth Care, http://www.prohealthcare.org/wellness/health-news/children/newborn-babies-feel-the-rhythm.aspx.
18. William J. Cromie, "Music on the Brain: Researchers Explore the Biology of Music," *Harvard University Gazette*, March 22, 2001.
19. Ibid.
20. Dess, "Music on the Mind."
21. Ibid.
22. Ibid.
23. "Developing Language for Life: News About Music and Child Development," National Literacy Trust, http://www.nationalliteracytrust.org.uk.
24. Liza Gross, "When Just One Sense Is Available, Multisensory Experience Fills In the Blanks," PLoS Biology, http://www.plosbiology.org/article/info%3Adoi%2F10.1371%2Fjournal.pbio.0040361.
25. Pierre Sollier, *Listening for Wellness: An Introduction to the Tomatis Method* (Walnut Creek, CA: The Mozart Center Press, 2005), 102–5.
26. Nobuo Masataka, "The Origins of Language and the Evolution of Music: A Comparative Perspective," *Physics of Life Reviews* 6, no. 1 (2009), 11–22.
27. Ibid.
28. Kathleen McGowan, "Songs of Experience: Overview of 'Neurosciences

and Music III,'" New York Academy of Sciences, http://www.nyas.org/Publications/EBriefings/Detail.aspx?cid=b87b940d-9e01-4502-aa56-27d15acc8679#.

29. Dess, "Music on the Mind."
30. Tim Radford, "Music Improves Brain Power—in Some Performers," *Guardian* (UK), September 12, 2003, http://www.guardian.co.uk/uk/2003/sep/12/health.research.
31. Ibid.
32. Lorna Duckworth, "Musicians Found to Have 'More Sensitive Brains,'" *The Independent,* June 17, 2002, http://www.independent.co.uk/news/science/musicians-found-to-have-more-sensitive-brains-645552.html.
33. Eric Nagourney, "Learning: In Tiny Part of the Brain, a Key to Foreign Tongues," *New York Times,* August 7, 2007, http://www.nytimes.com/2007/08/07/health/07lear.html.
34. Perri Klass, "Understanding 'Ba Ba Ba' As a Key to Development," *New York Times,* October 11, 2010.
35. Ibid.
36. Ibid.
37. Peter Banki, "The Poetry of Listening," Sydney, Australia, October 30, 2010, workshop presentation.
38. National Literacy Trust, "Developing Language for Life."
39. E. J. Mundell, "Sorry, Kids, Piano Lessons Make You Smarter," Forbes.com, http://www.forbes.com/2004/07/15/cx_0715health.html; "Music Expands the Mind," *Gazette* (Montreal), August 9, 2008.
40. Music Educators National Confence and the College Board, "Profile of SAT and Achievement Test Takers" (1998, 1996).
41. American Music Conference 2007, "Research Briefs: Did You Know?" NAMM Foundation, http://www.nammfoundation.org/.

Chapter Four: Rhythms of the Mind

1. University of Western Sydney, "Rockabye Baby: Research Shows Gentle Singing Soothes Sick Infants," ScienceDaily, http://www.sciencedaily.com/releases/2006/02/060213102134.htm.
2. University of Alberta Faculty of Medicine and Dentistry, "Music May Improve Feeding, Reduce Pain in Premature Babies," Children's

Neurobiological Solutions, http://www.cnsfoundation.org/site/News2?page=NewsArti cle&id=8591&security=1&news_iv_ctrl=-1.

3. Rebecca Grooms Johnson, "Perspectives in Pedagogy, Teaching the Young Child: An Interview with Lorna Heyge," *Keyboard Companion*, Autumn 2006, http://musikgarten.org.
4. Donna Brink Fox, "Music and the Baby's Brain: Early Experiences," *Music Educators Journal* 87 no. 2 (2000): 23–27, 50.
5. Carlos Rodriguez, "Children, Literature, and Music: Integrating Children's Literature in the Elementary General Music Classroom," *Iowa Music Educator*, April 1999.
6. Johnson, "Perspectives in Pedagogy."
7. Fox, "Music and the Baby's Brain."
8. Rosanna Wong Yick-ming, "Music in Education is Education for Life," *International Journal of Music Education* 23, no. 2 (2005): 107–9.
9. "With Additional Kodály Music Instruction, Math and Reading Scores Increase at Minneapolis Public Schools," *Gopher Music Notes*, Winter 1999.
10. Meg de Mougin, Marilyn Davidson, Cak Marshall, Wes McCune, and Alice Olsen, "What Constitutes Good Repertoire in Orff Schulwerk Instruction?" *Point-Counterpoint* 28, no. 3 (1996): 30.
11. Arthur Harvey, "Supporting Music Education," *Leka Nu Hou* 99, no. 2 (1999): 13–16.
12. Marie Forgeard, Ellen Winner, Andrea Norton, and Gottfried Schlaug, "Practicing a Musical Instrument in Childhood Is Associated with Enhanced Verbal Ability and Nonverbal Reasoning," *PLoS ONE* 3, no. 10 (2008): e3566.
13. Sharon Begley, "Music on the Mind," *Newsweek*, July 24, 2000.
14. Harvey, "Supporting Music Education."
15. Russ Cooper, "Music to Our Ears . . . and Our Minds," *Concordia Journal* 4, no. 5 (2008), http://cjournal.concordia.ca/archives/20081106/music_to_our_ears_and_our_minds.php.
16. G. Schlaug, "The Brain of Musicians. A Model for Functional and Structural Adaptation," *Annals of the New York Academy of Sciences* 930 (2001): 281–99.
17. Jeanne Wrasman Reynolds, "Music Education and Student Self-Concept: A Review of Literature," e-mail message to author, March 28, 2000.
18. Valerie Salvestrini, "Americans Overwhelmingly Want Music Education in

Schools," American Music Conference, April 21, 2003, http://www.amc-music.com/news/pressreleases/gallup2003.htm.

19. "Research: Music Training 'Tunes' the Auditory System," Newswise, http://www.newswise.com/articles/research-music-training-tunes-the-auditory-system?ret=/articles/list&category=latest&page=1&search[billing_institution_id]=91&search[sort]=date+desc&search[has_multimedia]=&search[status]=3.
20. Debby Mitchell, "The Relationship Between Rhythmic Competency and Academic Performance in First Grade Children," Ph.D. diss., University of Central Florida, 1994.
21. Gordon Shaw and Mathew Peterson, "Enhanced Learning of Proportional Math Through Music Training and Spatial-Temporal Training," *Neurological Research* 21, no. 2 (1999): 139–52.
22. Karen Lurie, "Arts Smarts," ScienCentral, http://www.sciencentral.com/articles/view.php3?article_id=218392326.
23. Paul Recer, "Researchers Monitoring Brain Activity Find Biological Evidence for Soothing Effect of Music," Associated Press, September 24, 2001, http://www.boston.com/news/daily/24/music.htm.
24. Eric Jensen, quoted in Dee Dickinson, "Music and the Mind," *New Horizons for Learning* (1993).
25. Robert Roy Britt, "Music Tickles Strong Memories," LiveScience, http://www.livescience.com/health/050526_music_memory.html.
26. Norman Weinberger, "The Neurobiology of Musical Learning and Memory," Musica, http://www.musica.uci.edu/mrn/V4I2F97.html#neurobiology.
27. Jayne M. Standley, "Does Music Instruction Help Children Learn to Read? Evidence of a Meta-Analysis," *Applications of Research in Music Education* 27, no. 1 (2008): 17–32.
28. Cromie, "Music on the Brain."
29. Northwestern University, "Music Training Linked to Enhanced Verbal Skills," ScienceDaily, http://www.sciencedaily.com/releases/2007/09/070926123908.htm.
30. Katie Rogers, "Elkhart Schools' Drum 2 Change Impacts Academic Performance, Develops Life Skills," Etruth, http://www.etruth.com/Know/News/Story.aspx?ID=438947.
31. Alex Doman, "The Brain Understanding Itself: ADHD or Auditory Pro-

cessing Disorder in Disguise?" http://alexdoman.com/2009/05/29/adhd-or-apd-in-disguise/.

32. Tara Parker-Pope, "Little-Known Disorder Can Take a Toll on Learning," *New York Times*, April 26, 2010.
33. Doman, "The Brain Understanding Itself."
34. Parker-Pope, "Little-Known Disorder Can Take a Toll on Learning."
35. Ibid.
36. Teri James Bellis, "Understanding Auditory Processing Disorders in Children," American Speech-Language-Hearing Association, http://www.asha.org/public/hearing/disorders/understand-apd-child.htm (accessed August 19, 2009).
37. Ibid.
38. Parker-Pope, "Little-Known Disorder Can Take a Toll on Learning."
39. Roland Haas and Vera Brandes, eds., *Music That Works: Contributions of Biology, Neurophysiology, Psychology, Sociology, Medicine and Musicology* (Vienna/New York: Springer, 2009).
40. Jane Richards, "Now Listen: Music a Medicine for Malady," *Sydney Morning Herald*, September 18, 2008, http://www.smh.com.au/news/entertainment/music/music-proven-to-soothe-body-and-mind/2008/09/17/1221330930106.html.
41. T. Wigram and C. Gold, "Music Therapy in the Assessment and Treatment of ASD," *Childcare, Health and Development*, 2005.
42. M. Boso, E. Emanuele, V. Minazzi, M. Abbamonte, and P. Politi, "Effect of Long-Term Interactive Music Therapy on Behavior Profile and Musical Skills in Young Adults with Severe Autism," *Journal of Alternative Complementary Medicine* 13, no. 7 (2007), http://www.ncbi.nlm.nih.gov/pubmed/17931062.
43. "DAD Launches Tour with Mobile Drum Therapy Center," Drummerszone.com, http://www.drummerszone.com/news/newsItem.php?n01ID=5148&type=C.
44. "Welcome to the Strong Institute," Strong Institute, http://stronginstitute.com/home.
45. "Beat the Odds: Social and Emotional Skill Building Delivered in a Framework of Drumming," UCLArts and Healing, http://uclartsandhealing.net/Images/Docs/Beat%20the%20Odds%20-%20An%20Evidence-Based%20Program.pdf.

46. Ibid.
47. Po Bronson and Ashley Merryman, "The Creativity Crisis," *Newsweek*, July 10, 2010.
48. Ibid.
49. Chris Roberts, "Educators Charge Arts Lag Under No Child Left Behind," Minnesota Public Radio, http://minnesota.publicradio.org/display/web/2007/03/13/nclbandarts/.
50. Bronson and Merryman, "The Creativity Crisis."
51. The College Board, "Profiles of SAT and Achievement Test Takers" (1998), quoted in "Give Your Children the Musical Advantage," AMC Music, http://www.amc-music.com.
52. "Texas Commission on Drug and Alcohol Abuse," *Houston Chronicle*, January 11, 1998.
53. "Arts Programs for At-Risk Youth: How U.S. Communities are Using the Arts to Rescue Their Youth and Deter Crime," Americans for the Arts, http://www.artsusa.org/NAPD/modules/resourceManager/publicsearch.aspx?id=9209.
54. Harvey, "Supporting Music Education."
55. Ibid.
56. *Journal of the American Medical Association* (September 1998), quoted in Harvey, "Supporting Music Education."
57. Bronson and Merryman, "The Creativity Crisis."
58. Ibid.
59. Ibid.
60. Greg Toppo, "Brain Scans Tune In to Personal Nature of Improvising Music," *USA Today*, March 4, 2008, http://www.usatoday.com/news/health/2008-03-04-musician-brain-scans_N.htm.
61. Ibid.
62. Dr. Paul Brewer (director of instrumental music, Aquinas College), author interview, October 24, 2010.
63. Charles B. Fowler, "The Shameful Neglect of Creativity," *Musical America*, September 1985.
64. Village Harmony of Vermont provides particularly rewarding group singing experiences for teenagers, with summer training camps and performance tours in the U.S. and in other countries around the world. For more information, see http://www.northernharmony.pair.com/.

65. Carma Haley Shoemaker, "The Sound of Music: The Influence of Music Education," PreschoolersToday.com, http://www.preschoolerstoday.com/articles/back-to-preschool-headquarters/the-sound-of-music-1073/3/.
66. Danielle Cronin, "Study Links Music to Teens' Mental States," *Canberra Times*, August 5, 2008, http://www.canberratimes.com.au/news/local/news/general/study-links-music-to-teens-mental-states/1235328.aspx.
67. Ibid.
68. Ibid.
69. Julie Deardorff, "Justin Roberts: 'Be Careful with Earbuds,'" *Chicago Tribune*, November 18, 2008, http://featuresblogs.chicagotribune.com/features_julieshealthclub/2008/11/justin-roberts.html.
70. American Academy of Audiology, "36 Million Americans Affected by Hearing Loss," Medical News Today, http://www.medicalnewstoday.com/articles/123248.php.
71. Ellie Harvey, "Alarm Sounds on Hearing Damage Among the Young," *Sydney Morning Herald*, June 10, 2008, http://www.smh.com.au/news/national/alarm-sounds-on-hearing-damage-among-the-young/2008/06/09/1212863545955.html.
72. Virginia Heffernan, "Against Headphones," *New York Times*, January 7, 2011.
73. Deardorff, "Justin Roberts: 'Be Careful with Earbuds.'"
74. American Academy of Otolaryngology, "Cell Phone Use Causes High Frequency Hearing Loss," Medical News Today, http://www.medicalnewstoday.com/articles/83116.php.
75. Harvey, "Alarm Sounds on Hearing Damage Among the Young."
76. Vishakha W. Rawool and Lynda A. Colligon-Wayne, "Auditory Lifestyles and Beliefs Related to Hearing Loss Among College Students in the USA," *Noise & Health* 10, no. 38 (2008), http://www.noiseandhealth.org/article.asp?issn=1463-1741;year=2008;volume=10;issue=38;spage=1;epage=10;aulast=Rawool;type=0.
77. Jon Hood, "Court Has Heard Enough in iPod Earbud Suit," ConsumerAffairs.com, http://www.consumeraffairs.com/news04/2010/01/ipod_earbud_suit.html.
78. Heffernan, "Against Headphones."
79. Ibid.
80. Tony Mickela, "Does Music Have an Impact on Students' Development?"

Children's Music Workshop, http://www.childrensmusicworkshop.com/advocacy/studentdevelopment.html.

81. Suda et al., "Cortical Responses to Mozart's Sonata Enhance Spatial-Reasoning Ability."
82. Peter Lavelle, "Depressed? Mr. Music Please!" ABC Health and Wellbeing, http://www.abc.net.au/health/thepulse/stories/2008/11/20/2416380.htm.
83. Ibid.
84. Patrice Madura Ward-Steinman, "The Development of an After-School Music Program for At-Risk Children: Student Musical Preferences and Pre-Service Teacher Reflections," *International Journal of Music Education* 24, no. 1 (2006): 85–96.

Chapter Five: The Harmony of the Body

1. Susan E. Mazer, "Music, Noise, and the Environment of Care: History, Theory, and Practice," *Music and Medicine* 2, no. 3 (2010), http://mmd.sagepub.com/content/2/3/182.
2. Ibid.
3. Joscelyn Godwin, *Music, Mysticism, and Magic: A Sourcebook* (UK: Arkana Paperbacks, 1987), 261, 263.
4. Maureen F. Cunningham, Bonnie Monson, and Marilyn Bookbinder, "Introducing a Music Program in the Perioperative Area," *AORN Journal* 66, no. 4 (1997): 674–82.
5. Amanda Gardner, "Joyful Music in Tune with Heart Health," HealthScout, http://www.healthscout.com/news/1/621243/main.html.
6. *Music Perception* (Fall 2000), quoted in Susan Brink, "Sing Out, Sister," *Los Angeles Times*, April 23, 2007, http://articles.latimes.com/print/2007/apr/23/health/he-sing23.
7. Marla Jo Fisher, "Joy of Singing in a Choir Could Be Preventive Medicine," *Boston Globe*, March 31, 2001.
8. Val Willingham, "The Power of Music: It's a Real Heart Opener," CNN.com, http://edition.cnn.com/2009/HEALTH/05/11/music.heart/index.html.
9. Dr. Alexander Mauskop, "Music Relieves Migraine Headaches and Pain," Headache News Blog, http://www.nyheadache.com/blog/?p=59.
10. Joanne V. Loewy, ed., *Music Therapy and Pediatric Pain* (New York: Satchnote Press, 1997).
11. Linda L. Chlan, William C. Engeland, Anita Anthony, and Jill Guttormson,

"Influence of Music on the Stress Response in Patients Receiving Mechanical Ventilatory Support: A Pilot Study," *American Journal of Critical Care* 16, no. 2 (2007): 141–45.

12. R. W. Lieu, P. Mehta, S. Fortuna, D. G. Armstrong, D. R. Cooperman, G. H. Thompson, and A. Gilmore, "A Randomized Prospective Study of Music Therapy for Reducing Anxiety During Cast Room Procedures," *Journal of Pediatric Orthopedics* 27, no. 7 (2007): 831–33.
13. Darcy DeLoach Walworth, "Procedural-Support Music Therapy in the Healthcare Setting: A Cost-Effectiveness Analysis," *Journal of Pediatric Nursing* 20, no. 4 (2005): 276–84.
14. Mauskop, "Music Relieves Migraine Headaches and Pain."
15. Anahad O'Connor, "The Claim: Humming Can Ease Sinus Problems," *New York Times*, December 20, 2010.
16. David Williams, "Get Your Sinuses Humming," *Alternatives* 9, no. 18 (2002), http://www.drdavidwilliams.com/DefaultBlank.aspx?ContentID=11682.
17. Eddie Weitzberg and Jon O. N. Lundberg, "Humming Greatly Increases Nasal Nitric Oxide," *American Journal of Respiratory and Critical Care Medicine* 166, no. 2 (2002): 144–45; M. Maniscalco, E. Weitzberg, J. Sundberg, M. Sofia, and J. O. Lundberg, "Assessment of Nasal and Sinus Nitric Oxide Output Using Single-Breath Humming Exhalations," *European Respiratory Journal* 22, no. 2 (2003): 323–29.
18. University of Groningen, "Tinnitus: Psychological Treatment and Neurostimulation Offer Hope," ScienceDaily, http://www.sciencedaily.com/releases/2008/11/081120175851.htm.
19. Nick Thomas, "Easing the Torment of Tinnitus," *Seattle Times*, June 25, 2007, http://seattletimes.nwsource.com/html/living/2003760030_tinnitus25.html.
20. Ibid.
21. University of Groningen, "Tinnitus: Psychological Treatment and Neurostimulation Offer Hope."
22. "Helping You Help Patients Take Back Control over Tinnitus," Neuromonics, http://www.neuromonics.com/professional/treatment/index.aspx?id=138&linkidentifier=id&itemid=138.
23. Garrison Keillor, "The Unknown Passenger at the Airport," *Chicago Tribune*, June 20, 2007, http://www.novamind.com/connect/nm_documents/

show_branch/Power/408AE3D6-02BB-4C9C-87CE-0E6399479327/1677461910.

24. Michelle Willard, "Music Pushes Critically Ill Teen to Recovery," *Murfreesboro Post*, May 4, 2008, http://www.murfreesboropost.com/news.php?viewStory=10793.
25. Tatiana Morales, "How Music Eases Asthma," CBSNews.com, http://www.cbsnews.com/stories/2003/11/04/earlyshow/living/main581686.shtml.
26. Anahad O'Connor, "Throat Exercises Can Relieve Sleep Apnea," *New York Times*, May 24, 2010.
27. "How the Didgeridoo Can Help Your Snoring," Articlesbase, http://www.articlesbase.com/sleep-articles/how-the-didgeridoo-can-help-your-snoring-560034.html#ixzz1CHCno18X.
28. M. A. Puhan, A. Suarez, C. Lo Cascio, A. Zahn, M. Heitz, and O. Braendli, "Didgeridoo Playing as an Alternative Treatment for Obstructive Sleep Apnoea Syndrome: Randomised Controlled Trial," *British Medical Journal* 332, no. 7536 (2006): 266–70.
29. "Home Remedies Put to the Test," Dr. Oz, http://www.doctoroz.com/videos/home-remedies-put-test.
30. Mitchell L. Gaynor, "Harness the Healing Power of Sound," Cancer Support Online, http://www.cancersupportwa.org.au/newsletter_article.php?news_id=102.
31. Mark S. Rider and Jeanne Achterberg, "Effect of Music-Assisted Imagery on Neutrophils and Lymphocytes," *Biofeedback and Self-Regulation* 14, no. 3 (1989): 247–57.
32. M. Smith, L. Casey, D. Johnson, C. Gwede, and O. Z. Riggin, "Music as a Therapeutic Intervention for Anxiety in Patients Receiving Radiation Therapy," *Oncology Nursing Forum* 28, no. 5 (2001), http://www.ncbi.nlm.nih.gov/pubmed/11421145.
33. Kristine L. Kwekkeboom, Molly Bumpus, Britt Wanta, and Ronald C. Serlin, "Oncology Nurses' Use of Nondrug Pain Interventions in Practice," *Journal of Pain Symptom Management* 35, no. 1 (2008), http://www.oncologystat.com/journals/journal_scans/Oncology_Nurses_Use_of_Nondrug_Pain_Interventions_in_Practice.html.
34. Gaynor, "Harness the Healing Power of Sound."
35. Barry Bittman, "Healing: To the Beat of an Inner Drummer," Remo, http://remo.com/portal/hr/article?id=13.

36. Anjali Joseph and Roger Ulrich, "Sound Control for Improved Outcomes in Healthcare Settings," The Center for Health Design, http://www.premierinc.com/safety/topics/construction/downloads/chd-issue-paper-sound-control.pdf.
37. Ibid.
38. Roger Ulrich, Craig Zimring, Xiaobo Quan, Anjali Joseph, and Ruchi Choudhary, "The Role of the Physical Environment in the Hospital of the 21st Century: A Once-in-a-Lifetime Opportunity," The Center for Health Design, United States Department of Health and Human Services, Office for Civil Rights (2004).
39. Joseph and Ulrich, "Sound Control for Improved Outcomes in Healthcare Settings."
40. Mazer, "Music, Noise, and the Environment of Care."
41. Barbara Blake Minckley, "A Study of Noise and Its Relationship to Patient Discomfort in the Recovery Room," *Nursing Research* 17, no. 3 (1968): 247–49.
42. D. Fife and E. Rappaport, "Noise and Hospital Stay," *American Journal of Public Health* 66, no. 7 (1976): 680–81; I. Hagerman, G. Rasmanis, V. Blomkvist, R. Ulrich, C. A. Eriksen, and T. Theorell, "Influence of Intensive Coronary Care Acoustics on the Quality of Care and Physiological State of Patients," *International Journal of Cardiology* 98, no. 2 (2005): 267–70.
43. Cromie, "Music on the Brain."
44. Hagerman et al., "Influence of Intensive Coronary Care Acoustics on the Quality of Care and Physiological State of Patients."
45. M. Slevin, N. Farrington, G. Duffy, L. Daly, and J. F. Murphy, "Altering the NICU and Measuring Infants' Responses," *Acta Paediatrica* 89, no. 5 (2000): 577–81; A. N. Johnson, "Neonatal Response to Control of Noise Inside the Incubator," *Pediatric Nursing* 27, no. 6 (2001): 600–605; J. de Traversay, "Premature Infant Responses to Noise Reduction by Earmuffs: Effects on Behavioral and Physiologic Measures," *Journal of Perinatology* 15, no. 6 (1995): 448–55.
46. David Barlas, Andrew E. Sama, Mary F. Ward, and Martin L. Lesser, "Comparison of the Auditory and Visual Privacy of Emergency Department Treatment Areas with Curtains Versus Those with Solid Walls," *Annals of Emergency Medicine* 38, no. 2 (2001): 135–39.
47. M. Topf and E. Dillon, "Noise-Induced Stress as a Predictor of Burnout in Critical Care Nurses," *Heart & Lung: The Journal of Acute and Critical Care*

17, no. 5 (1988): 567–74; W. E. Morrison, E. C. Haas, D. H. Shaffner, E. S. Garett, and J. C. Fackler, "Noise, Stress, and Annoyance in a Pediatric Intensive Care Unit," *Critical Care Medicine* 31, no. 1 (2003): 113–19; M. V. Bayo, A. M. García, and A. García, "Noise Levels in an Urban Hospital and Workers' Subjective Responses," *Archives of Environmental Health* 50, no. 3 (1995): 247–51.

48. R. Parsons and T. Hartig, "Environmental Psychophysiology," quoted in John T. Cacioppo, Louis G. Tassinary, and Gary Berntson, eds., *Handbook of Psychophysiology*, 2nd ed. (New York: Cambridge University Press, 2000), 815–46.
49. V. S. Murthy, K. L. Malhotra, I. Bala, and M. Raghunathan, "Detrimental Effects of Noise on Anesthetists," *Canadian Journal of Anaesthesia* 42 (1995): 608–11.
50. Joseph and Ulrich, "Sound Control for Improved Outcomes in Healthcare Settings."
51. Hagerman et al., "Influence of Intensive Coronary Care Acoustics on the Quality of Care and Physiological State of Patients."
52. E. Bailey and S. Timmons, "Noise Levels in PICU: An Evaluative Study," *Pediatric Nursing* 17, no. 10 (2005): 22–26; M. Buelow, "Noise Level Measurements in Four Phoenix Emergency Departments," *Journal of Emergency Nursing* 27, no. 1 (2001): 23–26; R. H. Baevsky, M. Y. Lu, and H. A. Smithline, "The Effectiveness of Wireless Telephone Communication Technology on Ambient Noise Level Reduction Within the ED," American College of Emergency Physicians Research Forum (Philadephia), October 23, 2000.
53. A. M. Yinnon, Y. Ilan, B. Tadmor, G. Altarescu, and C. Hershko, "Quality of Sleep in the Medical Department," *British Journal of Clinical Practice* 46, no. 2 (1992): 88–91; M. T. Southwell and G. Wistow, "Sleep in Hospitals at Night: Are Patients' Needs Being Met?" *Journal of Advanced Nursing* 21, no. 6 (1995): 1101–9; C. F. Baker, "Sensory Overload and Noise in the ICU: Sources of Environmental Stress," *Critical Care Quarterly* 6, no. 4 (1984): 66–80; Bailey and. Timmons, "Noise Levels in PICU."
54. Joseph and Ulrich, "Sound Control for Improved Outcomes in Healthcare Settings."
55. Cunningham et al., "Introducing a Music Program in the Perioperative Area."
56. Aubrey C. Patrick, "Patient Comfort: A Little TLC for MRI," *Medical Imaging*, February 2004.
57. Linda L. Chlan, "Music Therapy as a Nursing Intervention for Patients

Supported by Mechanical Ventilation," *AACN Clinical Issues* 11, no. 1 (2000): 128–38.

58. Esther Mok and Kwai-Yiu Wong, "Effects of Music on Patient Anxiety," *AORN Journal* 77, no. 2 (2003): 396.
59. Elizabeth Gillen, Francis Biley, and Davina Allen, "Effects of Music Listening on Adult Patients' Pre-Procedural State Anxiety in Hospital," *International Journal of Evidence-Based Healthcare* 6, no. 1 (2008), http://onlinelibrary.wiley.com/doi/10.1111/j.1744-1609.2007.00097.x/abstract.
60. H. L. Bonny and N. McCarron, "Music as an Adjunct to Anesthesia in Operative Procedures," *Journal of the American Association of Nurse Anesthetists* (February 1984).
61. U. Nilsson, N. Rawal, L. E. Unestahl, C. Zetterberg, and M. Unosson, "Improved Recovery After Music and Therapeutic Suggestions During General Anesthesia: A Double-Blind Randomized Controlled Trial," *Acta Anaesthesiologica Scandinavica* 45, no. 7 (2001): 812–17.
62. Penny Augustin and Anthony A. Hains, "Effect of Music on Ambulatory Surgery Patients' Preoperative Anxiety," *AORN Journal* 63, no. 4 (1996), http://findarticles.com/p/articles/mi_m0FSL/is_n4_v63/ai_19107109/?tag=content;col1.
63. M. F. Gatti and M. J. da Silva, "Ambient Music in the Emergency Services: The Professionals' Perception," *Revista Latino-Americana de Enfermagem* 15, no. 3 (2007): 377–83.
64. Karen Allen and Jim Blascovich, "Effects of Music on Cardiovascular Reactivity Among Surgeons," *JAMA* 272, no. 11 (1994), http://jama.ama-assn.org/cgi/content/abstract/272/11/882.
65. P. Thorgaard, E. Ertmann, V. Hansen, A. Noerregaard, V. Hansen, and L. Spanggaard, "Designed Sound and Music Environment in Postanaesthesia Care Units—A Multicentre Study of Patients and Staff," *Intensive and Critical Care Nursing* 21, no. 4 (2005): 220–25.
66. Y. Ullman, L. Fodor, I. Schwarzberg, N. Carmi, A. Ullmann, and Y. Ramon, "The Sounds of Music in the Operating Room," *Injury* 39, no. 5 (2008), http://www.ncbi.nlm.nih.gov/pubmed/16989832?ordinalpos=4&itool=EntrezSystem2.PEntrez.Pubmed.Pubmed_ResultsPanel.Pubmed_RVDocSum.
67. Ulrica Nilsson, "The Effect of Music Intervention in Stress Response to Cardiac Surgery in a Randomized Clinical Trial," *Heart & Lung* 38, no. 3 (2008), http://www.heartandlung.org/article/S0147-9563(08)00140-4/abstract.

68. Robert L. Routhieaux and David A. Tansik, "The Benefits of Music in Hospital Waiting Rooms," *Health Care Supervisor* 16, no. 2 (1997): 31–40.
69. Willingham, "The Power of Music."
70. Don Campbell, *The Mozart Effect* (New York: Quill, 2001): 60–61.
71. Maru E. Barrera, Mary H. Rykov, and Sandra L. Doyle, "The Effects of Interactive Music Therapy on Hospitalized Children with Cancer: A Pilot Study," *Psycho-Oncology* 11, no. 5 (2002): 379–88.
72. Ibid.
73. R. McCaffrey and R. Locsin, "The Effect of Music on Pain and Acute Confusion in Older Adults Undergoing Hip and Knee Surgery," *Holistic Nursing Practice* 20, no. 5 (2006): 218–24.
74. Institute for Music and Neurologic Function, "Success Stories: Trevor," Music Has Power, http://www.bethabe.org.
75. Whitney Holmes, "Music Heals Children," Newsplex.com, http://www.charlottesvillenewsplex.tv/news/headlines/9355391.html.
76. Chris Simnett, "Music Is a Powerful Pain Buster," *Calgary Herald*, May 29, 2008, http://www.canada.com/calgaryherald.
77. Christine Wicker, "What America Cares About: Healing Sick Kids Through Music," *Parade*, April 4, 2010, http://www.parade.com/news/what-america-cares-about/featured/100404-healing-sick-kids-through-music.html.
78. Dave Mason, "The Right Beat for Kids," *Santa Barbara News-Press*, July 29, 2009, http://www.newspress.com.
79. Simon Hooper, "Music a 'Mega-Vitamin' for the Brain," CNN.com, http://edition.cnn.com/2009/HEALTH/06/02/music.therapy/index.html.
80. T. Särkämö et al., "Music Listening Enhances Cognitive Recovery and Mood After Middle Cerebral Artery Stroke," *Brain* 131, part 3 (2008): 866–76.
81. "Applied Clinical Research: Auditory Sensorimotor Integration and Music-Supported Training of Motor Functions After Stroke," Institute of Music Physiology and Musicians' Medicine at the Hanover University of Music and Drama, http://www.immm.hmt-hannover.de/index.php?id=896&L=1.
82. Matthew Shulman, "Music as Medicine for the Brain," *U.S. News and World Report*, July 17, 2008.
83. Ibid.
84. Amy Price, author interview, November 15, 2010.
85. Oliver Sacks, quoted in Cindy Stauffer, "Music Used As Therapy for Par-

kinson's Sufferers," *Bay State Banner*, November 20, 2008, http://www.baystatebanner.com/health25-2008-11-20.

86. Shulman, "Music as Medicine for the Brain."
87. Ibid.
88. Mikhail Gorman, Margrit Betke, Elliot Saltzman, and Amir Lahav, "Music Maker—A Camera-Based Music Making Tool for Physical Rehabilitation," *Boston University Computer Science Technical Report No. 2005-032* (2005), http://www.cs.bu.edu/techreports/pdf/2005-032-music-maker.pdf.
89. Gary Graff, "Bret Michaels Adds New Chapter to 'Roses & Thorns' Autobiography," *Billboard*, June 17, 2010, http://www.billboard.com/news/bret-michaels-adds-new-chapter-to-roses-1004098825.story#/news/bret-michaels-adds-new-chapter-to-roses-1004098825.story.
90. Hooper, "Music a 'Mega-Vitamin' for the Brain."
91. Roslyn Sulcas, "Getting Their Groove Back, with Help from the Magic of Dance," *New York Times*, August 25, 2007.
92. Marc Shulgold, author interview, April 2009.
93. Dr. James Hopkins, "Pythagorean Harmonix Healing: About the Instruments," HarmonixHealing.com, http://harmonixhealing.com/Htm/Instruments.htm.
94. Ibid.
95. "Healing Through Sacred Sound and Music," Islamonline.net, http://www.islamonline.net/ar/Page/Home.
96. Jaakko Erkkilä, "Improvisational Psychodynamic Music Therapy in Depression Treatment—RCT-Outcomes and EEG-Data," Mozart & Science 2010, http://www.mozart-science.eu/en/speakers/erkkila-jaakko/Jaakko%20Erkkilae_Abstract%20%20%20%20.pdf/view.
97. Irving Kirsch, "Antidepressants and the Placebo Response," *Epidemiologia e Psichiatria Sociale* 18, no. 4 (2009): 318–22; Irving Kirsch, *The Emperor's New Drugs: Exploding the Antidepressant Myth* (New York: Basic Books, 2010): 101–102.
98. Sharon Begley, "The Depressing News About Antidepressants," *Newsweek*, January 29, 2010.
99. V. M. Brandes, D. Terris, C. Fischer, A. Loerbroks, M. N. Jarczok, G. Ottowitz, G. Titscher, J. E. Fischer, and J. F. Thayer, "Receptive Music Therapy for the Treatment of Depression: A Proof-of-Concept Study and Prospective Controlled Trial of Efficacy," *Psychotherapy and Psychosomatics* 79, no. 5 (2010): 321–22.

100. V. M. Brandes, D. Terris, C. Fischer, M. N. Schuessler, G. Ottowitz, G. Titscher, J. E. Fischer, and J. F. Thayer, "Music Programs Designed to Remedy Burnout Symptoms Show Significant Effects After Five Weeks," *Annals of the New York Academy of Sciences* 1169 (July 2009): 422–25.
101. Morris W. Brody, "Neurotic Manifestations of the Voice," *The Psychoanalytic Quarterly* 12 (1943): 371–80.
102. "U.S. Research Shows How Mantras Can Even Tackle Post-Traumatic Stress Disorder," Medical News Today, http://www.medicalnewstoday.com/articles/38783.php.
103. Silvia Nakkach, "Medicine Melodies. Emotional Magic and Music," Vox Mundi Project, http://www.voxmundiproject.com/medicine_melodies.htm#.
104. Garret Condon, "Making Noise, Getting Well," *Hartford Courant*, June 21, 2004.

Chapter Six: Let Music Ring

1. Garret Keizer, *The Unwanted Sound of Everything We Want: A Book About Noise* (New York: Public Affairs, 2010), 113–15.
2. Bill Sanderson, "Crying Out Loud!" *New York Post*, October 27, 2010.
3. Larry Dossey, "Quiet, Please: Observations on Noise," *Explore* 4, no. 3 (2008): 157–63.
4. George Prochnik, *In Pursuit of Silence*, 125–26.
5. Marin Allen, "A Call for Hearing Protection in Rural America," National Institute on Deafness and Other Communication Disorders, http://www.nidcd.nih.gov/news/releases/00/09_21_00.htm.
6. Tom Zeller Jr., "For Those Near, the Miserable Hum of Clean Energy," *New York Times*, October 5, 2010.
7. George Michelsen Foy, quoted in Ted Conover, "Noises Off," *New York Times*, May 28, 2010.
8. Garret Keizer, quoted in Conover, "Noises Off."
9. George Prochnik, quoted in Conover, "Noises Off."
10. Andy Coghlan, "Dying for Some Quiet: The Truth About Noise Pollution," *NewScientist*, August 22, 2007, http://www.newscientist.com/article/mg19526186.500-dying-for-some-quiet-the-truth-about-noise-pollution.html.
11. Roger Cohen, "Freedom's Blaring Horn," *New York Times*, June 17, 2010.

12. Dr. William H. Stewart, quoted in "Noise & Health Fact Sheet," Center for Hearing and Communication, http://www.chchearing.org/noise-center-home/facts-noise/noise-health.
13. Shauna Rempel, "When All Hope Is Gone, Sad Songs Say So Much," *Toronto Star*, June 19, 2008, http://www.thestar.com/living/article/445373.
14. Gunter Kreutz, "Using Music to Induce Emotions: Influences of Musical Preference and Absorption," Sage Journals Online, http://pom.sagepub.com/content/36/1/101.abstract.
15. Conrad Walters, "Smooth Operators, If the Groove's Right," *Sydney Morning Herald*, August 25, 2007.
16. Rempel, "When All Hope Is Gone, Sad Songs Say So Much."
17. Dossey, "Quiet, Please."
18. Ibid.
19. Tim Stelloh, "Gunfire Will No Longer Be Met by Silence," *New York Times*, December 10, 2010.
20. "Music Boosts Prisoners' Learning," BBC News, http://news.bbc.co.uk/2/hi/uk_news/education/7650466.stm.
21. Alice Wignall, "Keeping Body and Soul In Tune," *Guardian* (UK), August 26, 2008, http://www.guardian.co.uk/lifeandstyle/2008/aug/26/healthandwellbeing.fitness.
22. Brian Eno, "Freestyling," *Ode*, October 2008, http://www.odemagazine.com/doc/57/freestyling/.
23. Wignall, "Keeping Body and Soul In Tune."
24. Constantijn Koopman, "Community Music as Music Education: On the Educational Potential of Community Music," *International Journal of Music Education* 25, no. 2 (2007): 151–63.
25. Brink, "Sing Out, Sister."
26. Arizona State University, "Study Looks at Relationship Between Music, Mood," Arizona State University News, http://asunews.asu.edu/20080926_musicmood.
27. Doug Goodkin, "The Musical Community," *Orff Echo* (Summer 2001).
28. Christopher Small, "Whose Music Do We Teach, Anyway?" Music Educators National Conference, March 28, 1990, http://www.giarts.org/.
29. Peter Stampfel, "Freak Folk Origins, Part II," Perfect Sound Forever, http://www.furious.com/perfect/freakfolkorigins2.html.

30. Peter Stampfel, "Freak Folk Origins, Part I," Perfect Sound Forever, http://www.furious.com/perfect/freakfolkorigins.html.
31. "The FootnoteMaven's Tradition of Blog Caroling," FootnoteMaven, http://www.footnotemaven.com/2010/12/footnotemavens-tradition-of-blog.html.
32. Chorus America, "America's Performing Art: A Study of Choruses, Choral Singers, and Their Impact" (2003), http://www.chorusamerica.org/documents/2003chorstudy.pdf.
33. Wignall, "Keeping Body and Soul In Tune."
34. NIH Philharmonia, "NIH Philharmonia—About Us," NIHPhil.org, http://www.nihphil.org/about_us.htm.
35. "Making Music with Heart," Boston Minstrel Company, http://www.bostonminstrel.org/.
36. Kevin Sirois, "Boston Minstrel Company Sings in Homeless Shelters, Prisons, Hospitals," Wicked Local, http://www.wickedlocal.com/allston/archive/x297245654/Boston-Minstrel-Company-sings-in-homeless-shelters-prisons-hospitals.
37. Laura DeJoseph, "Making Music with Heart," Making Music, http://www.makingmusicmag.com/features_dev/show-feature.php?pageid=71.
38. Sirois, "Boston Minstrel Company Sings in Homeless Shelters, Prisons, Hospitals."
39. DeJoseph, "Making Music with Heart."
40. Mary Daniel Hobson, "AHN Interview: Rachel Bagby," Arts and Healing Network, http://www.artheals.org/news_2008/spring_2008.php.
41. "History of the Shropshire Music Foundation," Shropshire Music Foundation, http://www.shropshirefoundation.org/history/. For more information about the Shropshire Foundation, explore the organization's Web site, http://www.shropshirefoundation.org/.
42. Nancy Arcayna, "How Music Brings Peace," *Star Bulletin*, March 20, 2007, http://archives.starbulletin.com/2007/03/20/features/story01.html.
43. Anthony Ham, "Musicians for Peace," MusicalMissions.com, http://www.musicalmissionsofpeace.org/mm/arabworld.html.
44. "Peoples Musical Ambassador Projects," Musical Missions of Peace, http://www.musicalmissionsofpeace.org/Peoples%20Musical%20Ambassadors.html.

45. "Our Team: Christine Stevens," UpBeat Drum Circles, http://www.ubdrumcircles.com/about_team.html.
46. "Iraq Press Kit," UpBeat Drum Circles, http://www.ubdrumcircles.com/about_iraq_kit.html.

Chapter Seven: "Imagine You Are Humming to God"

1. Josie Glausiusz, "The Neural Orchestra," *Discover,* September 1, 1997, http://discovermagazine.com/1997/sep/theneuralorchest1227.
2. "Dr. Robin Sylvan: Music and the Brain," Library of Congress, http://www.loc.gov/podcasts/musicandthebrain/podcast_sylvan.html.
3. Jean During, *The Spirit of Sounds: The Unique Art of Ostad Elahi* (Cranbury, NJ: Cornwall Books, 2003).
4. James P. D'Angelo, "Tonality and Its Symbolic Associations in Paul Hindemith's Opera *Die Harmonie der Welt,* vols. 1 & 2," Ph.D. diss., New York University, 1983.
5. "Dr. Taoufiq ben Amor: Music and the Brain," Library of Congress, http://www.loc.gov/podcasts/musicandthebrain/podcast_benamor.html.
6. Alok Jha, "Favourite Music Evokes Same Feelings As Good Food or Drugs," *Guardian* (UK), January 9, 2011.
7. Ibid.
8. "Healing Through Sacred Sound and Music," Islamonline.net.
9. Edward Willett, "Breath Plus Space Equals Singing," *The Leader-Post* (Canada), October 24, 2007, http://www.canada.com/reginaleaderpost/news/arts_life/story.html?id=878514e0-f8a4-4dde-af1a-dbe077925c15&k=63309.
10. Ibid.
11. Nakkach, "Medicine Melodies."
12. Ibid.
13. Ibid.
14. Laurel Elizabeth Keyes and Don Campbell, *Toning: The Creative Power of the Voice* (Los Angeles: DeVorss & Company, 2008), 94-L.
15. Mark Rider and Mary Haas, *The Rhythmic Language of Health and Disease* (St. Louis: MMB Music, 1997), 103.
16. Medical News Today, "U.S. Research Shows How Mantras Can Even Tackle Post-Traumatic Stress Disorder."

Chapter Eight: The Melody Lingers

1. Oliver Sacks, "This Year, Change Your Mind," *New York Times*, December 31, 2010.
2. E. Lewis, "Gene Cohen Explains Why Brains Get Better with Age," Insights, http://www.umbc.edu/insights/2007/11/gene_cohen_explains_why_brains.html.
3. "The Mature Mind," ChangingMinds.org, http://changingminds.org/books/book_reviews/mature_mind.htm.
4. Ibid.
5. Ibid.
6. Gene Cohen, *Creativity in Later Life* (Burlington, VT: University of Vermont Osher Lifelong Learning Institute, 2008), online video, http://www.cctv.org/watch-tv/programs/creativity-later-life-dr-gene-cohen.
7. "New Horizons International Music Association: Concept and Philosophy," New Horizons International Music Association, http://www.newhorizonsmusic.org/home_page_items/concept_and_philosophy.html.
8. Eileen Elliott, "Residents Stretch Mind and Body with MMDG," *New York City Housing Authority Journal*, June 2008.
9. Sulcas, "Getting Their Groove Back."
10. For more information about New Horizons International Music Association, visit their Web site, http://www.newhorizonsmusic.org/nhima.html.
11. New Horizons International Music Association, "New Horizons International Music Association: Concept and Philosophy."
12. Lisa Jo Rudy, "Retirement Is a Great Time to Strike Up the Band," CNN Living, http://articles.cnn.com/2008-02-22/living/sr.musicians_1_roy-ernst-band-high-school?_s=PM:LIVING.
13. New Horizons International Music Association, "New Horizons International Music Association: Concept and Philosophy."
14. Kimberly Beauchamp, "Music Decreases Arthritis Pain in the Elderly," Bastyr Center for Natural Health, http://bastyrcenter.org/content/view/352/.
15. Carol Eustice, "Music Therapy Eases Arthritis Pain," About.com, http://arthritis.about.com/b/2006/06/06/music-therapy-eases-arthritis-pain.htm.
16. McCaffrey and Locsin, "The Effect of Music on Pain and Acute Confusion in Older Adults."
17. JD, "Arthritis and Playing Musical Instruments," Disabled World, http://

www.disabled-world.com/health/autoimmunediseases/arthritis/musical-instruments.php.

18. Gene D. Cohen, "The Creativity and Aging Study: The Impact of Professionally Conducted Cultural Programs on Older Adults," National Endowment for the Arts, http://www.nea.gov/resources/accessibility/CnA-Rep4-30-06.pdf.
19. Ibid.
20. Robert Ebisch, "Science of Hearing Loss Moving Near Speed of Sound," *Jewish Journal*, March 7, 2008, http://www.jewishjournal.com/so_cal_medicine/article/science_of_hearing_loss_moving_near_speed_of_sound_20080308.
21. Ibid.
22. Oliver Sacks, "The Abyss," *The New Yorker*, September 24, 2007.
23. Richard Alleyne and Lewis Carter, "Beatles Music More Than 'Auditory Cheesecake,' Scientists Find," *Telegraph* (UK), September 7, 2008.
24. Bob Herbert, "Thinking of Aretha," *New York Times*, December 24, 2010.
25. Jeremy Hsu, "Music-Memory Connection Found in Brain," Live Science, http://www.livescience.com/health/090224-music-memory.html.
26. Paul Recer, "Musical Memory Mystery Solved," Associated Press, December 13, 2002.
27. G. Shaw, "Sound Medicine: Music Therapy Plays off the Brain-Healing Power of Songs and Their Rhythms to Stimulate Memory and Movement," *Neurology Now* 2, no. 5 (2006): 26–29.
28. Cromie, "Music on the Brain."
29. Ross Peters, "Social Isolation and Loneliness," Centre on Aging, http://www.coag.uvic.ca/documents/research_snapshots/Social_Isolation_Loneliness.htm.
30. A. M. Kumar, F. Tims, D. G. Cruess, M. J. Mintzer, G. Ironson, D. Loewenstein, R. Cattan, J. B. Fernandez, C. Eisdorfer, and M. Kumar, "Music Therapy Increases Serum Melatonin Levels in Patients with Alzheimer's Disease," *Alternative Therapies in Health and Medicine* 5, no. 6, (1999), http://www.biomedexperts.com/Abstract.bme/10550905/Music_therapy_increases_serum_melatonin_levels_in_patients_with_Alzheimer_s_disease.
31. Willingham, "The Power of Music."
32. Jeff Pizek, "Mickey Hart: Unity, Healing Through the Beat," *Daily Herald*, July 4, 2008.

33. Cynthia Billhartz Gregorian, "Drumming Keeps Brain Humming," *St. Louis Post-Dispatch*, November 12, 2008, http://www.stltoday.com.
34. Barry Bittman, Karl T. Bruhn, Christine Stevens, James Westengard, and Paul O. Umbach, "Recreational Music-Making: A Cost-Effective Group Interdisciplinary Strategy for Reducing Burnout and Improving Mood States in Long-Term Care Workers," *Advances in Mind-Body Medicine* 19, no. 3–4 (2003): 4–15.
35. Patti Smith, *Just Kids* (New York: HarperCollins Publishers, 2010): xi–xii.
36. Ibid.
37. Charles Gourgey, "About Pastoral Music Therapy," Music Is Hope, http://www.musicishope.org/html/about.html.
38. Beth Ashley, "The Healing Harp," Therapy Times, http://www.therapytimes.com/content=0402J84C489E8884406040441.
39. "The Power of Sound: Healing in Practice. Important Qualities of Individualized Therapeutic Harp Music," Emerald Harp, http://www.emeraldharp.com/PDF/ihtp.pdf.
40. Ashley, "The Healing Harp."
41. Kathleen Burge, "Harpist Plays to Ease Pain at Final Gatherings," *Boston Globe*, November 9, 2008, http://www.boston.com/news/local/articles/2008/11/09/as_life_ebbs_healing_music_flows/.
42. "Hospice Music Program Brings Harmony to Patients and Families," *Homecare Connection*, Fall 2009.
43. John Flowers, "Song Eases Pain As the Lives of the Terminally Ill Near Their End," *Addison County Independent*, November 20, 2008.
44. Here, on the Web site of the Threshold Choir, you will find information on how to find and join a choir in your area, or create one yourself: http://www.thresholdchoir.org/index.htm.
45. Here, on the Web site of the Chalice of Repose Project, you will find a list of certified music thanatologists available to serve patients during their final months, days, or even hours: http://chaliceofrepose.org/.
46. Clare O'Callaghan, "Lullament: Lullaby and Lament Therapeutic Qualities Actualized Through Music Therapy," *American Journal of Hospice and Palliative Care* 25, no. 2 (2008): 93–99.
47. Flowers, "Song Eases Pain As the Lives of the Terminally Ill Near Their End."

Chapter Nine: A Soundtrack for Life

1. Victoria Dunckley, "Electronics and Sleep Disturbance in Children: Wired and Tired," EzineArticles, http://ezinearticles.com/?Electronics-and-Sleep-Disturbance-in-Children:-Wired-and-Tired&id=5181329.
2. R. Murray Schafer, *The Tuning of the World* (Philadelphia: University of Pennsylvania Press, 1981), 259.
3. Adapted from Rodger Graham, "A Cognitive-Attentional Perspective on the Psychological Benefits of Listening," *Music and Medicine* 2, no. 3 (2010): 171.

Further Reading

Beaulieu, John. *Music and Sound in the Healing Arts: An Energy Approach*. Barrytown, NY: Station Hill Press, 1987.

Becker, Judith. *Deep Listeners: Music, Emotion, and Trancing*. Bloomington, IN: Indiana University Press, 2004.

Bicknell, Jeanette. *Why Music Moves Us*. New York: Palgrave Macmillan, 2009.

Boyce-Tillman, June. *Constructing Musical Healing: The Wounds That Sing*. Philadelphia: Jessica Kingsley Publishers, 2000.

Campbell, Don. *The Harmony of Health*. Carlsbad, CA: Hay House, Inc., 2006.

Campbell, Don G. *Master Teacher Nadia Boulanger*. Washington, D. C.: Pastoral Press, 1983.

Campbell, Don. *The Mozart Effect®: Tapping the Power of Music to Heal the Body, Strengthen the Mind, and Unlock the Creative Spirit*. New York: Avon Books, 1997.

Campbell, Don. *Music: Physician for Times to Come*. Wheaton, IL: Quest Books, 1991.

Carey, Donna, Ellen Franklin, Judith Ponton, Paul Ponton, and MichelAngelo Fiacco. *Acutonics: From Galaxies to Cells*. Llano, NM: Devachan Press, 2010.

Carlson, Richard, and Benjamin Shield, eds. *Healers on Healing*. New York: Putnam, 1989.

Cohen, Gene D. *The Mature Mind: The Positive Power of the Aging Brain*. New York: Basic Books, 2006.

Crowe, Barbara. *Music and Soulmaking: Toward a New Theory of Music Therapy*. Lanham, MD: The Scarecrow Press Inc., 2004.

Davis, Dorinne S. *Sound Bodies Through Sound Therapy*. Landing, NJ: Kalco Publishing LLC, 2004.

Diallo, Yaya, and Mitchell Hall. *The Healing Drum: African Wisdom Teachings*. Rochester, VT: Destiny Books, 1989.

During, Jean. *The Spirit of Sounds: The Unique Art of Ostad Elahi*. Cranbury, NJ: Cornwall Books, 2003.

Eschen, Johannes Theodor, ed. *Analytical Music Therapy*. London: Jessica Kingsley Publishers, 2002.

Foy, George Michelsen. *Zero Decibels: The Quest for Absolute Silence*. New York: Scribner, 2010.

Gioia, Ted. *Healing Songs*. Durham, NC: Duke University Press, 2006.

———. *Work Songs*. Durham, NC: Duke University Press, 2006.

Goldman, Jonathan. *Healing Sounds: The Power of Harmonics*. Shaftesbury, UK: Element, 1992.

Hart, Mickey, and Fredric Lieberman, with D. A. Sonneborn. *Planet Drum: A Celebration of Percussion and Rhythm*. San Francisco: HarperCollins Publishers, 1991.

Hass, Roland, and Vera Brandes, eds. *Music That Works: Contributions of Biology, Neurophysiology, Psychology, Sociology, Medicine and Musicology*. Vienna: SpringerWienNewYork, 2009.

Horden, Peregrine, ed. *Music as Medicine: The History of Music Therapy Since Antiquity*. Aldershot, UK: Ashgate Publishing, 2000.

James, Jamie. *The Music of the Spheres: Music, Science, and the Natural Order of the Universe*. New York: Grove Press, 1993.

Jansen, Eva Rudy. *Singing Bowls: A Practical Handbook of Instruction and Use*. Havelte, Holland: Binkey Kok Publications, 1992.

Jenny, Hans. *Cymatics: A Study of Wave Phenomena and Vibration*. Translated by D. Q. Stephenson. Newmarket, NH: Macromedia Press, 2001.

Jourdain, Robert. *Music, the Brain, and Ecstasy: How Music Captures Our Imagination*. New York: William Morrow and Company Inc., 1997.

Kahn, Hazrat Inayat. *The Music of Life*. New Lebanon, NY: Omega Publications, 1998.

Karpf, Anne. *The Human Voice: How This Extraordinary Instrument Reveals Essential Clues About Who We Are*. New York: Bloomsbury USA, 2006.

Keizer, Garret. *The Unwanted Sound of Everything We Want: A Book About Noise*. New York: PublicAffairs, 2010.

Laderman, Carol, and Marina Roseman, eds. *The Performance of Healing*. New York: Routledge, 1996.

Lauterwasser, Alexander. *Water Sound Images: The Creative Music of the Universe*. Newmarket, NH: Macromedia Press, 2006.

Leeds, Joshua. *The Power of Sound: How to Be Healthy and Productive Using Music and Sound*. Rochester, VT: Healing Arts Press, 2010.

Levitin, Daniel J. *The World in Six Songs: How the Musical Brain Created Human Nature*. New York: Dutton, 2008.

———. *This Is Your Brain on Music: The Science of a Human Obsession*. New York: Dutton, 2006.

Machover, Wilma, and Marienne Uszler. *Sound Choices: Guiding Your Child's Musical Experiences*. New York: Oxford University Press, 1996.

Madaule, Paul. *When Listening Comes Alive: A Guide to Effective Learning and Communication*. Norval, ON: Moulin Publishing, 1994.

Mithen, Steven. *The Singing Neanderthals: The Origins of Music, Language, Mind, and Body*. London: Weidenfeld & Nicolson, 2005.

Montello, Louise. *Essential Musical Intelligence: Using Music as Your Path to Healing, Creativity, and Radiant Wholeness*. Wheaton, IL: Quest Books, 2002.

Patel, Aniruddh D. *Music, Language, and the Brain*. New York: Oxford University Press, 2008.

Prochnik, George. *In Pursuit of Silence: Listening for Meaning in a World of Noise*. New York: Doubleday, 2010.

Redmond, Layne. *When the Drummers Were Women: A Spiritual History of Rhythm*. New York: Three Rivers Press, 1997.

Sacks, Oliver. *Musicophilia: Tales of Music and the Brain*. New York: Knopf, 2007.

Sadler, Blair L., and Annette Ridenour. *Transforming the Healthcare Experience Through the Arts*. San Diego: Aesthetics Inc., 2009.

Sardello, Robert. *Silence: The Mystery of Wholeness*. Benson, NC: Goldenstone Press, 2006.

Scarantino, Barbara Anne. *Music Power: Creative Living Through the Joys of Music*. New York: Dodd Mead, 1987.

Sollier, Pierre. *Listening for Wellness: An Introduction to the Tomatis Method*. Walnut Creek, CA: The Mozart Center Press, 2005.

Sonnenschein, David. *Sound Design: The Expressive Power of Music, Voice, and Sound Effects in Cinema*. Studio City, CA: Michael Wiese Productions, 2001.

Steiner, Rudolf. *The Inner Nature of Music and the Experience of Tone*. Spring Valley, NY: Anthroposophic Press, 1983.

Storr, Anthony. *Music and the Mind*. New York: Ballantine Books, 1993.

Thaut, Michael H. *Rhythm, Music, and the Brain: Scientific Foundations and Clinical Applications*. New York: Routledge, 2005.

Tomatis, Alfred A. *The Conscious Ear: My Life of Transformation Through Listening*. Barrytown, NY: Station Hill Press Inc., 1992.

———. *The Ear and Language*. Norval, ON: Moulin Publishing, 2004.

———. *The Ear and the Voice*. Lanham, MD: The Scarecrow Press Inc., 2004.

Tourin, Christina. *Cradle of Sound*. Mount Laguna, CA: Emerald Harp Productions, 2006.

Index

Note: Page numbers in *italics* refer to tables. Page numbers followed by a *t* refer to text boxes. Page numbers followed by an *L* refer to Web links.